Global Television

For Julie, Emma and Kate

Global Television

An Introduction

Chris Barker

BLACKWELL *Publishers*

First published 1997

2 4 6 8 10 9 7 5 3 1

Blackwell Publishers Ltd
108 Cowley Road
Oxford OX4 1JF
UK

Blackwell Publishers Inc.
350 Main Street
Malden, Massachusetts 02148
USA

British Library Cataloguing in Publication Data
A CIP catalogue record is available from the British Library.

Library of Congress Cataloging-in-Publication Data
Barker, Chris, 1955–
    Global television : an introduction / Chris Barker.
        p. cm.
    Includes bibliographical references and index.
    ISBN 0–631–20149–1. — ISBN 0–631–20150–5 (pbk)
1. Television broadcasting—Political aspects. 2. Television broadcasting—Economic aspects. 3. Soap operas. 4. Television broadcasting of news. 5. Television Viewers—Psychology. I Title.
PN1992, 6, B35 1997
302.23'45—dc21

96–52330
CIP

Typeset in 10½ on 12½ Palatino by Grahame and Grahame Editorial, Brighton
Printed in Great Britain by T. J. International, Padstow, Cornwall

This book is printed on acid-free paper

Contents

Preface and Acknowledgements

While all cultural products are the outcome not of individual minds as such but of a matrix of social relationships and the shared resource of language, there is a very particular way in which this is not 'my' book. Rather, it is a text which attempts to summarize, popularize and evaluate the contributions of a select group of others, those who appear in the bibliography. I thank all of them and suggest only that this book is a document, and attempted documentation, of its time and place which aims to provide a resource for readers to develop a sense of what Media and Cultural Studies has to say about global television and to assist in the development of a critical appreciation of it.

I would also like to thank all those who form part of my personal network of social relationships and who have in various ways, and by definition, contributed to this book. These are thankfully numerous, but in order to limit the game of inclusion/exclusion I want to name only two. My mother for being my mother and Julie for continuing to love and support me. To anyone who reads this book I thank you for your time and interest.

This book attempts to cover a lot of ground which means that, given the sheer volume of literature, it is not possible to read and digest its entirety. Hence, this book represents a particular 'take' on general issues of globalization and television and is not always even-handed in its treatment of debates since it is clear that I have sympathy with authors who put forward arguments about global-ization, hybrid and reflexive identity positions, the active nature of audiences and postmodern cultural pluralism. All these arguments are disputed by other writers, and readers may like to pursue those debates in more depth.

The author and publishers wish to thank the following for permis-sion to use copyright material:

In chapter 4, I discuss some aspects of my own research into gendered identity. A much longer version of this material appears as 'Did you see? Soaps, teenage talk and gendered identity', in *Young: Nordic Journal of Youth Research*, vol. 4, no. 4, 1996. I would like to thank *Young* for permission to use the material in this book.

In chapter 6 I discuss further parts of my research in relation to ethnicity and hybrid identities. A much longer version is forth-coming as 'Television and the Reflexive Project of the Self: Soaps, Teenage Talk and Hybrid Identities' in *The British Journal of Sociology*. I would like to thank *The British Journal of Sociology* for permission to use the material in this book.

Some short extracts of taped conversation from the research are also set to appear in Danish as 'Gender, Ethnicity, Identity: soap talk amongst British Asian girls' in K. Drotner, and K. Klitgaard (in press) (eds) *Media, Youth, Television*, University of Copenhagen. I would like to thank the editors for permission to use the extracts.

Part I

The Global Institutions of Television

1

Modernity and Global Television

This is a book about television: its organizations, programmes and cultural influences across the globe. It is a legitimate subject for study because it is the major form of communication in many societies. Certainly within the economically 'developed' nations no other medium can match it for the sheer size of audiences. Williams (1974) argued that not only do people in Britain watch more drama on television than might have been seen in a year or even a life time in other historical periods, but we spend more time doing so than preparing and eating food.

While there have always been grounds for exploring the economic and cultural significance of television, the case is particularly acute at present because of changes in the patterns of global communications and global culture. Since the mid-1980s there has been a significant rise in transnational television both in terms of global ownership and in the use of the distribution technologies of satellite and cable to open up new markets. In turn, the globalization of the institutions of television raises crucial questions about culture and cultural identities for television is a major disseminator of cultural maps of meaning and a resource for identity construction.

Global television needs to be understood historically and sociologically in the wider context of the globalization of capitalist modernity, since global television is constituted by and constituting of the inherently globalizing nature of modernity. 'Society' as bounded by place and space is inadequate for the task of describing and evaluating television for we are part of a global post-traditional society from which there is no escape (Giddens, 1994). There is little doubt that television is a global phenomenon. According to Kellner (1990) there are in excess of 750 million television sets in more than 160 countries watched by 2.5 billion people per day. As table 1.1 illustrates, that figure has further increased by 100 million households in the space of a few years. The table also suggests that the number of television households is growing fastest in the developing world, with marginal growth in Europe and America compared with Africa and Asia, where the number of television sets has trebled, or Central America where the figure has doubled.

However, grasping the crucial developments in television across the globe is not just a numerical issue but is also concerned with the *changing character* of television, in particular the growing organization of television along commercial rather than public-service lines. Current developments in the political economy of television have been hastened by privatization and de-regulatory policies pursued by major western governments, which have favoured commercial television. Under these circumstances the future of traditional state television-services, particularly those funded out of public money and built on notions of public service, has been put into crisis. We will need to consider both how such television services are coping with the new challenges and what the cultural consequences of the emergent global television may be.

Table 1.1 *Television households (by region)*

Region	1984 ('000s)	1994 ('000s)
Africa	6, 691	21, 147
Asia	88, 861	302, 201
Australia/Oceania	5, 890	6, 665
Central America	12, 769	25, 732
European Union	109, 891	141, 382
Far East	51, 522	67, 175
Middle East	5, 948	10, 442
North America	93, 539	105, 346
South America	42, 378	67, 252
World	534, 604	854, 225

Source: Modified from *Screen Digest*, February 1995.

Further, it is arguable that the global expansion of television has been an uneven one favouring the institutions of the industrialized nations of the west in general and the USA in particular. Television as both technology and cultural form is a western-originated project and continues to be dominated economically by western and particularly American economic powers. However, globalization is not to be seen as a one-way flow of influence from the west to the 'rest', rather, globalization is a multi-directional and multi-dimensional set of processes. Indeed, the global spread of television may be inflected and configured in different ways under different local circumstances so that the production of the global and the local are the same process.

A recurrent theme in the book will be the relationship between economic imperatives, organizational practices and cultural meaning. The specificity of cultural practices demands that we do not reduce them to other practices so that culture is not to be 'read off', or to be explained by, the economic. Nevertheless, culture is a material force enacted under particular historical conditions. To be specific, while we would want to understand television programmes in their own terms as cultural products, we would also want to examine them in the context of their manufacture as commodities within capitalist forms of production and exchange. That is to say culture *is* bound up with economic production.

However, I am not arguing for economic determinism, by which is meant the idea that profit motive and class relations directly determine the form and meaning of cultural products. Economic determinism would mean that because a television company is privately owned and is driven by the need to make a profit, all the programmes made within that company will be pro-capitalist and supportive of the status quo. Most thinkers working in the field of cultural practices – including those within the tradition of 'cultural studies' – have rejected such a view as simplistic and failing to grant cultural practice any specificity of its own. While the analysis of economic determinants is necessary for any understanding of television it is not in its self sufficient. We will also need to examine cultural phenomena in terms of their own rules, logics, development and effectivity. Thus, as Stuart Hall has argued:

> We must 'think' a society or social formation as ever and always constituted by a set of complex practices; each with its own

specificity, its own modes of articulation; standing in an 'uneven development' to other related practices. (Hall, 1977, p. 237)

This suggests the need to understand economic and cultural phenomena as part of a complex totality of social relations. It points to the desirability of a multi-dimensional and multi-perspectival approach to the understanding of television, which would seek to understand the connections between economic, political, social and cultural dimensions of society without reducing social phenomena to any one dimension. Dahlgren (1995) uses the metaphor of the prism to grasp the complexity of understanding television. He argues that television needs to be understood as an industry, as a text and as a socio-cultural phenomenon. When we look through one side of the prism we may loose sight of the other dimensions. While it is beyond our cognitive abilities to grasp all the elements of television simultaneously, our understandings will always be partial; keeping all sides in view though our analysis will inevitably foreground some elements over others. To use the metaphor of television itself: we will use a variety of angles, close-ups, long shots, pans, and cut-aways to construct our picture of the medium. Our emerging vision, though it may arguably contain more or less veracity, will remain an interpretation to be debated and argued about.

An explanation of the organization of this book, the lenses through which television is understood, is thus required. In part I, *The Global Institutions of Television*, I seek to position television within the context of global modernity and suggest that global television is both a constituting element and consequence of the inherently globalizing nature of the institutions of modernity. This theme is taken up explicitly in chapter 1 where I elaborate on the concepts of globalization and capitalist modernity, but it recurs as an underlying theme throughout the book. In chapter 2 I tackle the question of what is meant by 'global television' and seek to map the changing nature of television across the globe, and to raise critical questions about the causes and consequences of these changes. The focus of this chapter is on the political economy of television.

The core argument of part I is that television is a global phenomenon on an institutional level involving both national systems and the development of transnational television. Advances in television technology have created new distribution mechanisms which, allied to political and industrial support for market solutions, has weakened national regulatory environments. New transnational commercial corporations have entered into the global television market creating serious competition for public service broadcasters which, while they continue to survive, have lost part of their audience to their competitors. There has been a rise in transnational and monopoly ownership circumventing national regulation so that global television is dominated by commercial multinational corporations.

In part II, *Prime-time Goes Global: Programmes and Audiences*, I analyse two crucial programme genres and follow this up with an exploration of what is known about audiences from current perspectives. Chapter 3 takes a fairly orthodox 'close-up' perspective and explores television texts in terms of genre, notably the globally significant forms of soap opera and news. The focus shifts in chapter 4 to theoretical and empirical understandings of audiences, centring on questions of cultural meaning and domestic routines. I draw upon research in this area from within the 'active audience' paradigm, again concentrating on soaps and news, to illustrate the arguments.

The core argument of part II is that television can be said to be global in that similar narrative forms circulate around the world: soap opera and news can be found in most countries. However, while we need to examine the similarities of soaps and news across the globe we will also note the difference between, say, western soaps and Latin American telenovelas, or between the news gathered by western agencies and the use made of that raw news material under local conditions.

Issues of representation and misrepresentation do matter and television is of ideological significance, albeit in a less coherent fashion than had been assumed by some critics since it is always a question of ideological competition rather than the imposition of a monolithic ideology. However, it will also be argued that heterogeneous global audiences are able to bring their own cultural competencies to bear and to decode programmes in ways which depart from the dominant textual ideologies. Since audiences can actively resist ideological formulations (though activity does not always involve resistance) the tensions between a centrally and commercially produced culture and an active knowledgeable audience are at the centre of an understanding of global television and of cultural conditions in general.

In part III, *The Cultural Politics of Global Television*, a wider angle lens is used to examine aspects of global television as a cultural form. Thus, chapter 5 explores questions of a 'television culture' which transcends or cuts across specific genres and, in particular, the way in which television can be said to constitute a 'promotional' and 'postmodern' culture. This is followed, in chapter 6, by a consideration of the consequences of global television for collective, notably national, identities. This is explored in conjunction with the debates about cultural and media imperialism. Questions of culture are always issues of power and politics (in its broadest sense) so the final chapter both attempts to draw together the arguments of the book and discusses some issues of political evaluation. This is because description and evaluation are inseparable, to ask questions about what is happening to television across the globe inevitably raises the issue of what we would want television to be like.

A core argument of part III is that the development of global television as a fundamentally commercial form has placed advertising in the visible forefront of its activities and that television remains the central vehicle for international advertising both in its multi-local and global-branding forms. Thus, television is central to the production and reproduction of a 'promo-culture' centred on the use of visual imagery to create value-added brands or commodity-signs.

Further, the global multiplication of communications technologies has created an increasingly complex semiotic environment in which television produces and circulates an explosive display of competing signs and meanings. This creates a flow of images which fuses news, views, drama and reportage so that a variety of juxtapositions of images and meanings creates a sort of electronic bricolage. Thus, the globalization of television has contributed to the construction of a postmodern collage of images from different times and places. Postmodern culture is a contradictory culture since it is an increasingly commodified culture but also an increasingly reflexive one.

The nation is not necessarily the most suitable level to understand the cultural impact of television. Rather, we need to consider various levels of cultural identification, action and influence. Post-traditional identity formation involves the production of multiple identities or identifications, many of which have little bearing on questions of national identity. It will be argued that television increases the sources and resources for identity production, which can lead to a range of hybrid forms of identity, though the defensive production of 'fundamentalist' identities is an equally significant outcome. Such arguments inevitably pose problems for nation-based ideas of cultural imperialism as we shall see in chapter 6.

Finally, it will be suggested that the critique of television is not best made in the name of aesthetic quality but rather in terms of the diversity of representation and the pragmatic consequences of discourses of power. Television can be educative, informative and entertaining as well as ideological and misleading. It is the cutting edge of advertising and consumer capitalism, but also of democracy, equality and a liberating form of hybrid identity politics. I contrast a vision of a plural and diverse 'public sphere' with the disciplinary power of modern institutions and the commodity orientation of capitalism. However, the vision of television as a diverse and plural public sphere is seriously compromised by its almost complete penetration by the interest-based messages and images of consumerism.

The organization of the book into its three component parts is not purely arbitrary but has embedded in it certain theoretical underpinnings which are worth elaborating on. On one level the organizational themes are clear: part I is about *institutions*, part II is about *programmes* and *audiences* and part III is about *culture* and *politics* which, though all these spheres are of course interrelated, maintains common analytical distinctions in relation to the subject matter. However, there is a further organizing principle centred on the concepts of modernity, postmodernity and postmodernism which requires clarification at the outset because these themes recur throughout the text. The intention at this stage is not to discuss them in depth, more will be said about these ideas later in the book, but to make clear how these concepts are being used.

The Modern and the Postmodern

A survey of any academic bookshop would confirm the renewed interest in the concept of modernity and its relatives postmodernity and postmodernism. While the proliferation of books on the subject may be an academic fashion it is also a response to substantive changes in the organization and enactment of our social worlds. Modernity and postmodernity are terms which refer to historical and sociological configurations whereas modernism and post-modernism refer to (a) cultural formations / cultural experience (e.g. postmodern culture), (b) artistic and architectural styles and movements (e.g. modernist and postmodernist architecture or film), and (c) a set of philosophical and epistemological concerns and positions (e.g. postmodern philosophers such as Lyotard).

Modernity, as theorized by thinkers such as Marx and Weber, is a historical period following the middle ages. It is a post-traditional order marked by change, innovation and dynamism. The institutions of modernity can be seen, at least in the account of Giddens (1990), to consist of:

- Capitalism (capital accumulation in the context of competitive labour and product markets).
- Industrialism (the transformation of nature: development of the created environment).
- Surveillance (control of information and social supervision).
- Military power (control of the means of violence in the context of the industrialization of war).

Logically, the concept of postmodernity suggests that the institutional trajectory of modernity has changed to such a degree that we now live in a post-industrial, post-capitalist order. While there are certainly suggestions of the former in the writings of Lyotard and Baudrillard none could seriously entertain the latter idea. That there have been changes in the way our institutions are organized is beyond doubt, but these are not best described as postmodernity (as institutional arrangements or as an historical period), but as a *radicalized modernity* (Giddens, 1990) by which aspects of modernity (e.g. the global spread of capitalism) have been accelerated. This Giddens calls high modernity.

Hence, in part I, *The Global Institutions of Television*, I take the position that television can be best understood in terms of the institutions and political economy of modernity using a discourse of the modern. There is also a sense in part II, *Prime-time Goes Global: Programmes and Audiences*, in which I see the genres of soap opera and news as carriers of modern ideas about time, space, linear causality and the self (as motivated and unified) which resonate with, and are reproduced by, audiences own understandings of themselves and their world.

However, I take a rather different position on the wider questions of culture and cultural practices, including meanings embedded in the flow of television. Though modernity has not yet passed (Habermas, 1987) and most of the elements described as postmodern were already existent in the modern (Giddens, 1990), there have been significant *cultural* changes which have often been best described in the language of the 'postmodern'. Given that these social and cultural changes are at the leading edge of society and are pointing to its future (or are already the dominant configuration) we may refer to living in a postmodern era. This postmodern era does not represent a sharp break but a transitional period of changing economic, social and cultural patterns which are shaping the contours of the future. In this sense it can be argued that we are living in a period that shows characteristics of both continuity with modernity and elements of rupture and change. Here the post-modern does not imply postmodernity but rather indicates a 'structure of feeling' (Williams, 1979; 1981) and a set of *cultural* prac-tices which need to be understood within a social, economic and political context. Postmodernism as a cultural form can be seen as a marker of 'radicalized modernity' and does not have to be regarded as coterminous with the concept of postmodernity as an historical period. I am using the term 'postmodern culture' to describe a quali-tatively different set of cultural concerns that have emerged in conjunction with the global time–space compression of late-modernity. Thus, postmodernism can be regarded as the cultural sensibility of high modernity.

Hence, in part III, *The Cultural Politics of Global Television*, I describe the culture of global television as postmodern in form and argue that the institutions of transnational television, which are institutions of modernity, are globalizing a postmodern cultural form. I also suggest that understanding global television through the modern concept of nation is not the best way forward. Rather, I argue in terms of a global flow of cultural discourses and a concept of multiple, shifting and hybrid identities, which, while not necessarily postmodern, certainly has a postmodern 'flavour' to it.

I also take a more postmodern than modern view of epistemology, that is, questions of truth and knowledge. I take the position that no universalizing epistemology is possible because all truth claims are formed within discourse and there is no 'God-like' discursive vantage point from which to evaluate claims neutrally. Further, language is fundamentally non-representational, it does not depict a world out there but, rather, is a human tool constituted by and constituting of the social world (Wittgenstein, 1957). Hence, there are no universal philosophical foundations for human thought and action, all truth is culture bound or 'ethnocentric' (Rorty, 1991). Indeed, 'truth' can be understood as a form of commendation and social agreement rather than a form of universal knowledge. As such, truth claims are always implicated in questions of inclusion/exclusion and power/knowledge (chapter 7).

Yet, a writer such as Foucault can be critical of universal claims to truth and the disciplinary consequences of modern knowledge and institutions, while also deploying modern concepts like capitalism, discipline, power and so forth. Likewise, Rorty (1991) who argues that knowledge is 'ethnocentric', and alongside the postmodern philosopher Lyotard is critical of 'meta-narratives', is a supporter of the institutions of liberal democracy and what he calls 'Postmodernist Bourgeois Liberalism'. He does this on the grounds of pragmatism, that is to say from his vantage point liberal democracies are the best social and political systems humans have yet come up with, because they reduce suffering, though this does not mean that we should not try to 'do better' in the future. Thus it is, I contend, perfectly reasonable to hold to a postmodern epistemology yet argue for the expansion of a diverse public sphere, itself a modern concept, in the name of difference and diversity.

Television programmes are not simple reflections of the world but specific constructions of it and thus represent forms of knowledge about the world. Within a postmodern epistemology neither television's truth claims nor its aesthetic judgements can be held universally, they are inevitably culture and interest bound. Therefore, we should be concerned with the pragmatic social and political consequences of constructing and disseminating specific discursive constructions of the world rather than abstract questions of absolute truth or aesthetic quality. Since all forms of knowledge, including aesthetic and political judgements, are contestable we should seek from television a wide variety of forms of understanding and these forms of understanding should be debated in the public sphere. This argument echoes, in cultural form, Rorty's defence of postmodern liberalism.

This requirement for diversity needs to be understood in two senses. First, in terms of *diversity of representations*, an issue connected with questions of textual construction. Second, in terms of *diversity of programme types,* an issue connected to questions of the organization of television systems. Diversity as a concept links postmodern ideas about knowledge to the modern conception of the public sphere, so that, paradoxically, I argue that the future of the public sphere could and should lie with the acceptance of postmodern cultural diversity. This forms the basis of the political arguments of chapter 7, *The Politics of Television.*

To summarize, the organization of the book into sections partly reflects a conceptual division of the subject matter into questions of (a) institutions/political economy, (b) programme genres, (c) audiences, (d) culture, and (e) politics, but it also represents a modern/postmodern distinction by which I take television to be institutionally bound up with modernity but view culture, identities and knowledge claims through more postmodern lenses.

The dynamism of modernity

Television constitutes, and is a consequence of, the inherently globalizing nature of the institutions of modernity. Television is globalized because it is an institution of capitalist modernity while at the same time contributing to the globalization of modernity through the world-wide circulation of images and discourses. The western-originating institutions of modernity (capitalism, industrialism, surveillance and military power) are dynamic and globalizing because, as Giddens writes:

> The dynamism of modernity derives from the *separation of time and space* and their recombination in forms which permit the precise time–space 'zoning' of social life; the *disembedding* of social systems (a phenomenon which connects closely with the factors involved in time–space separation); and the *reflexive ordering and reordering* of social relations in the light of continual inputs of knowledge affecting the actions of individuals and groups. (Giddens, 1990, pp. 16–17)

In chapter 4 we shall see how television is implicated in the time–space zoning of social life. For example, watching the soap opera *Neighbours* in the front room as a 'tea-time' family event can be understood in terms of the routines of daily life. Likewise, the introduction of television into China and rural India has arguably restructured the relationship between work time and leisure time in new domestic spaces (chapter 4). However, for the present we shall be more concerned with the relationship between the institutions of modernity and the concept of globalization. In particular, the development of abstract clock-time allows time, space and place (locales) to be separated from each other. Modernity fosters relations between 'absent' others, transactions are conducted across time and space and any given place is penetrated and shaped by social influences quite distant from it. This is interwoven with the disembedding or 'lifting out' of social relations from a local context and their restructuring across time and space. Giddens cites, in particular, symbolic tokens (e.g. money) and expert systems. Thus, the development of money and professional knowledge allows social relations to be stretched (or distanciated) across time and space, not least in the form of the stock market whereby financial experts conduct their business twenty-four hours a day across the entire planet using electronic communications as they abstract material resources into the numerical format of monetary transactions.

A number of factors can be seen to structure patterns of time–space distanciation (the processes by which societies are 'stretched' over spans of time and space), including the development of cities, changes in transportation and the expanded surveillance powers of the nation-state. The commodification of time, so that it becomes separate from lived experience, and the development of forms of communication and information control which separate presence in time from presence in space, is of particular significance (Giddens, 1985; 1990; 1991). For example, this is manifested by the midnight e-mail, arriving at 6 a.m. and stored until read, from a producer in London to an actor in New York. Further, television plays a direct role in this process as foreign programmes penetrate local meaning systems and display alternative understandings of time and space. In particular, the increase in live global coverage (e.g. CNN's of the Gulf War) and the emergence of the global totemic festival (Olympics, World Cup, Live Aid) may help to magnify a sense of global time and shrinking space. However, while the ease with which electronic media appear to create, through world-wide instantaneous activities and images, a sense of global time, it may, as Ferguson (1990) argues, be more a question of the overlaying of local notions of time–space with alternative definitions, thus relativizing both and creating new senses of ambiguity and uncertainty.

The dynamism of modernity is founded upon its reflexive nature, the continual re-evaluation of knowledge. Modern life involves the constant examination and alteration of social practices in the light of incoming information about those practices. On one level 'reflexivity' can refer to the continual monitoring of action, a process which is intrinsic to being human, since 'all human beings continuously monitor the circumstances of their activities as a feature of doing what they do' (Giddens, 1991, p. 35). Though 'routine reflexivity' of this type is not always 'held in the mind' during social activities (but is a 'taken-for-granted' aspect of 'pragmatic consciousness'), since agents are able to give reasons for their actions, reflexivity also has a more discursive meaning. Here reflexivity refers to the use of knowledge about social life as a constitutive element of it and refers to the constant revision of social activity in the light of new knowledge.

Both the discourses of television itself and the post-transmission talk of everyday life can be taken as forms of social knowledge in the light of which social life, including identity construction, takes place. Thus, a good deal of what most of us know about the globe and the vast array of human forms of life which inhabit our planet comes through television so that we can be world travellers even as we stay at home. News from the Persian Gulf, documentaries from the Amazon basin and music from Africa are all part of this process, as are the morality discourses of soap opera, the 'fly-on-the-wall' documentary about 'the state of marriage today' and *The Clothes Show* from the catwalks of Milan, all of which contribute to our conceptions of ourselves and our worlds, and in the light of which we construct and reconstruct ourselves. As we shall see later (chapter 6), the globalization of discourses about cultural life, in which television plays a signifcant part, increases the resources for identity construction and contributes to the development of hybrid cultural identities.

On a more institutional level television has been increasingly reflexive about its own status and production techniques. Television has a history and repeats that history within and across channels, this articulation of styles and histories contributes to the viewers understanding of TV history and thus 'television produces the conditions of an ironic knowingness' (Caughie, 1990). This includes the growth of self-conscious intertextuality, that is citation of one text within another, involving both explicit allusion to particular programmes and oblique references to other genre conventions and styles. This intertextuality is an aspect of enlarged cultural self-consciousness about the history and functions of cultural products including television. Thus, television contributes to our increasing reflexivity about ourselves, our culture, and the history, conditions and techniques of cultural production (chapter 5).

In contrast to this 'liberating' view of 'reflexivity' there is another version which puts more stress on the processes of discipline and control. The institutional terrain and the production of culture is increasingly commodified and controlled by transnational corporations so that western culture is almost completely a commercial one (chapter 5). The institutional reflexivity of global corporations who use television as a prime vehicle for advertising is part of the process by which modern organizations demand to know more about their own work-force and the purchasing practices of customers (who are television viewers). For Robins and Webster (1985), television is at the centre of a calculated strategy to control people's habits and routines. They place their analysis of television within the context of what they call the 'rationalization of control', by which is meant the increasing spread of calculative, methodical and deliberate means of conducting social affairs. Robins and Webster's contention is that the co-ordination of manufacture, distribution and marketing represents the extension of work-place discipline into all aspects of public and private life in a systematic and co-ordinated way. Television, they argue, is at the heart of this process emerging as it did in tandem with the expansion of consumer capitalism as the vehicle *par excellence* for advertising and the selling of consumer goods.

The Concept of Globalization

Not only is television self-evidently a global phenomenon in its production, exchange and consumption but it is part of popular consciousness that it is so. Globalization is constituted by a set of processes which are intrinsic to the dynamism of modernity and as a concept refers both to the compression of the world and the intensification of consciousness of the world as a whole (Robertson, 1992), that is, the ever increasing abundance of global connections and our understanding of them. As I have already suggested, the 'compression of the world' can be understood in terms of the institutions of modernity and thus globalization can be grasped in terms of the world capitalist economy, the nation-state system, the world military order and the global information system (Giddens, 1984; 1985), whereas the reflexive 'intensification of consciousness of the world' can be profitably viewed through more postmodern lenses.

On one level globalization is an economic phenomenon. One-half of the world's largest economic units are nations, the other half consists of transnational corporations. The top 200 transnationals, 89 of which are based in the USA and 25 in Japan, produce between a third and a half of world output. In the sphere of car production 22 firms produce 90 per cent of global production (Giddens, 1989). Such productive activity has to be financed and to do so an Australian-based company might consider Japanese loans arranged by a New York bank's London offices. These could be arranged at any time of the day or night with the aid of electronic communication. Globalization thus refers to economic activity on a global scale and is an aspect of time–space compression or the 'shrinking world'.

Global economic activity is not a new phenomenon and while scholars may differ over the precise historical dating we may at least agree that the sixteenth century saw an expansion of European mercantile trade beyond the borders of European nations to Asia, South America and the African continent. By the middle of the nineteenth century this mercantile period was giving way to a phase of more direct colonial control as the European powers scrambled to build an empire. In 1870 only one-tenth of Africa was under European colonial rule, by the end of the century only one-tenth was not so controlled. Colonial control involved military dominance, cultural ascendancy and the origins of economic dependency as colonial territory was turned into both a protected market for selected commodities from the imperial power and a provider of raw materials. Many colonial economies were reduced to a very limited range of commodity production. It is a matter of historical record that the early twentieth century saw a series of successful anti-colonial struggles and independence movements. By this time the economies of these countries were not only integrated into the world economic order (Wallerstein, 1974) but had been put in a position of dependency and 'underdevelopment' (Frank, 1967).

Economic globalization has been a process of creating a world economy, though one which has grown in an uneven way. Both 'world systems theory' (Wallerstein) and 'dependency theory' (Frank) in their protests against global inequality tend to obscure some of the differences between regions; we need to recognize degrees of incorporation into the world economic order and the various levels of economic development. There are, for example, not only differences between the western capitalist zone and the former eastern bloc nations, but also between newly industrializing nations like Brazil, Mexico, Taiwan, South Korea, Hong Kong, Singapore and the seven poorest nations on earth: Chad, Bangladesh, Ethiopia, Nepal, Mali, Burma and Zaire (Worsley, 1990).

Globalization is also concerned with issues of cultural meaning, including issues of texts, representation and identity. This is an enormous field of concerns which I do not intend to explore fully here. At this stage I simply wish to raise some interrelated issues. For example, Walter Benjamin (1973) pointed out the way in which 'originals' associated with the rituals of specific places (art galleries, theatres) were being outstripped by art made specifically for reproduction so that 'originality', in the historical sense, becomes the luxury preserve of the wealthy. The contemporary implications of this are manifold, but include the idea that culture can span time and place, that culture in the age of *electronic* reproduction will come to us via the screen, video, radio, etc. rather than us going to it in a ritualized space. Cultural artefacts and meanings from different historical periods and geographical places can mix together and be juxtaposed.

The values and meanings attached to place remain significant, but the networks in which people are involved extend far beyond their physical locations. The combination of historical population migration with the world-wide circulation of images has created new global identities so that, for example, black people in Brixton, Johannesburg or New York may have forms of solidarity and sympathy with each other far stronger than any they have with their next-door neighbour. Democratic forces world-wide may show solidarity with the students of Tiananmen Square by employing fax machines, and Greenpeace can come to form a globally-effective campaigning organization, not least through the strategic use of television images (Hebdige, 1990).

As Hebdige (1990) argues, cosmopolitanism is an aspect of day-to-day life. Diverse and remote cultures are becoming accessible today (as signs and commodities) via our televisions, radios, supermarkets and shopping centres. We may choose to eat 'Indian', dress 'Italian', watch 'American' and listen 'African'. However, such globalizing cultural tendencies need to be counterpoised to the re-emergence of the politics of place. Thus, attachment to place can be seen in the renewal of forms of Eastern European nationalism, neo-fascist politics and, to some degree, Islamic fundamentalism which, though itself having global aspirations, can be understood in part as a response to the spread and perceived threat of western modernity. All the examples above are to do with cultural difference and the creation of new alliances across national boundaries connected with those identities. Are we witnessing, then, the creation of regional or even global meanings shared by the majority of people? Is there in any sense a global culture? To the degree that there is, television is playing a significant role in international image and information flows.

If by 'global culture' we mean a unitary world culture, or a bounded culture connected to a world state, then we are a long way from such a scenario. As Smith (1990) has pointed out, cultures tend to be particular, time-bound and expressive of identities which historical circumstances have formed over long periods. Such cultural feelings and values refer to three components of shared experience: a sense of generational continuity, shared memories of specific events and people, and a common sense of destiny on the part of the collectivity. As yet, Smith argues, there is little in the way of shared world memories to underpin a global culture. On the other hand, we may be able to identify global cultural processes, of both cultural integration and disintegration, which are independent of inter-state relations. Some of these processes represent homogenization, particularly in the field of commodities and consumer culture, so that Coca Cola, the Big Mac and *Dallas* are known world-wide, while others involve ethnic resilience, fragmentation and the re-emergence of powerful nationalistic sentiments associated with the myths, memories and symbols of local places rather than global spaces.

Clifford (1992), amongst others, has argued that culture and cultural identities can no longer be adequately understood in terms of place, but are better conceptualized in terms of travel. This includes peoples and cultures which travel and places/cultures as sites of criss-crossing travellers. In one sense this has always been the case; consider Britain as at various moments populated by Celts, Saxons, Vikings, Normans, Romans, Afro-Caribbeans, Asians, etc. so that the 'English' language is a hybrid of words from all over the world. Likewise, the USA, home of native American Indians,

English, French, Spanish, Africans, Mexicans, Irish, Poles and too many more to mention. However, the accelerated globalization of late-modernity has increased the relevance of the metaphor of travel because all locales are now subject to the influences of distant places. Such influences include electronic communication like television, so that we can all be travellers from the comfort of our front rooms.

Further, at any given moment, identity of place, that is national identity, is only one competing subject position amongst many others. This is a stance underlined by Giddens (1985) when he argues that, for most people most of the time, national identity is not at the forefront of their minds. Identity and meaningful experience are much more likely to arise in the realms of the private spheres of family, friends and sexual relationships. Since day-to-day life is one geared to routine, national sentiments are not only distinct from them but tend to rise and fall according to circumstances.

While such processes are evident across the boundaries of nation-states the continued resilience and significance of the state is also a feature of our times. What we are seeing is a set of economic and cultural processes dating from different historical periods and with different developmental rhythms being overlaid upon each other, creating global disjunctures as well as new global connections and similarities. For example, the expansion of capitalism, the globalization of financial flows, the movements of ethnic peoples, the development of technology, the spread of the media and the diffusion of ideologies are not set in any inevitable or fixed relationship to one another: rather the need is to try and understand just exactly *how* they are related (Smith, 1990). The relationship between economic globalization and world cultural processes is thus not straightforward. Having said that, many of these issues *are* bound up with the economics of capitalism and consumer culture which represents a decisive though – not wholly determining – moment.

Capitalism and 'Global Television'

The globalization of television is an aspect of the dynamism of modernity inflected with the logic of capitalism. Capitalism is a system of commodity production premised upon the private ownership and control of the means of production whereby the owners of the means of production employ wage labour to produce commodities, which have exchange value, for sale in the market. The dynamics of capitalism stem from the pursuit of profit as the primary goal and a capitalist mode of production thus requires the constant production of new commodities and new markets so that capitalism is inherently expansionist and dynamic in its quest for those markets.

Television is bound up with capitalist modernity both as a set of economic activities and as a cultural force constituted by and constitutive of modernity. The rise of transnational television since the mid-1980s is, thus, an aspect of capitalist globalization whereby this essentially economically driven set of activities is *also* a set of cultural practices involving the circulation of ideas and images around the world. This expansion of global television as a set of economic and cultural practices has itself been enabled by technological and political developments which are re-structuring the world 'television order' (chapter 2).

While there is money to be made from the production and sale of television programmes these are also a means to sell the technological hardware of television, from satellites to sets, and to deliver audiences to advertisers so that television stands at the centre of wider commercial activities and is central to the expansion of consumer capitalism. Television is the vehicle *par excellence* for advertising and, thus, the selling of consumer goods. While advertisers initially aimed for the maximum number of viewers they increasingly target specific market segments and kinds of audiences. Though public service television, like the BBC, may sustain a degree of independence from the calculations of capitalist corporations, the increased commercialization of television, the apparent erosion of the public sphere, and the emergence of global communications networks, threatens its existence as television is increasingly part of a world-marketing strategy.

Herbert Schiller (1969; 1976; 1985) follows Wallerstein in describing a world economic system consisting of a global capitalist economy in which the core countries of the developed west dominate the peripheral 'developing' nations. Schiller emphasizes both the systematic and integrated nature of modern global capitalism and the critical role of the multinational and transnational corporations within it. He points to the global domination of the international communications industries by US-controlled corporations and to the interlocking between US television networks, defence sub-contractors and the Federal government. The picture he paints is one of US global economic dominance detrimental to the rest of the world and the developing nations in particular. Schiller extends the logic of his argument to make the case that the media fit into the world system of capitalism by providing ideological support for capitalism and the transnational corporations in particular. Though, as this book develops, we shall have reasons to doubt the coherence of Schiller's account, especially in relation to the concept of media imperialism, his description of global capitalism is a useful starting point.

Capitalism is not static, it is ever changing. Since at least the mid-1970s the economic globalization process has taken on a new dimension of time–space compression as leading transnational companies sought to boost profits in the face of saturated western markets, competition from newly industrializing nations, oil price rises and the failure to stabilize the world finance markets. In short, global recession hastened a renewed globalization of world economic activity involving the speed-up of production and consumption turnover assisted by the use of information and communication technology (Harvey, 1989). By time–space compression is meant the processes that change the qualities of space and time that we experience and our conceptions of it. Compression refers to the speed-up in the pace of life and the overcoming of spatial barriers (associated with the history and spread of capitalism) and is clearly a relative term involving comparison with previous conditions. In other words, it is bound up with our experience of a 'shrinking world'. In the sense used above, globalization refers to a set of related economic activities which are specifically to be understood as the practices of capitalism. Television as an economic phenomenon is clearly bound up with this process through the increased activity of transnational communications corporations, international co-productions and the global sale of television programmes.

The speed-up of production/consumption turnover has been enabled by new flexible production techniques and the use of telecommunications on a global scale. What is sometimes called post-Fordism,

> rests on flexibility with respect to labour processes, labour markets, products, and patterns of consumption. It is characterised by the emergence of entirely new sectors of production, new ways of providing financial services, new markets, and, above all, greatly

intensified rates of commercial, technological and organisational innovation. (Harvey, 1989, p. 147)

These flexible manufacturing systems are integrated with the 'customization' of design and quality, niche marketing and consumer 'life-styles'. An integral part of these developments has been a rapid expansion of communications technologies and a movement from viewing information as enabling commodity production to recognizing that information is itself a key commodity. Indeed, they are part of the restructuring of capitalism on a global scale which, for Lash and Urry (1987; 1994), is now a 'disorganized' set of global flows of capital, resources and people. Their analysis stresses the global nature of capitalism, the power of transnational corporations and the difficulties faced by states trying to regulate its operation. Place remains significant as an intersection or nodal point of global flows but in unpredictable ways.

Developments in television are part of a wider set of changes to communications industries as a whole. As Dyson and Humphreys (1990) note, four key ideas have dominated the communications sector: de-regulation, globalization, synergy and convergence. These interdependent and interconnected forces are applicable both to the manoeuvrings of corporations and the strategies of governments. They are interconnected because the forces behind the radical changes in telecommunications have been a combination of techno-logical developments and *market* change. This has contributed both to the creation of global communications giants and to the *convergence* (or erosion of boundaries) between sectors. Thus, tech-nological developments such as the unfolding of fibre-optic cable, satellite technology and digital-switching technology have opened up commercial possibilities which have led to telecommunications being hailed by corporation and state alike as *the* industry of the future.

The growth of telecommunications industries has been a matter not just of technology *per se* but of the demand for information. In particular, transnational companies have become dependent on telecommunications services to develop their own internal corporate communications on a global scale and to sell services and technology to others. The global scale of transnational capitalist organizations has put communications at the heart of world business. According to Schiller (1985), the development of the International Services

Digital Network (ISDN) is a mechanism both for servicing the information and communication requirements of transnational corporations and of further incorporating developing nations into the world economic order.

Associated with transnational global corporations is the pressure to *de-regulate* in all aspects of communications so that the influence of private companies begins to erode and eclipse the traditional public post and telecommunications organizations of Europe, Japan and Australia. De-regulation was seen by political forces as essential in order to compete in international markets, thus the Thatcher government in Britain and the new right of Reagan in the USA gave the whole economic process political and ideological reinforcement. The USA in particular has been at the forefront of such developments, not only in terms of de-regulation within its own borders, but in undermining international regulatory bodies such as the International Telecommunications Union and INTELSAT.

Corporations have sought to create *synergy* via vertical integration drawing together equipment manufacturers, information providers and transmitters. There has been a good deal of diversification by financial, computer and data-processing companies into telecommunications creating multi-media giants who dominate sectors of the market. New digital technology is one of the mechanisms driving a global communications shake-up making mergers between companies in the computer, entertainment and telecommunications sectors far more inviting. Further, companies need the financial power that can come from mergers to undertake the massive investment needed to be players in the global market. For example, in 1989 the merger of Time and Warner created the largest media group in the world with a market capitalization of $25 billion. This was followed in 1995 by Time-Warner's acquisition of Turner Broadcasting (CNN). In late 1993 the merger of Paramount communications, maker of such films as *The Firm* and *Indecent Proposal*, and Viacom, owner of MTV amongst other assets, saw the emergence of a $17 billion company making it the fifth largest media group behind Time-Warner, News Corporation, Bertelsmann and Walt Disney. We may note that four out of five of these companies are based in the USA, the exception being the German-based Bertelsmann. The Paramount–Viacom merger illustrates the commercial advantages of integration as it put a vast array of assets under one corporate roof: a Hollywood studio, cable systems, television and radio stations, and a book publisher. The preoccupation with combining software and hardware is well illustrated by the recent film *Last Action Hero*. This Schwarzenegger 'blockbuster' was made by Columbia Pictures, owned by the Sony Corporation. The soundtrack came from CBS, also owned by Sony and it was screened in cinemas with digital sound systems made by Sony. In addition, Sony produced virtual reality and video games based on the film.

Conclusions

The purpose of this chapter has been to elaborate on a number of the theoretical principles that are embedded in the remainder of this book and from which we can conclude the following:

- Global television needs to be understood historically and sociologically in the wider context of the globalization of capitalist modernity which itself is a set of economic and cultural phenomena operating unevenly across the planet. Globalization is constituted by a set of processes which are intrinsic to the dynamism of modernity and as a concept refers both to the compression of the world and the intensification of consciousness of the world as a whole. Of particular significance are the concepts of time and space separation, time–space compression, disembedding mechanisms and the reflexive ordering and reordering of social life.
- Television is bound up with wider social forces both as a set of economic activities and as a cultural force constitutive of and constituted by capitalist modernity. We noted the changing character of television, in particular the growing organization of television along commercial rather than public service lines. Developments in television are part of a wider set of changes to communications industries as a whole and we registered four key processes that have dominated the communications sector: de-regulation, globalization, synergy and convergence.
- Understanding global television requires a multi-dimensional and multi-perspectival approach which would seek to understand the connections between the economic, political, social and cultural dimensions of society without reducing social phenomena to any one dimension. While the globalization of the institutions of televison readily can be grasped in terms of 'modernity', the reflexive nature of contemporary culture has often been best documented in terms of postmodernism. Postmodernism as a cultural form is a

marker of 'radicalized modernity' and can be regarded as the cultural sensibility thereof.

- Television, which is at the heart of domestic life and public culture in the west, and is rapidly spreading across the globe, is a significant vantage point to illustrate wider global processes. Indeed, an examination of global television suggests that the notion of 'society' as bounded by place and space is increasingly inadequate for the task of describing and evaluating the condition of humanity as we enter the twenty-first century.

2

What is Global Television?

The concept of global television suggests two related phenomena. First, the term implies all the various configurations of public and commercial television which are regulated, funded and viewed within the boundaries of nation-states and/or language communities. A discussion of global television would therefore be concerned with British, American, Indian, and Australian television amongst others. It would also be concerned with Inuit and Aboriginal television. A second meaning of the term global television refers to television which in its technology, ownership, programme distribution and audiences operates across the boundaries of nation-states and language communities. Global television in this sense means transnational television.

The current interest in global television stems from the rise in transnational television and the perceived threats that it poses to the more bounded television services of nation-states. These 'threats' are described in terms of the economics of television, the regulation of television and the identities, particularly national identities, which are deemed to be in part the product of national television services. These concerns are cut across by another set of considerations, namely those of public service television counterpoised to commercial television. Much of the globe, for example, Europe, Australia and India amongst others, has a tradition of public service television funded and regulated by the state. In contrast, transnational television is commercial television driven by the profit motive. While there have been some, relatively weak, attempts at transnational regulation, for example, by the European Union, it is the ability of transnational television to escape or circumvent regulation that has caused concern to some commentators. These concerns are expressed in terms of programming range and quality, political and moral boundaries and the commodification of culture. In addition, transnational television has been associated with American finance, ownership and programming leading to accusations of poor quality, commercialism and threats to national identity. This was encapsulated in the then French Minister of Culture Jack Lang's well-known phrase 'wall-to-wall *Dallas*'.

The aim of this chapter is to map the political economy of global television with particular reference to the changing patterns of state public television and commercial transnational television. Where possible I have used up-to-date statistics to illustrate the patterns involved. However, this is a notoriously turbulent field subject to rapid change and I don't doubt that in the period between the writing and reading of this book these figures will have changed. Nevertheless, one would expect the broad patterns of transformation to be as described irrespective of modifications to specific details.

The Changing Face of Television: De-regulation and Re-regulation

One significant arena of change has been in the field of television regulation. As Michael (1990) remarks, there is very little in human life which is not subject to 'regulation' of one sort or another. If television was not regulated by public authorities, it would still be regulated by the laws of the market. Most television services have formal and informal rules regarding who has access to the means of production and distribution, not to mention the informal rules of who can say what in which particular style. Television is also regulated by the laws of the land in areas such as libel, obscenity, public order, ownership and free speech. The purpose of regulation has been to influence the range and quality of programmes and the degree of universalism attached to the service. Thus public service regulations have been enacted in order to ensure a · universal service together with a range of programmes designed to uphold the purposes of education, information and entertainment. Television systems with less public service regulation, for example, in the USA, have relied on the market to deliver what consumers want. The forms of regulation have varied across the television services of different nation-states. India has had, until recently, a regulatory system which has stressed the direct role of the state in controlling the development of television both economically and in terms of programme content. In contrast, the USA has developed a system which emphasizes First Amendment rights of free speech and private ownership alongside the economic primacy of the market place. The UK and Australia have traditionally had a regulatory environment which has given a major role to the state supplemented by a system of franchises to the commercial sector.

The initial regulatory frameworks for television were set up when over-the-air broadcasting was the only means of transferring signals from the broadcaster to the television set. State regulation was justified on the grounds of natural monopoly and the need, under those circumstances, to regulate frequency use to avoid general and military signal jamming, and to exert a degree of direction over content, either in terms of citizens rights to information or a state's interest in moral and political control.

The 1980s and early 1990s have been periods of de-regulation and re-regulation of television. This has been occasioned by a number of factors. The growth of 'new' communication technologies has invalidated the natural monopoly argument since digital technology allows frequencies to be further split and alternative delivery systems employed. They have also helped to make television an international medium requiring us to think in terms of transnational and regional regulation. Both these developments have been hastened by the transnational economic logic of commercial television. The legal rights to communicate and the adoption of diversity as a key public principle have been upheld by court rulings in various countries (Porter, 1989). This, allied to a new governmental enthusiasm for the market in the USA, UK and parts of continental Europe, has fuelled de-regulation. This de-regulation has mainly taken the form of relaxing monopolies and ownership rules together with increasing the number of television services available. This has been connected to the increased funding of television by commercial means in preference to forms of taxation.

The arguments of free marketers (Velganouski and Bishop, 1983) and de-regulators (Peacock, 1986) suggest that the public interest is best served by allowing the 'robust consumer' to identify and act in his or her best interests rather than have choices made by what they see as the cultural elitists of the media establishment. Indeed, Peacock not only views the broadcasting authorities as less able to ascertain viewers' interests, but as having been captured by producers' interests. Almost unlimited television channels regulated only by the price mechanism would give, it is argued, consumers 'sovereignty' because they will view only what they are prepared to pay for and producers, being profit seekers, will make programmes the viewers want. This unbridled commercialism would not only enable the making of programmes of broad appeal but also provide narrowcasting for devotees of the arts, for ethnic minorities and for community groups, since significant sections of the population would be prepared to pay for them.

The opposite view has been consistently put by Garnham (1980; 1983; 1990) who argues that the motive for change lies not with consumer choice but the needs of the electronics industries to find new markets. Further, he argues that real choice is not forthcoming because the capital costs of television, especially for the 'new' cable and satellite operators, is so high and the profit margins consequently tight that the temptation is to use low-cost programming of poor quality often imported or dug up from the archives. Garnham goes on to point out that advertising-financed media like the press have not maintained a position of multiple outlets but have tended towards near-monopoly ownership and similarity of content. The extreme logic of market-led television would be in the direction of pay-TV which, as Garnham argues, undermines the principle of universal access.

In his examination of the US television system, Blumler (1986) points out that an advertising-financed service develops pressures to maximize audiences and programme popularity above all else. The consequences for programming appear to be not an increase in range and quality but the reverse so that at any given moment the viewers' choice of programmes is limited. Formats across networks are very similar, programmes are pitched at a limited section of the population (excluding the poor), and certain programme forms such as arts programmes, single plays, documentaries and community programmes are limited or absent. This does not mean of course that American television does not make 'good' programmes, indeed there seems to be some evidence (Winston, 1986) that the increased competition faced by the networks has led them to seek 'cable resistant' programming of higher quality, rather it is a reflection on the lack of diversity.

De-regulation and commercial expansion have prompted widespread discussion about *new trends* in television. In Europe the 'old order' was marked by the subordination of broadcasting to public service goals set in the context of a broadly political process of regulation. Television was of a largely national character and was generally non-commercial in principle (McQuail, De Mateo, Tapper, 1992). Four interrelated developments have set in motion forces which have destabilized the old order and which may herald a new one (Sepstrup, 1989b). First, there has been a perceived growth in the technical possibilities of television, specifically computers, Direct Broadcast Satellite and fibre-optic cables. Second, there is an emergent desire to exploit these technical possibilities for economic profitability both on the part of commercial companies, notably transnationals, and on the part of nation-states wishing to fuel economic growth via the 'information society'. A third trend has been the enactment of new media policies in the light of other developments and, in particular, to de-regulate and re-regulate the television environment. A vogue for market solutions and the decline in government support for public service institutions has been in evidence. Lastly, there is an apparent consumer demand for more choice in television and a degree of dissatisfaction with the established order. This argument needs to be approached with caution since one can mistake the arguments and self-interest of transnational companies and free market politicians for a genuine public voice. The uptake of DBS and cable, for example, is very patchy and seems to be strongest where public service provision is of poor quality (Collins, 1990).

What is Happening to 'Public Service' Television?

While the 'public interest' does not necessarily imply state-regulated public service organizations, in practice the philosophy has been pursued through specific institutions like the British or Australian Broadcasting Corporations. A survey of public service television will reveal that there is no single model but there are identifiable themes which are described by Brants and Siune (1992) as:

- Some form of accountability to political representatives of the public via administrative organization.
- Some element of public finance.
- Regulation of content.
- A universal service which addresses citizens.
- A degree of protection from competition.

These elements of a public service model give rise to structural and institutional arrangements which were intended to offer account-ability, access, and adequacy or quality of programming (Kellner, 1990). In terms of what Blumler (1992) called 'vulnerable values', public service television would aim to offer a universal and compre-hensive service with balanced, impartial, accurate and diverse programming. The wider political and cultural implications being support for the integrity of political communication, the fostering of cultural diversity and identities, the maintenance of standards and the welfare of children. These, albeit contestable, concepts were seen to be outcomes of public support, namely, predictable revenues, universal availability, high audience reach and diversified programme and production capabilities (Hulten and Brants, 1992). Since the mid-1980s there have been radical changes in the global broadcasting order and high on the agenda of discussion amongst commentators has been the potential threat to public television that these developments pose.

The 'new order' in television is marked by the coexistence of public and commercial broadcasting, the deregulation of com-mercial television, the increasing emergence of multi-media transnational companies and pressure on public service television to operate with a commercial logic. The threats to public television are

Table 2.1   *Market share of public TV corporations (by share of viewing time)*

	1975 (%)	1990 (%)
Germany	100	69
Italy	91	46
France	100	33
Netherlands	100	58
United Kingdom	52	48

Source: The European Institute for Media: Adapted from Sanchez-Tabernero (1993).

in terms of finance, audience share, programme production/ acquisition and scheduling practices. The data in table 2.1 certainly suggest a decline, though not a terminal one, in the viewing figures for public television in Europe.

The commercialization of public television itself has taken the form of the introduction of advertising on public television (Italy and India), the increased involvement of public television in commercial merchandising (BBC and ABC), the greater use of outside independent production companies, and, most significant of all (but the hardest to quantify), the apparent drift of public television into more competitive scheduling practices. These strategies have been set against a background of financial stringency in public television. Global recession and ideological commitments have led governments to seek cuts in the costs of public television.

Overall, public service television is showing little sign of growing. Any growth in the television world is being done by commercial concerns. At the same time not much of public television has actually disappeared, it has proved resilient in the face of competition. Many public service television organizations have tried to retain a full range of programmes including programmes less attractive to the commercial sector; there is some evidence that this is successful. For example, in Australia the ABC has consistently improved its ratings, in Italy the combined RAI channels rate better than the combined commercial channels, in India the state-funded Doordarshan is fighting back against commercial opposition and in Britain the BBC looks set to remain a major player for the foreseeable future.

In the face of commercial competition public television would appear to have three distinct programming strategies. First, public television could choose to compete on the same ground and on the same terms as its competitors. This could only result in a 'dilution' of range and quality and a loss of distinctiveness for public television. This appears to be not only undesirable but suicidal. If public television is a copy of commercial television, what possible justification would there be for its existence let alone its public funding? The opposite strategy would be to go for a high quality, distinctive programming menu which catered for those programme types which commercial television had sidelined. This might include certain kinds of original drama and extended news and current affairs. The problem with this strategy is that while it might meet the needs of range and diversity across the system, it is a minority audience strategy which would lead the public service institutions into decline. It would require major and long-term political support which does not seem likely to be forthcoming. Besides which, it is a strategy which marginalizes both the institutions and the programmes. Perhaps the most viable strategy for public television is to maintain a full range of programme types from drama to quiz shows and sport to documentary but to establish a distinctiveness and quality by promoting the best of all kinds of programme.

Despite the *general* trend towards more commercial television and less regulated public service television the path of change has not been a uniform one. Different configurations are emerging within the context of different nation-states.

Case Studies: Australia, the Netherlands, India, the UK, the USA

Described below are the basic patterns of change in a number of countries. These are only brief 'thumb-nail' sketches of developments in order to highlight recent trends and emergent issues.

Australia

Australia has a dual system of public and commercial television. The National Service is provided by the non-commercial statutory body, the Australian Broadcasting Corporation. Commercial television is made up of a series of private stations, many of whom are organized into networks, particularly in the four major cities of Sydney, Melbourne, Brisbane and Adelaide. While the ABC remains the most extensive national network, much of Australia now has the commercial networks Channel 7, Channel 9 and Channel 10. The relative ratings of the networks fluctuate but in the early 1990s the ABC was taking between a 15 per cent to 20 per cent share of the audience alongside the lowest rated commercial network (Channel 10) with channels 7 and 9 out front sharing the remainder. Since 1980 a new player in the television game has been the Special Broadcasting Service (SBS) which serves the state capital cities and aims to provide multi-cultural television. SBS has attracted around a 2 per cent share.

The ABC is legally required to be both a broadcaster and a major producer of programmes. In this it is modelled on the British

Broadcasting Corporation. The commercial stations and networks on the other hand tend to act as publishers rather than producers. Programme schedules are made up of a combination of imports, station-produced programmes (usually news and game shows) and programmes brought in from 'packagers' who make and sell programmes. Over the years there have been many commercial packagers but the two largest and most consistent have been Crawford Productions and The Grundy Organisation. Indeed, the latter is not only a major supplier to the networks but one of the largest independent programme producers in the world.

The ABC is financed by a direct government grant rather than by licence fee which has led some to argue that the corporation is at the mercy of its political masters. The ABC does not carry advertisements, the main source of finance for the commercial stations, though it does carry out some commercial merchandising activities. The Corporation also seeks to sell programmes abroad or to enter into co-production agreements. Programme sales are of course the main financial objective of the 'packagers'.

Albert Moran (1985; 1989) argues that Australian television can be seen to have developed through three distinct phases. The first, from 1956 to 1965, was a period in which television can be seen as 'radio with pictures'. The second phase, 1965–75, saw the extension of local television production from game shows to the field of drama. The third period, taking us to the present day, is marked by the introduction of new technologies, the rise of media conglomerates, growing internationalization and an increasing overlap with the film production industry. In the first period of development stations were primarily concerned with the capital costs of running a station and gave little commitment to programme production other than in the cheapest form of variety show. Thus the screens tended to be filled with American- and British-originated programmes. The rise of network formation during the second phase meant that there was a shortage of imported programmes, this helped to prompt the expansion of more local production into drama. While the ABC continued to produce programmes in-house a good deal of the commercial stations screen time was made for them by 'packagers'. The third phase has seen the development of satellites as a significant technology, the buying and selling of the networks, a period of de-regulation and the emergence of the mini-series as a programme form.

The second half of the 1980s saw considerable changes of fortune in the Australian television scene. In 1986 the Hawke Labour government ended the two-station rule which restricted individual ownership of television stations in two of the five state capitals. Ownership would be restricted instead in terms of total audience reach of stations owned by the same company. This was originally proposed at 75 per cent but was enacted at 60 per cent. This de-regulation, combined with the launching of Aussat satellites in 1986 and 1987, made national commercial networks both technically and legally feasible as well as financially tempting. Simultaneously, cross-media ownership constraints were introduced to reduce the common control of newspapers, television and radio. These developments triggered a spate of station buying and selling. Between December 1986 and September 1988, 12 out of the 15 stations in capital cities changed hands leaving an increased concentration of station ownership (Murdock, 1990; *The Listener*, 21 June 1990).

Meanwhile, there has been something of a change in fortune for the ABC. From the mid 1970s to the mid-1980s the ABC was subject to annual financial revue and consistently saw its budget eroded. The corporation lost key creative staff to commercial television, output fell, particularly in the field of expensive drama, and the ratings followed. Under 'new management' the corporation has been able to regularize its finances, increase its production of locally produced drama, cut its costs to a level where it is competitive with outside production houses and, above all, increase its ratings from a low point of a 10 per cent share in the 1970s to a high point of 20 per cent (*Variety*, April 1990; *The Times*, 12 May 1992). After a major de-regulatory period public television has fought back to attract an audience fed up with the increase in American imports which followed the commercial networks shake-up.

There is a sense in which Australian television has been subject to internationalizing influences since its inception. The institutions were modelled on those of the UK and USA, and programming has always involved a substantial level of imports from those countries. At the same time Australia has adopted measures to encourage Australian production and established itself as a viable exporter of programmes (most famously in the field of the serial with *Neighbours, Home and Away, Sons and Daughters, Prisoner* and *A Country Practice*). Perhaps more significant is the relatively successful strategy of the public service ABC after a period of financial stringency and falling ratings left it wallowing in the doldrums. This strategy has crucially involved a deliberate policy of producing Australian drama about Australian issues in an Australian context while attempting to retain high production values. The Corporation also has plans to extend its news service across the globe including link-ups with foreign news channels. Despite increased programme success the Corporation still faces financial problems and complains of $A 120 million lost off its budget in ten years. In Australia, as elsewhere in the world, the continued success of public television depends on the political will to make it happen.

The Netherlands

As a relatively small nation the Netherlands is particularly vulnerable to transnational pressures. Smaller countries tend to suffer from problems of dependence, resource shortage, market size, vulnerability and corporatism (Meier and Trappel, 1992). There are three major trends in Dutch television. First, is a general extension of programming hours; second, is the general commercialization of public television; and third is the growing penetration of satellite stations.

Dutch public service regulations stress the need for freedom of expression, diversity, individual preference and the protection of Dutch culture. This translates into television as an organizing principle by which stations are run by social, cultural, political and religious movements. In the early days of Dutch television there was a strict 'pillarization' of broadcasting and only broadcasters with ties to the 'main streams in society' could operate. Thus television was dominated by VARA for the socialists, KRO for the Catholics, NCRV and VPRO for the Protestants, and AVRO for the commercial–liberal sphere. The 1969 Broadcasting Act weakened the pillar system but did not abandon it. Rather, it was opened up to other interests as long as they aimed 'at satisfying cultural, religious or spiritual needs felt amongst the population' and added to the existing pluriformity. They are also required by law, as are all TV corporations, to offer a range of programme types (to which minimum percentages are now attached). In addition, a Dutch Broadcasting Foundation (NOS) was founded to act alongside existing organizations and to be both more independent and supply programmes not otherwise produced.

There are eight main broadcasting organizations in Holland who share three public TV channels. The division of air-time is operated on the basis of public membership levels with the exception of NOS who, with no membership, are allocated twice the broadcasting time of even the largest of the other organizations. Class A broadcasters receive twelve hours television time a week and this covers the 'committed' VARA, KRO, NCRV, and the popular more entertainment led AVRO, TROS and VOO. Class B broadcasters, the liberal/progressive VPRO and the evangelical EO, are allocated seven hours per week. The channel divisions, reorganized in 1992, find KRO, NCRV, EO and AVRO on Nederland 1. TROS, VOO, VARA and VPRO are located on Nederland 2, with NOS and a few small non-membership channels on Nederland 3. At present over 93 per cent of Holland is cabled and viewers often have a choice of up to 19 public channels including those from the Netherlands, Germany, Britain and Belgium, as well as a local cable channel. Despite this apparent choice the ratings during the early 1990s are dominated by RTL4 (26%), the commercial satellite channel and the public channels, Nederland 1 (20%), Nederland 2 (19%) and Nederland 3 (12%).

National broadcasting in the Netherlands is funded from the licence fee (65%) and advertising revenue (35%). The national broadcasting organizations also receive an independent income from sales of their guides and membership fees. Anyone who owns a television has to pay the licence fee. The minister responsible decides how much money is to be made available to broadcasting and the Media Authority then distribute this money on the basis of a fixed hourly rate and the amount of air-time allocated. Local cable is funded by a combination of municipal funds, subscriptions, donations, membership fees and advertising. All advertisements on public channels are handled by the non-profit Radio and Television Advertising Association (STER) and have been traditionally placed in fixed blocks outside of programmes. Up to 15 per cent of advertising can now be placed outside of the fixed blocks, that is, beside different programmes, and some spot advertising within programmes is expected. Money spent on advertising is some 15 per cent below the European average and a rise in the amount and influence of advertising is likely. The revenues from advertising are distributed proportionally to the broadcasting organizations by STER though some goes to the press as compensation for loss of advertising revenue (4%) and some to a special fund to stimulate Dutch cultural productions by public broadcasters.

The Netherlands has had a public broadcasting regulatory system for the entirety of its television history. Until 1991 television stations were not permitted to operate on a commercial basis over the airwaves. During 1990 the government introduced a bill to permit commercial broadcasting though at time of writing no national commercial network has emerged. The Netherlands is unusual in its recently planned introduction of a third public channel intended to counter the threat of commercial satellite television. In this, one would have to say, it has not been notably successful.

In 1986 there were some 12 foreign channels being received in Holland with potential reception rates of between 84 per cent and 24 per cent with the average viewer able to pick up six of them (Bekkers, 1987). At the time, the consistent viewing of Dutch channels over foreign channels seemed to give the public service institutions grounds for optimism. Since then the arrival and immense success of RTL4 has made the situation rather more dramatic. RTL4 a Luxembourg-based (partly Dutch owned) satellite television channel has captured a quarter of the viewing audience since its inception in 1989. In this, it has been assisted by the fact that Holland is one of the most densely cabled countries in Europe and it is not necessary to own a DBS dish to receive RTL4.

The general picture in the Netherlands has been one of tension between the increased commercialization and 'liberalization' of television and the protection of the existing public service. Ang (1991) discusses some of the problems this has posed for VARA, the socialist broadcasting organization, with its necessary commitment to public television. Her argument is that in its early days VARA had a 'direct and reciprocal' relationship with its audience, it was the ordinary people's television station and ordinary people were members of its association. On the one hand VARA needed to maintain its socialist stance or lose its distinctiveness and, along the way, the committed section of its audience. On the other hand the association needed to attract a large enough audience to secure its financial future. With the developments of television during the 1970s and 1980s the idea that VARA had a natural and loyal audience was increasingly cast into doubt by the emergence of the popular television organization TROS. TROS was successful in building up a large audience at the expense of VARA and other associations by employing a clearly commercial strategy. In short, the combination of technology, commercial pressures and wider social shifts is irrevocably changing the face of Dutch television.

India

India is a vast country of some 835 million people with diverse cultures, languages and customs. However, broadcasting in India has not been marked by diversity but by the domination of the state-owned and -funded television service Doordarshan. The service has been described as one of 'the most boring ... in the world, dominated by stories of ministers and officials attending seminars or inaugurating projects' (*The Economist*, 29 August 1992). However, there is recent evidence that the Indian television scene is in the process of change, towards a more pluralistic and entertainment-oriented set-up.

Television started in India as an experimental service in 1959 with a limited three day a week transmission. A more regular provision had to await 1965. The Indian television service was initially a fairly limited one both in transmission hours and territorial coverage. The real expansion in Indian television came in the early 1980s with the launching of INSAT 1, a programme of transmitter building across the country, the introduction of a limited national programme service, the arrival of colour, and the introduction of a second channel into Delhi, Bombay, Calcutta and Madras. Between 1971 and 1985 the signal reach of Indian television expanded from a half a million people to 396 million or 60 per cent of the population. Indian ministry sources more recently put the figure at 78 per cent of the population (Ministry of Information and Broadcasting, 1991). This expansion of television in India, at a cost of millions of dollars, has had government support and can be seen as an aspect of national, social and economic development. It has also been seen, however, as deliberate political aggrandizement by the Gandhi family linked to the wooing of both a growing Indian middle class and the economic might of multinational electronics companies (Pendakur, 1991).

Broadcasting is financed directly from government funds rather than from a licence fee, though in recent years an increasing level of spot advertising and programme sponsorship has developed. Chatterji (1991) argues that the government maintains a tight control of the expenditure of Doordarshan and that the powers of the

Director-General are, thus, limited. It is commonly argued that Doordarshan is an outdated rather rigid bureaucracy suffering from low morale and a lack of imagination and creativity. Rajagopal (1993) argues that this is, at least in part, a vestigial colonial orientation towards society; a result of an inherited and embedded bureaucracy within a deeply inegalitarian society. There have been attempts to redirect aspects of Doordarshan and to link its perceived educational and social role with entertainment through so-called 'pro-development' soaps, for example *Hum Log* (Us Folks). In the end, under pressure from advertisers and sponsors, the writer of *Hum Log*, Joshi, felt that 'entertainment won out over education'. Subsequent developments led to the establishment of a more entertainment-based, commercially sponsored prime-time television oriented to middle-class earners. In 1984–5 two-thirds of Doordarshan's revenues were earned from six multinational companies (*Countermedia*, 1(2), 1986). Thus, reform of a rather static state institution along more progressive and democratic lines began to give way to the commercialization of Doordarshan, later to be outstripped by developments in the truly commercial sector.

India's ability to support a more commercial and entertainment-oriented service was indicated by the rapid spread of VCRs in the early 1980s when a primarily middle-class market bought over 300,000 machines between 1981–3 with a further estimated growth of 20,000 purchases a month (Ninan and Singh, 1983). More recently, the state service has met competition from satellite television in the form of the Hong Kong based Star TV. The initial transmissions in English (including MTV and the BBC's World News Service) and Chinese created an audience of some eight million, and with the launch of a new Hindi channel the owners hope to attract some 20 to 30 million people (*The Economist*, 29 August 1992). More recent reports put the figure at 18.8 million (*The Guardian*, 23 October 1993). The Hindi channel which began with a three-hour transmission expects to extend this to 24-hour provision. Star TV has been acquired by Rupert Murdoch's News Corporation and can be expected to be part of global satellite link-up. At present the most popular channel broadcast by Star is the Hindi-language Zee-TV. Star also carries three English-language channels (including CNN), Dubai television, Asian Television Network and a regional Malayalm-language channel, Asianet. Satellite television is rapidly becoming very popular and profitable, siphoning off both audience and advertisers from Doordarshan. Exactly how Star will develop remains to be seen, though Murdoch is likely to want to use his vast array of US programming already available to Fox and Sky, alongside a set of global ceremonial and sporting events. Equally, one of the attractions of Star to Murdoch is its library of Indian and Chinese films, since locally-oriented programming is important to satellite television in building up and retaining its audience. This is, in part, why the BBC's news service on 'Star' was, until removed, well-received in India. 'People didn't want CNN which was just the US. They wanted a global news service and this caused CNN to revamp its whole outlook' (Neil Blackley, *The Guardian*, 13 October 1993). The need for local programming has also led the Pearson organization to consider launching a rival Hindi-language channel (*Screen Digest*, April 1995).

At first Doordarshan tried to disregard the changes but could ignore them no more if they wished to survive. Thus the Indian government has decided to open the broadcast television industry up to private companies. The organization of commercial TV would be on a regional basis, to prevent monopoly, and would require companies to desist from screening programmes seen as a threat to the unity of the country or which would offend ethnic or social morals. The basis on which the right to broadcast in specific areas would be granted has not been made clear but doubtless multi-nationals will await the opening up of a potentially massive and lucrative market. Furthermore there are plans for Doordarshan to launch five satellite channels and to screen amongst other things *Dallas* and Disney. In contrast, the *Ramayana* and the *Mahabharata*, two epics serialized by Doordarshan and based on classic mythic tales, have been the most popular television, ever, in India. While a new media revolution would appear to be about to sweep across the continent a degree of caution must be retained. Doordarshan seems to be 'fighting back' though it will be unable to turn the tide. Changes in Indian television towards a more commercial and pluralistic system are unlikely to be reversed.

United Kingdom

The organizational field of British television has been dominated by the British Broadcasting Corporation (BBC) since its birth in the 1920s. The BBC is a public corporation run as a quasi-independent body. From its inception, the BBC has been stamped with a public service philosophy both legally and practically by successive Director-Generals. The BBC, unlike many television companies across the world, has always been a programme producer as well as a distribution network. Indeed, the BBC can arguably be said to be the biggest television production company in the world.

In 1954 the BBC monopoly of television services was broken when the Television Act brought commercial television into being. 'Commercial' has always been something of a misnomer when applied to Independent Television (ITV) since it has been supervised by a public body (the Independent Broadcasting Authority), subject to public service obligations and to a degree sheltered from the harsh realities of market competition. There has been only one ITV company in most regions and the network arrangements have been the outcome of agreements not competition. The 1954 Act obliged ITV companies to adopt norms of quality and balance, which were in essence those of public service as developed by the BBC. Channel Four, set up in the early 1980s, was conceived as an innovation for British TV both in structure and content. Unlike the BBC or ITV, Channel Four is primarily a publisher and does not make pro-grammes. The programme supply to Channel Four has originated from a combination of ITV companies, independent producers and imports. The channel has been given a statutory remit to extend the range and diversity of broadcasting by offering a suitable proportion of programmes not generally catered for by ITV and to experiment with form and content.

The financing of television in the UK has reflected a dual system of production and distribution. The BBC has received public money via the collection of a licence fee levied on all television sets while commercial television has raised revenue through the sale of ad-vertising time. The BBC, along with many commentators, has often felt that the Corporation was underfunded by the level of licence fee and open to governmental pressure during the times of its periodic renewal. The ITV sector has generally done well from advertising. Ownership of a television company was seen in its early days as a 'licence to print money'. Even into the mid-1980s the press reported 'ITV profits soaring' (*Television Today*, November 1984). However, in the light of more recent developments, concern has been expressed in some ITV quarters about future profitability. This is an aspect of recession and an outcome of recent changes in the organization of television.

Cable has had limited impact in the UK though its performance is improving. DBS has a growing foothold in the television market with BSkyB using the Astra satellite. The penetration rate is growing, from 12.4 per cent in August 1994 to 14.8 per cent in mid-September 1995 (*Screen Digest*, August 1994 and September 1995). In August 1992 the BSkyB audience share was 4.8 per cent (*The Guardian*, 12 August 1992) but this has risen to 8.5 per cent (*Screen Digest*, June 1995). However, the main changes in UK broadcasting are located in the field of terrestrial broadcasting and have been brought about by political rather than technological forces.

The Thatcher government set up the Peacock Committee in 1985 to look at the possibilities of the BBC being part funded by advertising. The Committee rejected this idea but put forward a conception of television based on the market and consumer choice which did not necessarily require a public service institution. The welfare of the consumer and the principles of public service were to be met by the market. The outcome was a de-regulatory White Paper (1988), the Broadcasting Act (1990), and a review process surrounding the BBC charter renewal in 1996. Within the terms of the 1990 Act, commercial terrestrial television, domestic British satellite television and cable TV are the responsibility of the newly-formed Independent Television Commission (ITC). This body will regulate commercial television in a much lighter way than the IBA and its decisions can be challenged in court. The ITV franchise holders still have some public service obligations but they are much more generalized and weaker than before. Although they are meant to retain quality there is, for example, no specific requirement for them to broadcast current affairs in prime time.

The ITV franchises were awarded on the basis of a bidding system which has left some of the successful bidders with enormous costs to carry, threatening their commercial survival. Three 'old' ITV companies have been replaced by three new companies who are to be publishers rather than producers of programmes. There has been strong pressure from the more powerful companies to relax the restrictions on take-overs and allow the network to shrink to fewer, richer companies. This is argued on the grounds that (a) some weaker companies may otherwise go bankrupt and (b) larger, strong companies are required to compete in the international market place. Politicians have partly yielded to this pressure by allowing a limited relaxation of ownership rules. This led to almost immediate announcements of the take over of Central Television by Carlton and speculation that London Weekend Television (LWT) was poised to take over Yorkshire–TyneTees. The concern is that the new commercial imperatives will fuel an audience maximization strategy and reduce the range and quality of the ITV schedules.

The future of the BBC remains in doubt, but a recent government Green Paper and the BBC's own discussion document suggest that the corporation will continue to be funded via a licence fee and remain a public service institution. At the same time the government has made it clear that it is looking for more 'efficiency' and cuts in 'bureaucracy'. The BBC's discussion document about the Corporation's future, a response to the Green Paper, argues that it will focus on performing a set of clearly-defined roles that complement the commercial sector. These are:

- Providing comprehensive impartial news and information for a fair and informed national debate.
- The development and expression of British culture and entertainment.
- The provision of programming and services which create opportunities for education.
- Stimulating the communication of ideas and cultural practices between Britain and abroad.

The BBC says that it is not intending to retreat into a cultural ghetto of minority areas but will continue to produce a full range of programmes. The official explanation is that the Corporation will be producing the best of each programme type. It is also argued that the BBC will complement commercially-funded television by providing programmes that the market will not. It is difficult not to read into this that the BBC's strategic position will be one of a slightly smaller scale, more distinctively upmarket, public service broadcaster.

Much of the controversy surrounding the BBC has been about the introduction of commercially-driven mechanisms of operation. Central to this is the notion of 'Producer Choice' that allows producers to buy in required services from outside, as well as operating an internal market. It also demands that producers maintain rigorous financial control. The rationale for producer choice is that it allows the BBC to cost all its activities and cut out inefficiencies. Opponents of producer choice point to what they see as the grotesque bureaucracy which accompanies every transaction. There is also a great fear that it may see the erosion of the BBC as a craft base and the slow disintegration of one of the last vertically-integrated television organizations.

The USA

American commercial television is organizationally complex, including several different sets of institutional players. Traditionally, the main players in the organizational field are the television stations, the networks and the production companies. Television stations, of which there are over 700, usually serve particular geographical locations acting as purchasing and transmitting organizations. Few stations produce programming, apart from local news, so that programmes are either supplied by the networks to their affiliates or are purchased from production companies. Local television stations make their money from the fee received from the network, plus the opportunities they are given to sell local and national advertising. In addition to the network affiliate stations there are a significant number of independent stations who dispose of all their own advertising time, purchase programmes and offer counter schedules to the networks. Independent stations often rely on syndication and strip scheduling.

The centre of power in American television has traditionally been the networks. During the 1960s and 1970s over 80 per cent of the television audience was watching a network programme (Cantor and Cantor, 1992). The networks originate and commission programmes, research audience reactions, construct schedules, distribute programmes to the stations, perform a censorship role in the guise of 'standards and practices' and, above all, sell advertising space. Like the stations, the networks produce only a small amount of programmes, mainly news, sport and soap opera. Indeed, they are prevented by law from producing much prime-time material. The networks buy and commission programmes from production companies who can be categorized as major Hollywood film studios, major independent producers and minor independent producers.

The prime driving forces of American television are not to be found in rules and regulations but in the financing of the system. With the exception of the public broadcast service (which reaches only 2–3% of the audience and in any case depends in part on sponsorship and donations), the majority of television institutions are privately-owned companies whose prime purpose is to make a profit which they do either by selling advertising space or programmes. Blumler (1986) argues that few in the industry dispute the central power of the 'bottom-line' commercial ethos throughout the system. At every level the transactions of US television are about selling. For both the networks and the programme makers maximum profit is associated with audience maximization. For the former this comes through advertising revenue, for the latter it is connected to higher payments from the networks and, more significantly still, higher syndication fees.

There have been three major trends in US television in recent years: de-regulation, increased outlets for programmes and an apparent decline in the power of the networks. Aspects of these changes are connected with expansion in delivery systems to include not only terrestrial transmission but cable, satellite and microwave technologies.

The 1980s saw significant de-regulatory moves which included:

- Relaxing the restrictions on the ownership of stations (from seven to twelve).
- The abolition of the 'Fairness Doctrine' which aimed to ensure balance.
- The elimination of cable regulations including the 'must carry' rule (which ensured that cable television carried the broadcast networks).

The possible regrouping of the non-network affiliate stations which the '12' ruling prompted, cable penetration of 40 per cent in 1986 (Sartori, 1986) rising to 68.23 per cent in 1994 (*Screen Digest*, April 1995)) plus the increased use of VCRs caused a decline in network power. NBC, ABC and CBS saw their share of viewers drop from 85 per cent to 73 per cent during the mid-1980s along with levels of advertising revenue. While some loss of network audience and power seems to be permanent there is also evidence that the situation has now stabilized. The DBS experiment was a failure, cable penetration rates have slowed, there is Congressional pressure to re-regulate cable, and the networks are even beginning to increase their combined ratings again. On the other hand, Fox Cable TV has emerged as a virtual fourth television network.

In summary the broad developmental directions of television which have been encountered thus far and which have occurred within a variety of states across the globe include the weakening of national regulatory environments underwritten by political and industrial support for market solutions. This has enabled the emergence of new commercial entrants into the television market creating serious competition for public service broadcasters who have suffered not only a decline in legitimacy but also lost some of their audience to commercial competitors. However, while there has been a general rise in commercial television channels and broadcasting hours public service television has not withered away and, indeed, in certain quarters has made something of a 'comeback'.

The prevailing winds of change have blown with varying degrees of strength and with distinct consequences in different contexts so that in the USA an already commercial system has merely seen adjustments leaving its fundamental balance and drives intact, while in India and the Netherlands there has been a substantial and decisive shift away from state funded and regulated television towards more commercial structures and motivations. In the UK and Australia, already mixed systems of publicly- and privately-funded television have been maintained though with the scales tipping towards commercial television and away from public service television.

An exploration of international television state by state is a legitimate approach to take and it illuminates some of the critical changes taking place, but, as I suggested at the beginning of the chapter, some aspects of global television need to be understood in terms of *transnational trends* such as international programme flows, transnational distribution technologies and an emerging pattern of transnational ownership. It is to these issues that we now turn.

The Rise of Transnational Television: International Television Flows

It has been argued (Dyson and Humphreys, 1990) that we can expect a doubling of broadcast programme hours in western Europe between 1986 and 2000. The western European television programme market was set to grow from $10.6 billion in 1988 to $16 billion in 1998. But where are the programmes and associated advertising to come from? The fear amongst many European politicians and commentators was that the market would be dominated by the Americans who hold the top three positions in terms of global turnover for both traditional television companies and the world film industry. This European concern with the potential domination of the audio-visual market (see Mattelart; Delcourt, and Mattelart, 1984) is one that has been echoed world-wide.

The empirical evidence regarding international television flow has been characterized by Sepstrup (1989a) as limited in volume and weak in theoretical and conceptual clarity. In particular, a restricted range of studies has been used to generalize in an unsustainable manner and draw universal conclusions which then form the basis of global cultural theories. Most notably, the conclusion is drawn that the international trade in television programming is dominated by the USA and that following from this we can speak of media and/or cultural imperialism (chapter 6).

The work of Varis (1974; 1984) is commonly cited as illustrating US dominance in programme flows. His early work found that the USA accounted for over 40 per cent of all programme hours exported world-wide, including 44 per cent of hours imported by western Europe. The USA was found to import only one per cent of its commercial television programming and 2 per cent of its public service programming, less than all the countries in the 50-nation study apart from China. The 1984 update showed little substantive change in world trade patterns apart from a degree of regionalization of imports. In terms of programme hours, Varis gives the US share of exports as 77 per cent for Latin America, 44 per cent for Western Europe, 42 per cent for Arab countries, 47 per cent for Africa (south of the Sahara) and 70 per cent for Canada.

Such evidence, convincing though it seems to be, does tend to obscure some of the subtleties of the debate. Thus, while 44 per cent of all imported television hours to western Europe came from the USA, Sepstrup (1989b) argues that what is more relevant is that 73 per cent of the total national supply in all of Western Europe was domestically produced, 13 per cent came from the USA and 12 per cent from other western European countries. It can thus be argued that in the EU, US television has a minor role compared to western European produced television or that its role has at least been exaggerated. It is unwise to over-generalize on the basis of these figures since they obscure the differences between large and small nations within Europe (the latter tend to import more), between programme types (American programme supply is heavily concentrated in fictional programmes) and the levels of consumption (American programmes seem to be heavily concentrated in prime-time hours).

The US penetration of a given television market or national

boundary varies widely and depends on income per capita, total resources, shared languages, the national levels and quality of programming, and the degree of commercial activity. While the USA can claim 'at least 75% of the worldwide television programme exports' (Hoskins et al., 1995), there has been a distinct move towards *regionalization* of markets on the basis of shared language, culture and historic trade links. For example, in chapter 3 I discuss 'Telenovelas' (Latin American soap opera) which forms the core of a Spanish-language (and Portuguese-language) trade covering not only Latin America but the US cable networks and European countries such as Portugal, Spain and Italy. In the same chapter we encounter a degree of pan-European, pan-African and pan-Asian co-operation in news production. This argument is reinforced by Waterman (1988) who shows that, during the 1980s, 80 per cent of US overseas distribution was going to seven countries: Australia, Canada, France, Germany, Italy, Japan and the UK. These are, by global standards, wealthy countries who have their own production facilities and whose screens cannot really be said to be dominated by US television.

According to Cantor and Cantor (1992), in examining inter-national television flow we need to distinguish between those countries who have no need to import programmes because they have their own production facilities (UK, Brazil, Japan), those who need to top up domestic production (Canada, Australia) and those who, by virtue of having little domestic production, are dependent on external supply (most of South America, Africa and Asia, though not India). We also need to distinguish between types of flow: the national, bilateral and international (Sepstrup, 1989a). The global picture is, therefore, considerably more complex than a view which can only see US dominance of the world's television sets.

That said, the USA remains *the* major player in the world television programme market. Hoskins and Mirus (1988) go some way to giving us an explanation for this with their concept of 'cultural discount'. According to this hypothesis a programme rooted in one culture will have a diminished appeal elsewhere as viewers find it difficult to identify with the language, style, values, beliefs and insti-tutions represented. As a result, all things being equal, fewer people will watch a foreign programme than a domestic programme of the same type and quality, and hence the value to the broadcaster will be less. The percentage difference in value to the broadcaster is the cultural discount on the foreign programme. The authors point out that this explains why trade is predominately in entertainment, especially drama, where the size of the discount is minimized. The argument is developed by showing that all things are not equal and that the there is low cultural discount applied to US programme exports and high cultural discount applied to programmes imported by the US.

This account of the international trade in television has concentrated on the sale of programmes to national broadcasting systems. However, global television also trades in television formats, for example the game show or soap opera which is copied and domesticated for local consumption. Co-production and co-financing are also increasingly manifestations of international television as is the international trade in programme merchandise. Though still relatively modest, intra-European co-productions are on the increase (table 2.2). The advantages of co-production are seen to be financial pooling and access to foreign markets. The disadvantages are increased co-ordination costs and a loss of both control and cultural specificity (Hoskins et al., 1995).

Is 'Global Television' Driven by Technology?

A number of the changes in the patterns of television described thus far have been underpinned by technological developments which have enabled a phenomenal increase in available television channels. The prime developments in these distribution technologies lie with cable and satellite.

Satellites are able to offer a much increased number of TV signals either directly or via head stations of cable systems. Despite high start-up costs, satellites have the potential to offer high-quality picture and sound on a much increased scale. The television

Table 2.2 *European Union co-productions*

	1992	1993
+ EU	123	150
+ Rest of Europe	45	29
+ Central and East Europe	28	28

Source: *Screen Digest*, August 1994.

Table 2.3 *European cable and satellite reception equipment 1994 (percentage of equipped households)*

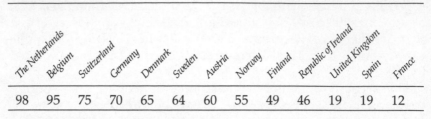

The Netherlands	Belgium	Switzerland	Germany	Denmark	Sweden	Austria	Norway	Finland	Republic of Ireland	United Kingdom	Spain	France
98	95	75	70	65	64	60	55	49	46	19	19	12

Source: Modified from *Cable and Satellite Europe*, September 1995.

potential of satellites was brought to prominence in the mid-1970s when Home Box Office in the United States used satellites as a means of delivering television to cable systems across America and demonstrated its profitability. It was not long before Europe, Australia, India and others were developing satellites for television usage. Table 2.3 shows penetration levels of cable and satellite reception equipment in western Europe.

The technology and politics of satellites are intimately connected. From the beginning, satellite technology has been dominated by the USA. INTELSAT, the international satellite governing body, was set up and controlled by the Americans even though at a later date other western powers were to become influential partners. For the

Table 2.4 *Cable Connections (by region)*

Region	Homes subscribing ('000s) 1991	Homes subscribing ('000s) 1994	Penetration of TV households (%) 1991	Penetration of TV households (%) 1994
Asia	N/A	57,850	N/A	19.14
Central America	343	2,109	1.52	8.20
European Union	23,620	31,888	17.46	22.51
Far East	7,834	12,586	12.48	18.74
North America	65,939	72,508	63.71	68.83
South America	2,690	4,845	4.46	7.20
World	108,958	189,000	15.79	22.11

Source: Modified from *Screen Digest*, April 1995.
N/A = Not available

Table 2.5 *Cable Connections (by selected countries)*

Country	Homes subscribing ('000s) 1991	Homes subscribing ('000s) 1994	Penetration of TV households (%) 1991	Penetration of TV households (%) 1994
Brazil	40	300	0.11	0.77
China	N/A	40,000	N/A	17.58
India	N/A	17,500	N/A	909
The Netherlands	5,225	5, 800	88.98	93.49
United Kingdom	267	909	2.75	4.05
USA	59,329	64,277	63.73	68.23

Source: Modified from *Screen Digest*, April 1995.
N/A = Not available

majority of its existence international satellites have been owned and operated by national governments and their agencies but in recent times the American 'free skies' policies led them to allow private companies to own and operate satellites. In Europe, EUTELSAT, the 'Post, Telephone and Telecommunications industries' satellite' foundation, has tried to develop a 'European' strategy based on European technology. This venture was based on the idea of DBS and was conceived within an internationally-agreed notion of national territorial footprints. This strategy has been left stranded by technological and commercial developments which have meant that the cheaper medium-powered satellites (e.g. Astra) are able to be picked up by small dishes across a wide geographical area. The Astra satellite from which the Murdoch-controlled BSkyB channels operate is based on American technology and financed from private sources. Its Luxembourg registration has allowed it to evade certain national regulations.

Unsurprisingly, there is still extremely unequal development of global cable penetration rates as the tables 2.4 and 2.5 suggest. Most of the present cable systems are based on the copper based coaxial specification. However, the future of cable will lie with the use of fibre-optics cable with its far greater capabilities both in terms of numbers of channels and the potential for interactive programmes. Indeed, it was cable which seemed to promise, both in America and Europe, a vision of participation and democracy on a local level. The development of cable was seen at one and the same time as the basis of national industrial policy and as a consumer controlled two-way form of communication. Little of that vision seems to be left now that cable is seen, primarily, as a distribution network for satellite-fed, centrally conceived, programming.

Looking to the future, we may expect to see television linked to computers via cable to form a 'super information highway'. The current model of such a development is the Internet. The Internet is a communications infrastructure of linked but de-centred computer terminals. Set up originally by the US military, it is now based in universities across the globe and has no central regulatory authority. In January 1995 there were around 4.8million Internet host computers with probably 24 million users (*Screen Digest*, April 1995). The Internet has a number of different levels of use: e-mail, news groups, world-wide webs sites and on-line services. The last two of these are the most rapidly expanding and of most interest to commercial concerns.

Traditionally, the Internet has involved free access but this is beginning to change. A number of multinational corporations are developing subscription services and web sites or are looking at setting up their own 'super information highways'. For example, Microsoft produced the software package Windows which is used on over 50 million computers and which, if linked together, could allow them to develop and control their own Internet (*Screen Digest*, April 1995). Rupert Murdoch's News Corporation has open ambitions to develop its own super information highway. Partners in the venture include British Telecom and Cellnet (telephone lines); Comstream (satellite data compression), along with the News Corporation owned News Datacom (Pay-TV subscription management); Delphi Internet Services (news and information services); and

Table 2.6   *Growth in the number of world-wide web sites*

	Sites	Monthly Growth %
June 93	130	
Dec 93	623	29.8 %
June 94	1, 265	12.5 %
Dec 94	11, 576	44.6 %
Feb 95	27, 000	52.7 %

Source: Screen Digest, April 1995.

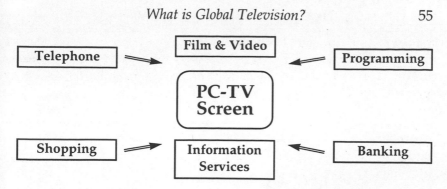

Figure 2.1 Television as a visual terminal

of course the programme archives and distribution expertise of BSkyB and Twentieth Century Fox. Time-Warner and Viacom/Paramount are also in a position to develop such convergence. In this 'future world', television would be the visual terminal in which a whole range of services and activities would converge. (See figure 2.1)

Through Me-TV, as this scenario is sometimes known, one could order and pay for shopping; transfer e-money; keep an eye on one's bank account; call up a selection of films, videos and programmes; and search the world-wide web for information. Future developments might also include the visual phone and high definition wall-sized screens. Such a television service would undoubtedly be flooded with adverts and other promotional forms. However, Smart-TV will target viewers with promotions aimed specifically at them. This will be based on information gathered through television-viewing patterns, purchasing patterns and socio-economic status. The component parts of this picture are already being put in place in the USA where 34 per cent of the population have PCs and 40 per cent of these have modems (required to access the Internet). It is estimated that by the year 2005 there will be 25 million interactive cable households in the USA and some 22 million in Europe (*Screen Digest*, October 1994). On a global scale, it is clear that the twenty-first century and the pre-modern are about to coexist in the form of high-tech New York and rural Bangladesh.

In addition to cable and satellite, a third critical technology widely applicable to television is the video recorder (VCR). This technology has become significant both for its ability to offer cinema films a longer shelf-life through video release and, even more importantly, the audience to time-shift the programmes watched. Ownership of

Table 2.7   *VCR households (by selected countries)*

Country	Homes ('000s) 1990	Homes ('000s) 1994	Penetration of TV households (%) 1990	Peentration of TV households (%) 1994
Australia	3,316	3,712	64.6	69.8
Brazil	40	80	21.1	27.7
China	1,215	14,810	1.4	6.5
India	2,989	5,329	22.8	15.2
The Netherlands	2,831	3, 834	48.8	61.8
United Kingdom	14,271	16,730	67.0	74.5
USA	57,688	78,125	62.6	82.9

Source: Modified from *Screen Digest*, August 1995.

a VCR can allow an audience more easily to construct its own viewing patterns quite separately from the TV companies' schedules. This is especially the case when used in conjunction with cable/satellite television. World-wide VCR ownership has risen from 10 million in 1980 to 300 million in 1994 with a global penetration rate of television households of 38.2 per cent. (*Screen Digest*, August 1995). The distribution of VCR ownership remains globally variable (table 2.7).

One cannot understand technology in isolation. Differences between television systems are not the outcome of technology alone, but of its development within specific social, economic and cultural contexts. The same point needs to be made regarding the 'new' technologies. Certainly the capabilities of these technologies to deliver more channels, avoid state control and turn the TV set into a place for shopping, banking and game playing are significant developments, but the driving forces are commercial and political rather than simply technological. As Smith has argued:

> The present 'revolution', if such it is, is one of investment rather than technical innovation, of transformation of scale more than of technological horizon. (Smith, 1993 p. 20)

Technology does not in and of itself create a push towards market solutions, rather it has been used by vested political and industrial interests to justify such a move. The ultimate configuration of the emergent television systems will be the outcome of the strategic moves of transnational companies and political forces more than anything else. This helps to account for the fact that the technologies which are leading a television revolution, cable and satellite delivery systems, have developed in *distinct ways in different countries.*

In the UK, cable television has not yet made any significant inroads and Britain has one of the lowest cable density rates in Europe. By contrast, the Netherlands is one of the most heavily-cabled countries in Europe with over 90 per cent of households connected to a cable system. Cable struggled in the UK during the 1980s despite the government's attempts to encourage its development, but with a new wave of recent American investment in British cable and its use as a carrier for satellite programmes a gradual expansion during the 1990s seems likely. In the USA, cable expanded at a considerable rate during the early 1980s (indeed, Fox-TV is effectively a fourth network) though the latter part of the decade saw a considerable slowing of penetration rates. It seems unlikely that cable will be able to further erode the networks standing but most cities have cable systems offering over 20 channels and these do dominate the screening of movies and the syndication market.

In India, it is the development of commercial satellite television that threatens state-owned television's (Doordarshan) dominance and has forced the government to entertain the idea of commercial broadcasting. In the UK, the satellite channels of BSkyB have had some success in creating a niche for themselves, especially in relation to sport, but the audience share of 8 per cent has some way to go before it can be seen as a serious threat to the BBC or ITV stations. In contrast, the Luxembourg-based RTL4 satellite station has made decisive inroads into the Dutch market.

Since many of the 'new' stations are not producing programmes but recycling old ones, they are often unable to compete with the production values of the established broadcasters where, as in the UK and USA, the 'old' broadcasters are strongly entrenched. Where the older services have been weaker and or dull then cable and satellite have been more successful. This appears to be the case in India, Holland and Germany and to some extent Canada. In any case, the ownership of the production and distribution facilities is the decisive context in which technological developments take place.

Who Owns 'Global Television'?

The significance of television ownership lies with issues of constraint and independence related to diversity or monopoly control. Thus, there is an argument that diversity of programmes is related to diversity of ownership and control. We may make a distinction between allocative and operational control (Murdock, 1982). The former is concerned primarily with the setting of overall organizational goals and the deployment of resources. Those with allocative control are able to formulate broad policy, expand or cut back in certain areas, and control basic financial policy and distribution of profit. Such control rests with the boards of companies and corporations. Those in operational control, the broadcasters, have traditionally had a fair degree of autonomy in programme production within the limits already set. Direct proprietorial control is usually not required since the operations managers are fully aware of the constraints put upon them by allocative controllers. The degree of operational autonomy granted will of course vary from one situation to another. For example, the evidence appears to be that operational autonomy has traditionally been greater in the UK, especially within the BBC, than in the USA where advertiser and network influence on programme production has been strong or in India were direct state interference has been a marker of the system.

Murdock and Golding (1977) have argued that the ownership of communications by private capital is subject to a *general* process of concentration via conglomeration. This produces multi-media and multi-industry corporations who are part of a wider process of capital conglomeration. Thus, many commercial television companies have investments in both media and non-media interests or are part of organizations that do.

On the basis of their core activities Murdock (1990) distinguishes three basic kinds of conglomerates operating in the communications field: industrial conglomerates, service conglomerates and communications conglomerates. Alan Bond's *industrial* conglomerate was the owner of Channel Nine in Australia, General Electric bought the American network NBC, and the Italian industrial giant Fiat has major press holdings. Also based in Italy is the Berlusconi-owned Fininvest, a *service* conglomerate centred on real estate, financial services, newspapers, cinemas and retailing in addition to ownership of the three main Italian commercial television networks. In the

UK, Granada television is part of the larger Granada group with interests in a range of leisure services, investment and insurance, motorway services and television rental. In contrast to these diversified structures, the major interests of communications conglomerates are centred on media and information industries. A well-known example would be Rupert Murdoch's News Corporation. On a less grandiose scale it would also include the Australian-based Grundy Organisation or the UK-based Carlton Communications. The recent de-regulatory trend has led to a flurry of selling and buying in Europe, Australia and the USA, the outcome of which has largely been an increased concentration of ownership and the transformation of the market by transnational companies operating both locally and globally (Mazzoleni and Palmer, 1990). As Murdock (1990) argues, this is significant because of the potential of leading communications corporations spanning continents and industries to influence contemporary cultural life.

Case studies in global media ownership

Rupert Murdoch, head of the globally-influential News Corporation is reported to have argued that, 'The days of the media baron are over' (the *Observer*, 5 September 1993), by which he meant that the expansion of media channels enabled by digital technology would open up the media world to multiple ownership. One can only assume that Murdoch had his tongue firmly in his cheek when he said this as the recent expansion of his own cross-media ownership belies his words. Indeed, in the very same speech he puts the position more clearly:

> I would see us buying world-wide sporting events that will go right around the world, great musical events, making programmes for a world audience. We will need local programming as well of course, but synergies will exist in special events . . . This is encouraged by the spread of world-wide marketing companies, the toy companies, car companies, food and soft drink companies who we can provide a one-stop shop for.

The acquisition by News Corporation of the Hong Kong based Star TV for $525 million has given Murdoch a satellite television footprint over Asia and the Middle East with a potential audience of 45 billion viewers. When allied to his other television interests – BSkyB (UK), Seven Network (Australia), Fox TV (USA) – his organization's

Table 2.8 *Star TV penetration in Asia*

Country	Homes Feb. 1993 ('000s)	Homes Nov. 1993 ('000s)	Change Feb–Nov. (%)	Penetration (%)
China	4,800	30,363	+533	34.6
Hong Kong	307	331	+8	22.5
Indonesia	36	50	+39	0.2
India	3,300	7,278	+121	50.7
Israel	410	621	+51	86.0
Korea	19	184	+868	1.8
Kuwait	13	31	+138	6.5
Pakistan	60	77	+28	2.6
Philippines	137	187	+36	4.3
Saudi Arabia	–	369	–	9.1
Taiwan	1,980	2,376	+20	53.2
Thailand	25	143	+472	2.3
UAE	73	117	+60	75.5
Total	11,160	42, 127	+277	–

Source: Screen Digest, April 1994.

television interests alone have a global reach of some two-thirds of the planet. He would thus be able to relay his programmes around the world virtually unchallenged since both business and technological developments seem to move faster than the thinking of regulators (though China is trying to ban Star and Iran has banned satellite dishes).

What is significant in looking at the News Corporation 'empire' (see figure 2.2) is not just the spatial breadth of ownership but the potential link-ups between elements of the media industries. In Twentieth Century Fox and Star TV, Murdoch acquired a huge library of film and television material which he can now channel through his network of distribution outlets. It would appear that Murdoch hopes to create a lucrative global advertising market. Should he run into any local difficulties with rivals and politicians, he is arguably able to influence, or attempt to influence, the political climate through his newspapers. It is perhaps no coincidence that prior to the launch of his British-based Sky satellite channels it was Murdoch-owned newspapers that led a series of attacks on the rival BBC.

One aspect of current developments is the array of deals and partnerships that Murdoch is putting together. For example, Murdoch has at various times co-operated with both the BBC and CNN who, interestingly, are potential rivals to Murdoch's own ambition to run a global news service. We have a situation where the BBC and News Corporation are rivals in the field of news (indeed

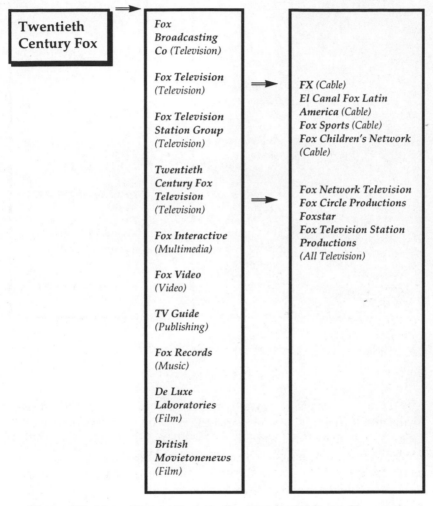

Figure 2.2 News Corporation: wholly-owned subsidiaries (Twentieth Century Fox, News Corporation, News International UK)
Source: Modified from *Screen Digest*, January 1995.

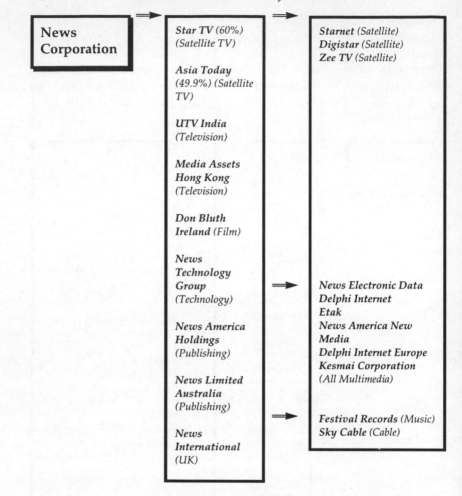

Figure 2.2 (*continued*)

Murdoch removed BBC news from Star-TV) but are co-operating in terms of UK football coverage and the BSkyB broadcast channel UK Gold (which uses BBC archive material). On a technological front, News Corporation is working with British Telecom and Cellnet to develop the means by which to link satellites with telephone networks to create what Murdoch has called the digital 'super-highways of communication'.

Figure 2.2 is a condensed version of the Murdoch empire which *Screen Digest* (January 1995) describes as 'arguably the most global

News International (UK)	British Sky Broadcasting (40%) (Satellite)	Sky Movies The Movie Channel Sky Movies Gold Sky Sports Sky Sports 2 Sky One Sky News Sky Travel Channel Sky Soap (All Satellite)
	Broadsystem (Technology)	
	News Datacom (Technology)	
	News Group Newspapers (Publishing)	QVC Europe (20%) Nickelodeon (50%) Sky Radio (71.5%) Vox Germany (49.9%)
	Times Newspapers Holdings (Publishing)	Partners: NAP TV Hungary (Television) Grupo Zeta Spain (Publishing) who own Renvir Spain (Television) and Antena 3 Spain (Television)
	News Multimedia (Multimedia)	
	News UK (Publishing)	

Figure 2.2 (continued)

of all "Hollywood majors" '. Time-Warner is in size, scope and capital value the worlds largest media corporation. Through a process of merger and take-overs Time-Warner has developed into a sprawling multi-media group of immense scope. Its tentacles reach into every corner of the globe and includes feature film production and distribution, television production and distribution, pay-TV, cable TV, satellite systems, publishing, theme parks, stores and electronics. Time-Warner itself is 15 per cent owned by Canadian drinks conglomerate Seagram. Time-Warner Entertainment is owned by Time-Warner (63.27%), Toshiba & Itochu of Japan (5.61%) and US West (25.51%), a telecommunications group. Since the construction of figure 2.3 Time-Warner have acquired Turner Broadcasting which runs CNN. The organization also has an immense array of partnerships and alliances which extends its influence far beyond that shown by wholly-owned subsidiaries. Those clearly related to

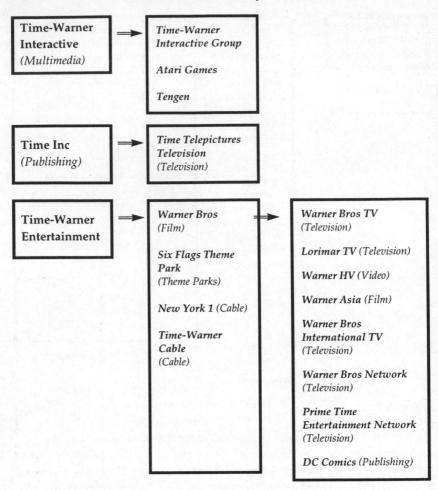

Figure 2.3   Time-Warner – wholly-owned subsidiaries
Source: Modified from *Screen Digest*, January 1995.

television are shown in table 2.9 though there are many others.

Tucked away in the corner of the Time-Warner global corporate map is a small film company called Savoy Pictures in which Time-Warner has a 3 per cent stake. The other stakeholders are Mitsui & Co, Chargeurs and Carlton Communications. The London-based Carlton Communications is a minnow compared to Time-Warner or News Corporation, yet it too has global connections. Even small companies have had to 'go global'. Carlton is best known to the gen-

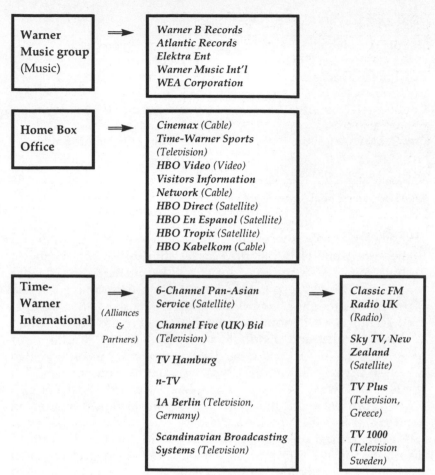

Figure 2.3 (*continued*)

eral public in the UK as the commercial television licence holder in the largest ITV region (London weekday) reaching some 11 million viewers. Less widely known is that Carlton has a 20 per cent holding in Central Television, the UK's second largest ITV regional licensee and in GMTV breakfast television. Although this is the public face of Carlton communications its longer-term business has been in relation to technical communications services within the film and television production industries. Thus, 'Technicolor Video Services' is a market leader in the production of pre-recorded video cassettes operating in the USA, UK, Netherlands and Italy. The film arm of

Table 2.9 *Time-Warner: some partners and alliances*

Viacom/Paramount (50%)	Viacom Television (50%)
Cable y Television (Spain)	Citadel Entertainment
Newhouse Broadcasting (10%)	Carlton Communications
EKO Turkey	VueScan
Continental Cable (10%)	Kablevision (Sweden)
Canal Plus	Chinese Cable j.v
Cox Cable (10%)	HBO: Hungary; Pacific; Brazil; Czech; Asia
Anglia Television (UK)	US Cable j.v

Source: Modified from *Screen Digest*, January 1995.

Technicolor has laboratories in Hollywood, New York, London and Rome and is one of the world's largest film processors. Some of Technicolor's clients in both film and video include the globally-recognized Disney Corporation, Home Box Office, and Columbia Pictures. Through 'Pickwick Video' (based in Europe) and 'Technicolor Distribution Services' (based in the USA) Carlton is able to market and distribute tapes. During 1992 Carlton was responsible for 35 per cent of the distribution of pre-recorded video cassettes in the UK. In the 'Moving Picture Company', 'TVI', 'Carlton Broadcast Facilities', 'Complete Post' and 'Post Perfect', Carlton competes in the post-production facilities market in London, Los Angeles and New York.

A geographical breakdown of Carlton Communications profit distribution is interesting because it shows both a degree of global reach and the importance of North America as the main source of profit (table 2.10). Though differing in terms of scale and influence,

Table 2.10 *Carlton Communications: source of profits by region*

Geographical Location	Pre-tax Profits	Profit as a percentage of total
North America	£56.4m	55
United Kingdom	£32.0m	32
Europe	£7.6m	7
Japan	£4.0m	4
Asia and others	£2.2m	2

Source: *Carlton Communications plc: Annual Report*, 1992.

News Corporation, Time-Warner and Carlton Communications all illustrate the emergence of global networks of ownership and control. This is of particular importance with regard to the distribution networks which, within a commercially-driven system, are of paramount significance. Distributors control not only what gets broadcast but also what is made since few companies will wish to spend large amounts of money making programmes that have not secured distribution agreements. It follows, given the global domination of transnational corporations, that a very real problem is the lack of production and distribution facilities outside the hands of the major production centres.

Alternatives: Channels of Resistance?

Despite the overwhelming predominance of transnational corporate control of production and distribution there are nevertheless signs of alternative productions taking place, albeit on a rather limited scale (Dowmunt, 1993). Thus, Batty (1993) describes the development of 'alternative' television in Ernabella, a remote Aboriginal community located in the semi-arid regions of northern South Australia. Here the Pitjantjatjarra people, having already some considerable experience of asserting their rights, decided to establish a media committee to monitor developments within satellite and video television. The project began as a small-scale project producing video programmes for the Ernabella community but soon expanded to take in the surrounding Pitjantjatjarra communities to become the local channel. This outlet was used to distribute news about local cultural, political and sporting events, as well as to educate the younger members of the community in the traditions of the past. As the project developed, and the members became more confident, they began to stitch together locally-produced programmes with some from the national ABC network which they accessed via a satellite dish. The success of this venture, argues Batty, is based on the adaptation of international technology by local people for local needs and funded from local sources. He contrasts this with Imparja, an Aboriginal-owned and run station set up within the context of Australian commercial television. Imparja won the franchise as the 'Remote Commercial Television Service' serving central Australia with its substantial Aboriginal population. However, the fact that a substantial part of the audience is not Aboriginal and that the station must make money through advertising has undercut its original cultural and political project and left the station with only a weak Aboriginal presence both in terms of personnel and programming.

While Ernabella television was in the remote Australian outback, 'Deep Dish' was a project conceived in the heartland of America. Lucas and Wallner (1993) describe how, in the midst of the Gulf War, a group of media activists became discontented with the lack of serious discussion or questioning in the mainstream American media. In response they launched the 'Gulf Crisis TV Project' with the express purpose of producing alternative programmes. A core group of activists, having alerted colleagues nation-wide, were able to gather and edit a vast amount of footage shot on easily available video cameras into a series of shows critical of US-government Gulf policy. They were able to persuade a number of access cable channels and PBS stations to screen the programmes which were distributed nationally by hiring satellite time. Thus, the very commercial availability of television technology was being put to quite a different purpose.

Conclusions

The key changes in the political economy of global television as described in this chapter can be summarized as follows:

- Advances in television technology creating new distribution mechanisms.
- A weakening of national regulatory environments.
- Political and industrial support for market solutions.
- A rise in television channels and broadcasting hours.
- A degree of loss of legitimacy for public television.
- The emergence of new entrants in to the global television market creating serious competition for public service broadcasters.
- A degree of loss of audience by public television to commercial competitors.
- A rise in transnational and monopoly ownership circumventing national regulation.

These trends conjure up a picture of transglobal television dominated by commercial multinational corporations, with public service television confined to the sidelines of minority interest. There is indeed grounds for painting such a picture. However, public service television has not yet disappeared, the global television market is not yet dominated by one American corporation and the patterns of television business are complex involving global, regional and local flows.

A complementary and alternative approach to that of political economy, which has formed the basis of this chapter, is to examine the programming strategies of global television. Are there global genres? Do programmes travel well across borders? These are questions which we can begin to tackle in the next chapter.

Part II

Prime-time Goes Global: Programmes and Audiences

3

Global Soaps and Global News

Television is primarily a narrative form, that is to say a story-telling form. The appeal of global television lies in its ability to tell stories in ways and about subjects that have resonance with its audience. Indeed, the transition to electronic media has involved the proliferation of narrative form so that today we may see television as the prime 'story-teller' of western societies taking over the role Benjamin assigned to the fairy-tale, 'the first tutor of children' (Benjamin, 1973).

Narratives are 'the way in which this society speaks to itself, the way in which the individual must live to be accepted there' (Sollers, cited in Laing, 1978, p. 99). Narratives thus provide explanations for the way things are. They supply answers to the question: how shall we live? They offer us frameworks of understanding and rules of reference about the way the world is constructed. Of course, stories have story-tellers and it is always best to ask the questions, who is speaking? From what perspective? Does one voice silence another? Since stories both constitute and are constituted by wider social relations we need to know which particular interests are being promoted by specific narratives. Further, the significance of global television lies not only in its discursive content but also in the global spread of particular narrative forms in which are embedded western scientific and realist assumptions about the appearance of physical reality and the plausibility of action.

In this chapter I will be describing and discussing two of the most prominent narrative forms of global television: soap opera and news. While global television certainly promotes other televisual forms – sport and music television are perhaps the most high profile – nevertheless, soaps and news are amongst the most enduring and watched forms of television.

To subsume different programmes under the same heading 'soap opera' or 'news' suggests that we think they have something in common, that they are part of the same genre. Ryall has argued that:

> The master image for genre criticism is the triangle composed of artist/film/audience. Genres may be defined as patterns/forms/ styles/structures which transcend individual films and which supervise both their construction by the film maker and their reading by audiences. (Ryall, 1975, p. 28)

All production operates within constraints but Ryall's notion of 'supervision' is useful because it suggests patterns of meaning which are shared by the different programmes inside the same genre. There is a sense in which this represents a constraint because limits have been set within which producers and writers must work. On the other hand, genre can offer creative possibilities because the notion of 'supervision' introduces the sense of a shared meaning between writers, producers and audiences so that the use of a genre form does not necessarily imply a conservative and formulaic work. Thus playwright Trevor Griffiths argues that 'the plays which set the deepest are plays which are aware of their own conventions, or other conventions and which manage to spring the unexpected within those conventions' (in Pike, 1982, p. 37).

Genres structure the narrative process and contain it, they regulate it in particular ways using specific elements and combinations of elements to produce coherence and credibility. Genre thus represents systemizations and repetitions of problems, and solutions in narratives. They must also involve sufficient difference to generate meaning and pleasure (Neale, 1980). Thus, genre concerns patterns of similarity and difference for, as Neale argues:

> Genre can perhaps best be characterised as one of repetition and limited difference, it should, however be stressed that the element of difference is not only real but fundamental. The notion that all westerns (or all gangster films or all war films or whatever) are all

the same is not only just an unwarranted generalisation, it is profoundly wrong; if each text within a genre were, literally, the same, there would simply not be enough difference to generate either meaning or pleasure. (Neale, 1980, p. 49–50)

In a discussion of genre study, Jane Feuer (1992) distinguishes between three different approaches to the study of genre which she calls the *aesthetic* approach, the *ritual* approach and the *ideological* approach. The first of these defines genre in terms of a system of conventions that permits expression within certain bounds. The second sees genre as an exchange between industry and audience on a shared and negotiated terrain, while the third case stresses the role genre plays in policing meaning and reproducing ideology.

Traditional genre studies drawn from a literary base have tended to stress the aesthetic elements and to delineate the parameters of a genre in theoretical terms. However, television studies have tended to take their categories from historical usage so that a critic's list of television genres is unlikely to differ vastly from either that of the industry or the audience. While aesthetic considerations need to be brought to bear in the study of television there is a considerable element of ritual because of the production and scheduling techniques involved. It suits the television industry to be able to produce a standard product since this both cuts costs and helps to 'deliver an audience'. Genre offers a way for the television industry to control the tension between similarity and difference inherent in the production of a cultural product.

Western Soaps: Form and Content

Though soap opera is American in origin, the name deriving from the sponsorship of serial narratives on radio by US soap producers such as Colgate and Palmolive, it has now become a world-wide genre. Soap opera is a global form in two senses: it is a narrative mode *produced* in a variety of countries across the globe and it is one of the most exported forms of television *viewed* in a range of cultural contexts. Soap operas are also local to the degree that they can encompass the history, culture and specific problems of particular local conditions.

We may make a broad distinction between soaps that are of an essentially local, regional or international character. Local soaps are those which are only seen within a national setting, for example many of the US daytime soaps or locally-produced soaps like *Generations*, a South African production for the home market. Others have a broader regional appeal, in particular those which serve a specific language community. Thus the UK-produced *Coronation Street* has built up a sizeable audience in English-speaking countries such as Australia, New Zealand and Canada, as has *EastEnders* (which has also been seen in Norway, Holland, Belgium, Denmark and Spain), though for cultural rather than language reasons both have had only limited impact in America. TV Globo, the Brazilian network, has been very successful in exporting its 'soaps', known as 'Telenovelas', throughout the Spanish-speaking world (and beyond, especially into Portugal, Italy and the USA).

Finally, there are the internationally-known soaps which have been seen across the globe wherever a TV set is to be found. In this category we could put the American prime-time soaps *Dallas* and *Dynasty*, the US daytime soaps *Days of Our Lives* and *The Bold and the Beautiful*, the youth-oriented *Beverley Hills 90210*, and increasingly the Australian-produced soaps such as *Neighbours*. I was reminded of the global circulation and contemporary significance of soap opera when, during September 1996, I was able to watch an array of soaps on South African television. These included *Days of Our Lives*, *The Bold and the Beautiful*, *The Young and the Restless*, *Beverley Hills 90210* and *Santa Barbara* from the USA, *Neighbours* and *Home and Away* from Australia and the locally-produced *Generations*. Doubtless there were others available that I missed.

Drawing in particular from the work of Geraghty (1981; 1991), Allen (1985; 1995) and Ang (1985) I shall trace the broad formal conventions of prime-time soap opera and analyse their central themes and ideologies. This immediately raises problems for some critics who see the daytime soap as the defining form. Daytime soaps tend to be slower in pace with lower production costs compared to the more lavish and action-oriented night-time programmes. Nevertheless, they both share certain formal characteristics, most notably an open-ended narrative and an orientation towards a female audience. Further, the prime-time versions are very much characterized as soaps within the popular discourse on the subject as illustrated in the tabloid press.

According to Geraghty, the soap opera form involves a distinctive use of time and space. The soap, as a long-running serial, has a potentially unlimited time period in which to tell its stories so that there is not the sense of closure which is more commonly a feature of the film or the 13-episode series. Soap operas do not encourage expectations of an ending. This means that the sense of time in the narrative, rather than being subordinated to plot considerations, takes on the characteristics of real time. We are meant to assume that events in the soap world are continuing unabated between episodes so that, as Geraghty argues, the ideal soap would be a daily event. On rare occasions, usually involving family rituals or communal disasters, we will be presented with a more elongated sense of the present and a whole episode may be devoted to one event. American soaps tend to have less of a sense of real time than their UK or Australian counterparts.

Most soaps establish a sense of geographical space that the audience can identify with and to which the characters return again and again. Thus, *Dallas* is not only set in its namesake city but more specifically on the Southfork ranch, *Neighbours* utilizes the Melbourne suburbs, while both *Coronation Street* and *EastEnders* are set in working-class areas of major British cities, Manchester and London respectively. These programmes also employ regularly repeated interiors including front rooms, dining areas, shops and public places. Most UK soaps, with the exception perhaps of *Brookside*, utilize the corner shop, public house and street or square as public spaces where characters meet and talk. This is both a plot function, any character can meet any other character; an economic necessity, sets are repeatable; and a factor in establishing a sense of community. This communal space is partly employed in Australian soaps, witness the cafe in *Neighbours*, but hardly at all in American prime-time soaps which tend to display grand individual houses like Southfork or the Carrington mansion in *Dynasty*. Thus, British soaps are noticeably more committed to the use of public space than their American counterparts.

The narrative structures of soaps involve the intertwining of multiple strands within a given episode and these strands will continue across a number of episodes for a period of many weeks. Some of these narrative themes are more or less permanent, for example, JR's feud with Cliff Barnes in *Dallas*, others come and go. In any case, they deal with the inevitable disruption of the status quo since, by definition, a long-running serial cannot allow stability to reign. While the story-lines may deal with change it is also part of the staple diet of soaps to include a regular group of familiar characters around which the stories revolve. Of course, soap operas rely on the audience's accumulated knowledge about the serial which adds depth and subtlety to their understanding, though they must also allow the casual viewer to quickly identify character traits and thus employ serial types who occupy status positions. These positions are commonly associated with the single/married dichotomy enabling such characters to be deployed in family crises and romantic attachments. That is not to say that characters never change; the trick is, as with genre, to handle the movement between similarity and change. Similarity allows for familiarity and predictability; change adds interest and moves the narrative forward. In addition, the soap's ability to deploy a wide range of characters allows for both multiple plots and for multiple identifications by the audience who can endorse some characters but not others or be torn between characters according to the circumstances.

Soaps are often structured by the tension between the conventions of realism and melodrama. The realist approach is particularly marked in the British soaps and follows a tradition of equating realist conventions with 'quality'. Realism refers here to a set of conventions by which the drama appears to be a representation of the 'real world' with motivated characters, recognizable locations and believable social problems. The narrative techniques deliberately hide and obscure their own status as constructs in order to deny their artificiality and present the narrative as 'real'. When it was launched in the 1960s *Coronation Street* was very much part of this realist tradition representing the emergence of a voice for the northern working class in British film and television. It purported to deal with the real problems of real people in a working-class context in a way which was recognizable and understandable to the people it addressed. Some 20 years later *Brookside* was set in motion with a similar appeal to present the world 'as it really is' and in doing so denied that *Coronation Street* was any longer adequate to the task, the world having passed it by. While located in London rather than the North of England, *EastEnders* shares a focus on a regional working class and upon a gritty realism. It has set out to represent a range of contemporary characters and to engage in social issues like AIDS, race, gender, homosexuality, unemployment, etc.

It is a critical distinguishing factor that British soaps are primarily, though not exclusively, oriented around realist conventions while American soaps play much more openly with those of melodrama. Melodrama is about a heightened sense of the dramatic, a focus on emotions and 'life's torments' where characters may appear to have insufficient motivation from a 'realist' point of view. Rather, the characters seem to act as icons for a particular emotional stance or dilemma which is carried forward by both the narrative and the *mise-en-scène*. Reinforced by the use of a certain elevated acting style, dramatic music and lingering close-up shots, the story-lines contain a variety of twists and turns which would stretch the credibility of a realist narrative and that propel the viewer along a roller-coaster ride of emotional ups and downs.

It would be incorrect to see any given soap as operating exclusively within either realist or melodramatic conventions. Rather they are a mixture of conventions so that a distinguishing feature of a given soap is the balance of conventions which are deployed. Thus, *EastEnders* and *Dallas* use both realist and melodramatic conventions but the former is more obviously realist while the latter leans towards melodrama. Additionally, as Geraghty argues, part of the appeal of soaps is the way in which they use the values and conventions of light entertainment. For example, the American prime-time soaps frequently revel in a spectacle of extravagance and opulence. Shows like *Dallas* and *Dynasty* are infused with a sense of glamour and style through the use of luxurious locations and decorative characters. The Australian soaps like *Neighbours* and *Home and Away* make extensive use of the 'great Australian outdoors' where the sun always shines and swimming costumes, T-shirts and shorts are obligatory so that, for the British viewer, life in Australia seems like one long summer holiday. The realist conventions of British soaps make the deployment of such techniques more problematic though they often contain an element of subdued female glamour. There can also be an overlap with light entertainment forms like the sitcom: *Coronation Street* has, over the years, moved away from its realist origins and begun to resemble a wry comedy with its tongue-in-cheek humour.

Soaps are a specific genre of television not only in terms of their narrative form but also with regard to their pivotal themes which centre on the sphere of interpersonal relationships. Marriages, divorces, break-ups and coming-togethers, alliances, arguments, acts of revenge and acts of caring are at the core of the soap opera and provide the narrative dynamic and the emotional interest. This concern with the personal sphere, it is often claimed, gives soaps a unique orientation towards the traditional domain of women, both in the obvious domestic sense, but also in terms of women's interest and competence in the private and personal world. The narrative concerns of soaps frequently centre on women characters and are structured in a way which encourages a sympathetic understanding from a woman's point of view. The actions of women are both central to the stories and are validated rather than marginalized or caricatured. This is one reason for the increased academic interest in soaps, much of the work pioneered by women writers from a feminist perspective. This is not to say that soaps do not, to varying degrees, incorporate aspects of the public sphere, rather it is to suggest that where the public sphere is dealt with, for example the machinations of the US oil industry or the ravages of unemployment, they are handled in terms of their implications for characters' personal lives or as indicators of character traits.

Given the stress in soaps on the personal sphere it is understandable that 'the family' is at the heart of soap opera stories. A great deal of soap talk centres on who is in a relationship with whom, which marriage is in trouble and which children are causing heartache, while a significant part of the 'action' takes place in typical family circumstances: the dining room, the front room, the bedroom. The family is the mythic centre of the soap opera. It is mythic because only a limited number of characters actually live in a conventional nuclear family, the imaginary ideal of which is constantly shattered by the arguments, affairs and divorces which are so necessarily part of the soap opera. Nevertheless, most of the characters are in some way positioned in relation to the family, available in plot terms for a marriage, divorce, relationship, birth, death or tragedy. Not that the treatment of the family is the same in all soaps; Geraghty draws attention to differences between US and British soaps. The former, she argues, adopt a patriarchal model of the family which centres on men's efforts to hold the family together in the face of crisis, since the family is intimately connected to questions of property, power and money. This kind of family is about the continuation of a dynasty which is threatened, sometimes by the poor judgement of men, but more commonly by the movement of women in and out of the family. In British soaps, where there is a tradition of strong women characters who offer selfless support to others, most notably a breed of feckless men, the moral and practical task of family survival falls on their shoulders.

British soaps are markedly different from their American prime-time counterparts in their treatment of 'community' and 'social issues'. If one critical set of locations for the soap is the family house, the other, at least for UK soaps, is public spaces, such as the public house, the corner shop, the street corner and the square. In addition to the narrative and economic advantages this offers (repeated use of the same sets in which any combination of characters could conceivably meet and talk) it contributes to a sense of community which forms part of a unifying ideal in soaps such as *Coronation Street* and *EastEnders*. This sense of community is further constructed (it is always a precarious sense of community threatened by internal conflicts) through set-piece communal occasions, weddings, birthdays, funerals and celebrations, and the continual reference to a communal history. *Brookside* is perhaps the exception to this in the UK, being more concerned with the discourse of class than community, though it does retain the sense of distinct geographical region which is characteristic of the UK soap. Little of this sense of community is evident in American prime-time soaps, for while the city of Dallas may be a recognizable geographical location and characters meet in public places, these attributes alone do not function to create a sense of the value of community. Further, American soaps do not engage with the class, community and regional history characteristic of British soap opera.

One criticism of British soaps has been the representation of community as, on the whole, exclusively white, heterosexual and working class. For the majority of its existence *Coronation Street* has had few black characters, somewhat odd for a programme with realist pretensions located in multi-cultural Manchester. Nor, rather surprisingly, have American soaps *Dallas* and *Dynasty* much of a track record in terms of the representation of that country's multi-ethnic population, and when black characters have appeared it has often been in roles which have brought 'trouble' to the family and community. However, during the 1980s there was some expansion of the boundaries of representation in soaps. *EastEnders* in particular has tried to portray a wider cross-section of ethnic communities and characters without demanding that individuals be the sole carriers of the black experience within the programme. That is not to say that such representation has been without its justified criticism, for example treating racism as a personal issue of illiberality rather than structured inequality or giving insufficient attention to the specificity of black culture. The 1990s has also seen an increase in representations of economically independent career women in both American and British soaps with the increased use of plots involving business and career women.

Class has been a problematic area for soaps to address, in part because class conflict would cut across the ideal of community. Further, class is in a sense a defining notion of the community in British soaps, that is to say the communities are working class. Where middle-class characters appear it is often to reinforce the boundaries of the community through the marking of difference. There is a sense in which the exclusive focus on a particular class is also a characteristic of American soaps, since they often centre on the comings and goings of an extremely rich section of the corporate business world, most commonly the US oil industry, though the economic power of multinational business is presented in terms of family conflicts and personal ambition rather than those of class. In Britain, the soap that has most obviously tried to address questions of class has been *Brookside* where the 'close' is populated by a range of characters from different class positions. Class is seen both as a motivating factor for those characters, that is to say it is in terms of class that we are often asked to understand them, as well as a source of conflict between characters. *Brookside*, thus, avoids the collapse of class into discourses of community, and narrative themes frequently return to issues of unemployment, trade unionism and government economic policy. For example, Gottlieb (1993) discusses an episode of *Brookside* which centres on 16-year old Damon's hopes of employment after he has done well on a Youth Training Scheme and the subsequent disappointment and disillusion when those hopes are dashed. It was a public criticism at the time that the government-initiated YTS was a cynical exercise in manipulating the unemployment figures more than a real opportunity for young people to train and work. This connects of course with the realist conventions of *Brookside* which involve low-key acting, flat minimalist camera work and the use of a 'real' housing estate.

While the increase in the range of characters in soaps and the expansion of story-lines to include wider social issues are to be welcomed, Geraghty expresses concern that the increasing role of male characters and the entrance of the teenager as a key soap concern may be upsetting the particular orientation of soaps to women viewers and disrupting the pleasures they can gain from them. For example, the courting of the male audience has led to an increased use of conventions from the crime series and, Geraghty suggests, a shift in the representation of women towards pleasing the male eye.

What kind of an ideological analysis of soap opera could we make? What 'world visions' are crystallized therein? Any answers to such questions must of course be qualified, for while there are similarities of theme across a number of soaps there are also marked differences in terms of emphasis. Secondly, within a single soap we are likely to find contradictory ideological impulses.

Let us consider the issue of the addressing and representation of women, a central issue in the examination of the soap opera since it is frequently argued that soap opera is a woman's space in which women's motivations are validated and celebrated. It can be argued that soap operas address issues in the personal sphere which speak to women's competencies and from which many women take pleasure. It is also apparent that many soap operas deploy a variety of strong- and independent-minded woman characters. However, while the private sphere may be celebrated, women are frequently confined to it so that the financially-independent woman in the soap is a relatively recent and limited phenomenon. Additionally, the use of glamour and the physical appearance of women to enhance soaps is subject to the criticism that the representation of women is for the male gaze. Women may be strong in soaps but that strength is frequently put at the service of the family and the men within it. As commentators have argued, there is both protest and acceptance by women in soap opera.

The family, which as we have noted represents the mythic centre of soap opera life, is also handled in a contradictory way – it is idealized yet shown to be tearing itself apart. Women are both the victims of the claustrophobia of family life and in a sense the saviour of that which is valuable about it, that is the care and concern. This emphasis on the family may lead to the general exclusion of the public sphere, an ideological implication of which is that personal and family relations are deemed more important than wider social and structural issues. If we are happy in the family nothing else matters, or it matters only in terms of its private implications for individuals.

Whether it be in response to such criticism or not, soaps have begun to engage with public issues like racism, AIDS, crime, unemployment and so forth for which they might be praised, especially to the degree that they perform an educative role. Of course, soaps have always had some level of engagement with the public sphere; in the case of British soaps the core realm of the community and in the case of American prime-time soaps the world of the corporate business, and we might want to argue that the representation of 'community' is a valuable ideal. After all, it not only encapsulates values of care and concern it also celebrates the life of otherwise under-represented segments of society. However, one might also ask whether the community represented is not a myth, and, furthermore, a myth which obscures the fundamental realities of structured inequality in terms of class, gender and ethnicity. That such inequalities are obscured in American prime-time soap seems incontestable since they glamorize and legitimize multinational capitalism and big business in general. Voices which might potentially challenge such a view simply do not appear so that it would not be difficult to read *Dallas* as a celebration of the American way of consumer capitalism albeit presented in terms of a primordial kinship drama.

In summary, I am suggesting that *contradictory* textual meanings are available to viewers. Which of these meanings are activated by the audience is another issue and one which we will examine in chapter 5.

Latin Soaps: A Challenge to the US?

As Allen (1995) argues, it has been the Latin form of the soap – *Telenovelas* – and in particular the Brazilian (TV-Globo) and Mexican (Televisa) production centres that have benefited most radically from the increased demand for the serial form in the 1980s. For example, TV-Globo makes annual profits of US $20 million on its exports of telenovelas to over 100 countries. As Allen suggests, this represents an apparent reversal of the assumed flow of television from north to south, centre to periphery. During the 1980s telenovelas became the dominant Latin American television export, representing 70 per cent of the total of hours exported. Within Latin America they consistently get higher ratings than their imported American rivals (Rogers and Antola, 1985).

Telenovelas form the core of Latin American television production and consumption, the success of which has allowed some Latin American producers to develop the economic, professional and technical infrastructure to thrive despite their proximity to the US centres of production. Telenovelas are both a daytime and a prime-time phenomena and appeal to large audiences across the class and gender divides, and do not have the association with a female audience that soaps have acquired in the USA and Europe.

Telenovelas are a dominant genre in a way no single genre can claim to be in the entertainment programming of the United States, and they have a large following in all Latin American countries. (McAnany and La Pastina, 1994)

It is common for Latin American networks to broadcast nine to fourteen telenovelas each day five or six times a week (Rogers and Antola, 1985). For example, in Venezuela they are transmitted by the commercial networks in two blocks: 13.00–15.00 and 21.00–23.00 on Mondays to Saturdays inclusive (Barrios, 1988).

McAnany and La Pastina (1994) argue that it is important to understand the economic context of telenovelas and suggest three reasons why this is the case. First, the prime-time popularity of telenovelas allied to their export potential make them crucial to the prosperity of media production and distribution organizations. Second, the centrality of Brazil, Mexico and Venezuela as production centres contributes to the dominance of these national genres across Latin America. Third, telenovelas are seen by many commentators as a vehicle for consumer culture through product placement and advertising. Indeed, for many writers it is not just consumer culture that is at stake but modernity itself in so far as telenovelas provide a medium for the appropriation of attitudes consistent with the coming of modernity (Martin-Barbero, 1995; Mattelart and Mattelart, 1992).

Telenovelas have family resemblances with Anglo-American soap operas. Both are long-running serial narratives produced for television, and both, with varying degrees of emphasis, employ melodramatic narrative modes. Further, soap operas and telenovelas share a history of origination and sponsorship by US-based soap companies like Colgate and Lever Brothers. However, as Lopez (1995) reminds us, telenovelas have distinctive features which make them a specific genre. Whereas the soap opera is distinguished by its open-ended, potentially limitless, narrative form telenovelas have a specific number of episodes (often 100) that encourages narrative closure through definite endings. In this sense telenovelas have more in common with prime-time US soaps than the mainstream daytime soap operas. However, the narrative closure involved in telenovelas are not ones that necessarily structure the text from its inception since they continue to be written as they are screened and are continually subject to revision. In Brazil, TV-Globo puts considerable resources into audience monitoring and makes the development of telenovelas plots subject to audience feedback. At its most simple an unsuccessful programme will be cut short and a successful one will be extended thus demanding additional plot material. More subtly the endings of telenovelas can be altered to fit in with popular demand and to this extent telenovelas remain open-ended texts.

In general, telenovelas are a melodramatic form based on the representation of polarized moral forces expressed through dialogue and personalization. Telenovelas employ standard conventions and devices of melodrama while locating social and political issues firmly in the domestic domain. A common plot device involves the mystery and confusion which surrounds the secret identity, and unknown parentage, of a key character. Telenovelas represent for Martin-Barbero a moment in the evolution of the Latin melodrama, from its location in an oral story-telling tradition through its newspaper and radio serializations to its cinematic grammar, which 'speaks of a *primordial sociality*, whose metaphor continues to be the thick, censored plot of the tightly woven fabric of family relationships' (Martin-Barbero, 1995, p. 277). An emphasis which telenovelas share of course with soap operas. However, just as there are differences between the two genres so there are distinct cleavages within the telenovela form. Martin-Barbero suggests two distinct models. The first he defines as a '*serious* genre' centred on primordial feelings and passions in which tragic suffering predominates. The central dramatic conflicts of this form have to do with kinship and the form relies on a certain reduction of characters to signs. References to times and places are blurred and melodrama remains the organizing narrative principle. This model is to be seen in Mexican and Venezuelan productions, though the former tends towards baroque *mise-en-scène* in contrast to the primary orality of the latter. The second model, exemplified by Brazilian and Colombian telenovelas, incorporates a degree of everyday realism and national specificity into its format whereby the particularities of class, nation, gender and age emerge and characters, released from the need to be moral signs, are incorporated more into the routines and rhythms of everyday life. This allows telenovelas to represent the transformations of modern life including new social relations and moral conflicts. According to Lopez:

> The differences are so marked that almost anyone familiar with telenovelas can provide a general ahistorical sketch of the characteristics of the various national manifestations of the genre. (Lopez, 1995, p. 261)

She suggests, not unlike Martin-Barbero above, that Mexican telenovelas are 'notorious for their weepiness', Brazilian telenovelas are more cinematic and realist, while Colombian telenovelas attempt to occupy a middle ground between these two positions. The significance of this lies with the fostering of a televisual 'national' in which the 'imagined community' of the nation is organized around specific images of itself and the sense of living the nation through simultaneous viewing. In the case of the US Spanish-speaking market 'the telenovelas is making "nation" where there is no coincidence between nation and state' (Lopez, 1995, p. 266). Through the Spanish-language networks, Univision and Telemundo, telenovelas have helped promote a shared sense of Hispanic or Latino cultural identity amongst the US-based Spanish Diaspora.

However, telenovelas do not unambiguously promote national identity and Martin-Barbero highlights a developmental tension within telenovelas between national, Latin American and international themes. On the one hand, the introduction of a realist strand into telenovelas allowed for the representation of specific places; notably characteristics of particular nation-states – Brazil, Peru, Argentina, Mexico, etc. – while on the other hand, there has been a trend towards Latin American integration through the use of standardized sounds, rhythms and icons which promoted the export of telenovelas throughout the continent. The internationalization of the telenovela through its export to Portugal, Spain, Italy, Poland, Japan and other countries furthered a 'progressive neutralisation of the characteristics of Latin American-ness' since 'production for a global market implies the generalisation of narrative models and the thinning out of cultural characteristics' (Martin-Barbero, 1995, p. 283).

Brazilian Telenovelas

Brazilian telenovelas have received particular attention from scholars for three reasons. First, Brazil is the main exporter of telenovelas in the international market. Second, the rise of the dominant television company, TV-Globo, is intimately connected with the development of telenovelas, and third, because the social, economic and political situation in Brazil has been refracted through changes in the genre's format. What started life as a dependent relative of the American soap opera has now become an independent entity and the 'pre-eminent form of Brazilian popular culture' (Straubhaar, 1982).

Television in Brazil began in 1950 in São Paulo and rapidly spread to other cities. At first television was aimed at an economic elite, the upper and middle classes, but later oriented itself to a mass audience with telenovelas spearheading the populist drive. Telenovelas began as a cheap form of programming bearing the marks of American influence both in terms of programme format (American radio and television soap opera) and funding (the US-based transnational Time-Life helped to finance TV-Globo) with the main source of revenue being US advertisers. However, during the 1960s Globo began rejecting Time-Life programming advice in favour of its own populist strategy and was supported in this by the Brazilian military government who wanted to reduce imported programmes and promote Brazilian national identity via the 'Brazilianization' of television. Key to Globo's success in developing its own programming, reducing imports and increasing audiences were the telenovelas (Straubhaar, 1988).

A decisive moment in the transition of telenovelas into a populist form with more Brazilian content came in 1968 with the transmission of the telenovela *Beto Rockefeller*. Ironically, *Beto Rockefeller* was produced by TV-Globo's main rival TV-Tupi, but it was Globo that learned the lessons of its success (aided by its close alliance with the military dictatorship which refused to renew TV-Tupi's licence!). The significance of *Beto Rockefeller* lay in its adoption of a more realist style, the language being more colloquial and the story development less obviously formulaic, which became the model for the development of Brazilian novelas. Less studio bound than previous television drama, this telenovela was also more visually interesting with outside locations and a faster narrative pace. More filmic in style it actually relied on video technology to achieve this editing effect. *Beto Rockefeller* was a telenovela with a self-consciously modern feel deploying a central character who was no longer only a 'sign for good' but a more ambivalent, modest and insecure person with an eye for social mobility. The concerns of the urban middle class became embedded in the Brazilian telenovelas (Mattelart and Mattelart, 1992).

While there are always dangers of misrepresentation in reducing the complex development of telenovelas to thematic trends it does give us a feel for this dramatic form. Vink (1988) has provided an analysis of 24 Brazilian telenovelas broadcast between 1971 and 1987 the main points of which can be summarized thus:

- The average novela consists of 30–40 characters.
- While good and evil characters retain an influence there is a tendency to blur the boundaries in search of a more realist representation.
- Like the soap opera, the core of the telenovela's universe is interpersonal relations though this has not prevented it from incorporating more social realist themes which are understood in terms of their impact on the personal sphere.
- Brazilian novelas have a penchant for 'supernatural' personages.
- Telenovelas have moved out of the studio and involve a variety of outside locations with an urban, particularly Rio de Janeiro, bias.
- Settings are an important indicator of class with the rich living in big houses with swimming pools while the working class live in houses which connote bad taste. The depth of real poverty in Brazil is not shown and class is depicted as a question of consumption rather than production and place of work.
- The central discourses of telenovelas in Brazil concern interpersonal relations and class.

This final point requires some elaboration. The core of the telenovela's discourse is the achievment of happiness through heterosexual love. Ideally, this is to be found in marriage, but the realist orientation of the novelas means that this is not necessarily so. Marriage is sometimes seen as an economic and social arrangement which does not depend on romantic love which may be pursued elsewhere. While the presentation of women in traditional domestic and subordinate roles is the norm, a degree of social change is reflected in the increasing number of independent women seeking happiness through their own means. Personal conflicts between the pursuit of love and the constraints of social role form central themes in many telenovelas so that the discourses of love connect with those of class. Thus, a number of significant 'loves' are between characters of different social classes involving conflicts between social position and the pursuit of the loved one. Social mobility through marriage is a common novelas' theme. The juxtaposition of class life-styles is also core to a number of novelas with the rich marked by conspicuous consumption and the characters often treated unsympathetically. The rich are seldom happy and frequently cast as the 'bad' characters. The working class, who are depicted in terms of their plain life-style and colloquial language rather than their work, are treated with more sympathy but in a rather patronizing and stereotyped way. Novelas vary in the degree to which working-class characters accept this situation with resignation or seek ways out through struggle or social mobility. According to Vink, it is the professional middle class and their world which is depicted with variety and objectivity so that it is their social, economic and political aspirations, for example personal freedom and consumerism, which are the forms of change most often presented and sympathetically treated. Rarely do the collective industrial and political struggles of the working class reach the screen.

The danger with summarizing the themes of telenovelas in this way is that they appear as closed formulaic productions. While the above does represent a degree of formula it is not as rigid as it may at first appear, rather, novelas embrace competing and conflicting discourses. Thus, women are presented on the one hand as adjuncts of men, they are economically and socially dependent on men and daughters are directed to marry according to the father's wishes, while on the other hand telenovelas often show women denouncing and resisting such domination in a variety of ways. Such resistance is underpinned by a philosophy of individuality, personal freedom and choice.

The discourses of freedom and choice are philosophic elements of modernity, the spread of which is the key to all telenovelas in Brazil. In addition to notions of personal freedom, social change, mobility, economic 'development' and Brazilian national identity, all core themes of the modern telenovelas stress consumption as both the route to happiness and the markers of class 'taste' and 'distinction' (Bourdieu, 1984). Stress within the stories on happiness through consumption (one character was represented in tearful joy on the acquisition of a refrigerator) is paralleled by the Brazilian practice of 'merchandising' or product placement within the texts. Merchandising represents a larger source of revenue for TV-Globo than the more familiar spot advertising and entails the use of branded goods (cars, fridges, telephones, food) by the characters alongside lingering shots of the product which are presented as desirable and socially prestigious. Advertising is, thus, a core component of viewers' experience in Brazil where television is dominated by a commercial ethos which echoes the American system on which it was, in part, modelled. Every 12 minutes or so a dramatic break must be arranged to facilitate the adverts, the significance of which lies, as Mattelart and Mattelart (1992) argue, not just in the promotion of consumerism, the government (the largest advertiser) or TV-Globo itself, but in a specifically modern experience of time. They suggest that the novela 'combines two temporalities: alternating long periods and short periods'. The long period is that of the serial, the story developed over months or even years which has no real beginning or end. The time of the 'long durée' is one of emotion, pathos and family life and coincides with traditional popular narrative forms. The short period is that of the rapid mixture of shots (long and short) which combine to push the narrative forward in conjunction with the periodic interjection of adverts. This is a modern, perhaps postmodern, rhythm so that telenovelas are a mixture of the traditional and the modern.

To describe telenovelas as both traditional and modern raises interesting questions about the relative influence of national and foreign cultures within Brazilian television. These broader questions of cultural identity and cultural imperialism are discussed more fully in chapter 6, but some observations are in order here. Straubhaar (1982) has argued, using data from a content analysis during the 1970s, that the manifest content of Brazilian telenovelas, the stories and themes, show little signs of foreign influence but are clearly Brazilian. However, he does acknowledge what he calls the latent or underlying themes of youth culture, consumerism and capitalist economic values but argues that these are not foreign as such, since Brazil is increasingly a consumer society, and Brazilian television is clearly a commercial phenomenon. This prompts difficult questions about what is or is not Brazilian.

Herold (1988) argues that to talk of 'Brazilianization' acknowledges that the original forms were not Brazilian and goes on to argue that North American–Brazilian hybrid forms are effectively American not Brazilian in their plots, formats, production styles and themes. But how can a form such as the telenovelas, which is extremely popular in Brazil and contains Brazilian settings and characters, not be Brazilian? Herold seems to be in pursuit of some kind of pre-modern authentic 'Brazilianness' whereas it may be more profitable to see telenovelas as emblematic of the articulation of the global and the local. The underlying content being that of capitalist modernity in a Brazilian context.

However, capitalist modernity is marked by unequal development and unequal power. Both Brazilian society and Brazilian television can be argued to be in a structurally subordinate relationship to foreign, notably American, economic and media dynamics. Thus, Sinclair (1990) argues that the export of telenovelas to the USA does not mask the reliance of the Spanish-language networks on American capital and advertisers. While the cultural impact of the Spanish language networks and their broadcasting of telenovelas across the USA may promote a form of pan-American Spanish identity it has not broken the reliance on American capital, which has a substantial ownership stake in these channels, nor on US transnationals such as Coca Cola, McDonald's and Proctor & Gamble, who supply most of the advertising revenue. It is not the commodities and life-styles of Brazilian capitalism which are dominant but those promoted by American-based transnationals. This can be seen to involve a more lasting form of dependence though one which in its specifics is paradoxically still Brazilian.

The 'Global Appeal' of Soap Opera

Anglo-American soap operas and Latin American telenovelas share a number of features with each other and indeed with other soap operas around the world. These include a long-running serial form with interweaving multiple story strands mainly operating with a sense of real time and set in distinct geographical locations. While community, class and social issues all play their part in the thematic make-up of soap opera the core of the stories always revolves around interpersonal and family relationships. We also noted differences both between telenovelas and their Anglo-American counterparts and within the British, American and Latin American forms themselves. In particular, we recognized that soap operas mix the conventions of realism and melodrama in varying degrees so that British soaps are known for their realist orientation when compared to the more melodramatic form of many US soaps, and Mexican melodramatic-oriented telenovelas can be contrasted with the more realist Brazilian form.

Though telenovelas share many characteristics with soap opera they are also different in some respects, notably in their commitment to a specific number of episodes in contrast to the never-ending openness of the narrative in Anglo-American soaps and in their greater stress on class, social mobility, freedom, choice, consumption and other themes of modernity. All this reminds us that genre is concerned with the management of similarity and difference wherein lies the explanation for why soap opera has emerged as one of the most popular world-wide television forms, that is to say its ability to explore apparently global themes in more specifically local ways.

Hence, the global attraction of soap opera can be partly attributed to the apparently *universal* appeal of particular open-ended narrative forms, the centrality of the personal and kinship relations and in some circumstances the emergence of an international style embedded in the traditions of Hollywood. Liebes and Katz identify the key *cross-cultural* components of *Dallas* in terms of its *primordial kinship drama* and its *serial* narrative techniques.

> We are led by viewers to two dimensions of the *Dallas* genre, the semantic dimension, which draws so heavily on primordial themes of human relations, and the syntactic dimension of seriality, which regularly combines and recombines this set of basic relational elements to tell endless variations of the same story. (Liebes and Katz, 1988, p. 117)

However, the success of the soap opera can also reflect the possibilities offered to audiences of engaging in *local* or regional issues and problems located in recognizable and 'real' places. The tensions between the poles of the global and the local are highlighted by, on the one hand, the enormous global popularity of soaps like *Neighbours* and *Dallas* and on the other hand the failure of these very same soaps in particular countries (e.g. *Neighbours* in America, *Dallas* in Japan). Crofts' (1995) discussion of 'Global Neighbours' is illuminating in this respect since, as he argues:

> lest it be imagined that *Neighbours* has universal popularity or even
> comprehensibility, there remain some 150 countries to which it has
> not been exported, and many in which its notions of kinship
> systems, gender relations, and cultural spaces would appear most
> odd. (Crofts, 1995, p. 102)

He goes on to outline the factors that made *Neighbours* popular in some countries, notably the UK, but a relative failure in others, specifically the USA and France, and suggests a range of textual features which account for the success of *Neighbours*. Central to the appeal of *Neighbours* is its location in everyday experiences, particularly domestic experiences, which is a characteristic it shares with other soaps. This domesticity is specifically suburban allowing the representation of an enclosed private sphere of leisure, family and suburban sensibilities (crime and violence are 'out there') together with 'wholesome neighbourliness'. Within this suburban world 'differences are resolved, dissolved or repressed' and conflict minimized so that differences of class, gender and ethnicity are blurred and social problems displaced onto characters outside of the 'inner circle'. This is the comfortable world of the 'depoliticized middle class'. It is Croft's contention that *Neighbours* relies on 'feel-good characters' to sustain itself, allied to a specific appeal to the teenage audience with representations of young, vital, sexually attractive and unrebellious youth.

While such textual elements help to explain the success of *Neighbours* in general terms we must add the specific institutional and cultural conditions which prevail in given countries and which were instrumental in determining the programme's actual reception. Thus in the UK, *Neighbours* was relatively cheap to buy and supportively scheduled (it was the first programme to be stripped over five weekdays in the UK) by the BBC. In addition, the UK 'mediascape' had encouraged a 'broad familiarity' with Australian soaps having already screened *Prisoner: Cell Block H*, *A Country Practice*, *Flying Doctors* and other programmes of Antipodean origin. Interest was further fuelled by continuous media publicity given to the programme, particularly by the tabloid press, stoked up by the celebrity status of Kylie Minogue and Jason Donovan. Crofts goes on to argue that the sunny weather, spacious homes and myth of

Australian egalitarianism allowed British audiences living through a drab climate and economic depression to project their fantasies onto the programme. Differences of accent and idiom were slight enough to be assimilated, but great enough to encourage an exotic view of Australian life-styles.

Most of the textual elements discussed above ought to have promoted the success of *Neighbours* in the USA as well as in Britain, and Crofts notes a certain suburban similarity between *Neighbours* and *Beverley Hills 90210*. However, a number of factors worked against this. First, the everyday naturalism of *Neighbours* was not attuned to the greater melodrama of US soaps to which audiences were accustomed. Second, the ethnocentric American 'mediascape' far from acclimatizing audiences to imported programmes has consistently denied them access. Third, though *Neighbours* was screened it was not given the scheduling position or length of run needed to promote success. Likewise in France, where the domination of small-screen drama by American soaps, British costume drama and French mini-series did not provide fertile soil for *Neighbours* to put down roots.

Crofts' discussion of *Neighbours* helps us to understand that the global success, and failures, of soap opera depends on both the specificities of soap opera as a televisual form and the particularities of the conditions of reception. The dialectic of the global and local is illustrated by the fact that on the one hand there has been the emergence of an international prime-time soap opera style, while on the other many soaps retain a local setting and regional language audiences. To the degree that an international style exists it has the following characteristics:

1 High production values. That is to say a fairly glossy and expensive look.
2 Pleasing visual appearances from the glamour and wealth of *Dallas* to the adventurous and sunfilled landscape of Australia.
3 More action and physical movement than would be encountered in traditional soaps. In other words a faster-paced programme.
4 Hollywood-style narrative modes with which the global audience is familiar.
5 Elements of melodrama over realism as the dominant narrative style.

Nevertheless, there is widespread understanding that given a choice audiences prefer home-grown soaps to imports so that while the international soap makes big waves it is less impressive than an indigenous soap in local conditions. The generic soap opera form appears to have global appeal, most national television networks show soaps, but no particular soap opera has achieved such status.

As noted above, one of the reasons for the success of *Neighbours* in Britain was its strip-scheduling five days a week in the 'tea-time' slot. This strategic positioning boosted the audience not only for *Neighbours* itself but, through an intentional-scheduling manoeuvre, the audience for the programme that followed it, namely the *Six O'clock News*. News is of course one of the principal genres of televison; it appears in one form or another on just about every television network across the globe, often during 'prime-time', and is the subject of whole globally-distributed channels such as Cable News Network (CNN). 'If journalism were a philosophy rather than a trade' reflects one of the central characters in E. L. Doctorow's novel *The Waterworks*, 'it would say there is no order in the universe, no discernible meaning, without . . . the daily paper'. Therein lies the essence of the debate about news, that it serves as a significant source of the narrative frameworks for making sense of our world.

News Narratives

The production of 'news' holds a strategic position in debates about television for its presumed, and often feared, influence on public life, a concern that has been heightened by the emergence of global cross-border television. For example, it is a commonly-held belief that the western news media played a significant role in the revolutions in eastern Europe and the fall of the Berlin Wall in particular. The attempts by the Chinese government to prevent the reception of western news transmitted across its borders by Star TV's satellite system has become symbolic of the panic that the advent of global news can initiate. However, we would be mistaken if we imagined that such fear is only the preserve of undemocratic governments vainly trying to stem the inevitable tide of western liberal democracy since many democratic non-western nations have concerns about the cultural impact of western-originated news on traditional life-styles. Underlying these concerns is the perception that global news production and dissemination are an unbalanced affair very largely in the hands of western agencies. These fears are further fuelled by the open ambition of CNN, News Corporation, Reuters and the BBC to build global news services and to occupy the strategic heights of global news and information flows. Western nations also hold a philosophical and practical interest in television news as exemplified by undoubted attempts to censor and control news output in the perceived interest of the state. Finally, the population of the globe has grounds to fear not so much the free flow of news but its restriction and control by less than half-a-dozen global news organizations, themselves sub-sets of transnational corporations.

News is not of course a reflection of reality so much as 'the putting together of reality' (Schlesinger, 1978). It is not an unmediated 'window-on-the-world' but a selected and constructed representation of 'reality' and the criteria for such selection tell us about the ideological world-view that is being assembled and disseminated. The first selection concerns the topics that news covers which Hartley (1982) identifies, for Anglo-American news, as politics, the economy, foreign affairs, domestic affairs, sport and 'occasional' stories. These topics define the news paradigm, the significant omission being the domain of the personal/sexual. A second selection concerns the constitution of the topic so that politics, for example, is defined as being about government and mainstream political parties with a stress on personalities. The economy is circumscribed as being about the city, trade figures, government policy, inflation, money supply and so forth. Foreign affairs means intergovernmental relations while domestic news is subdivided into 'hard' stories – conflict, violence, industrial disputes – and 'soft' human interest stories. The category of 'sport' has traditionally been constituted by male professional sport. For the manufacture of a story within a topic, we can turn to Galtung and Ruge's (1973) pioneering work on 'news values' where they identify four prime news values of the western world: reference to elite nations, reference to elite persons, personalization and negativity. While the unexpected has significant news value it has even more so if it has negative consequences involving elite persons of an elite nation. Overall, as Schlesinger (1991) argues, what is required is thus:

> a recognition of the crucial importance of the contested processes
> of definition and interpretation in political culture. Or, in an idiom
> which is now out of fashion, of ideological struggle and its contexts.
> (Schlesinger, 1991, p. vii)

For instance, it can be argued that in the UK the whole terrain of state power and parliamentary politics is reproduced and legitimated by political reporting (Hall et al., 1978). Connell (1981) reports the privileging of governmental definitions of the workings of the economy while Hartley (1982) discusses 'trial by semiotics' in which there is a closing of the multi-accentuality of the sign to indicate how an event should be interpreted. Example, an industrial dispute is structured as an action by strikers rather than a dispute between two parties. Likewise the Glasgow University Media Group (1976; 1980; 1982) have consistently presented evidence to suggest a similar privileging of employer definitions over those of trade unions.

A brief discussion of Anglo-American news values cannot hope to deal adequately with all the issues of news coverage or the complexities of global television news. The questions we need to ask are whether such values are globally significant and whether the essential nature of news is the same whatever its origins. Straubhaar (1992) concludes (based on a cross-cultural study involving the USA, USSR, Japan, West Germany, Italy , India , Colombia and China) that 'what is news' is 'fairly consistent' from country to country and that the format of 20–40 minute programmes anchored by presenters was a common feature. In particular, 'politics' and 'economics' were consistently the main news topics. However, there were differences of emphasis in the treatment of those topics. For example, while US news contained the highest levels of criticism of government and issues of human rights they were also the most prone to 'sensationalism' and concentration on accidents, disasters and crime. Unsurprisingly, television in India and China contained more 'development news' but also, in the case of the latter, a more positive approach to science and technology. In contrast, Madden (1992) puts the case for the cultural specificity of news. Her analysis of the Inuit Broadcasting Corporation's news output suggests that it differs from western news in both content and style. There is, in contrast to western news, a stress on consensus over conflict, personal privacy over the public's 'right to know' and multi-vocal construction rather than the privileged voice of the news-reader. That Straubhaar should have found similarity over difference may reflect not so much a universal conception of news but 'the drift towards an international standardization of basic journalistic discourses' (Dahlgren, 1995, p. 49).

Gurevitch, Levy and Roeh (1991) carried out a study to ascertain the degree to which television news could be said to have 'gone global'. Their general case for regarding news as a global phenomenon rests on the establishment of news exchange arrangements whereby subscribing news organizations exchange news material with a particular emphasis on the sharing of visual footage. Data collected by Gurevitch et al. about the Eurovision News Exchange and the 36 countries which regularly use it suggests that the availability of common news footage and a shared professional culture led to 'substantial, but not complete' convergence of news stories. Across a two-week period up to 20 of the lead items were the same with a particular concentration in relation to foreign news so that news about other countries is more uniform than domestic news. However, the fact that much of the material exchanged is visual does mean that different interpretations of events can be added leading to what Gurevitch et al. call the 'domestication' of global news. They regard this as a 'countervailing force to the pull of globalisation'. For example, the same footage of a speech by the then Soviet president Gorbachev was given quite different treatments by US and British television. The former was highly sceptical about the intent of Gorbachev's speech while the latter took a much more sympathetic line. The overall picture is, thus, a mixed one with a tendency towards the establishment of global news partly countered by its insertion into local meaning structures and contexts. However, the globalizing trend remains of particular significance since, as we shall see later, western news agencies appear to dominate global news agendas.

In this respect, a trend in western news of global significance is the elevation of 'Islam' to the role of chief bogeyman. Much recent news coverage in the west has been devoted to the Gulf War and Saddam Hussein in particular; to the states of Iran, Iraq and Libya (with a special emphasis on their alleged sponsoring of terrorism); and to Salman Rushdie's book *The Satanic Verses* and the fatwa declared by Ayatollah Khomeini. As Said (1981) has argued, western media have represented Islamic peoples as irrational fanatics led by Messianic and authoritarian leaders. While there are of course political and ethical questions to be debated around the practices of Islam, western media coverage has not promoted the *dialogic* approach required for cross-cultural understanding but has taken sides against Islam with little understanding or explanation of what meanings are involved.

key !!!

Television news is constituted not only by its choice of topics and stories but also by its verbal and visual idioms or modes of address. Presentational styles have always been subject to tension between an informational and educational purpose and the need to engage and entertain us televisually. While current affairs programmes are often 'serious' in tone with adherence to the 'rules' of balance, more popular programmes adopt a friendly, lighter idiom in which we are invited to consider the impact of particular news items from the perspective of the 'average person in the street'. Dahlgren (1995) argues that increased commercial competition in global television has tilted the balance in favour of the latter and cites increased use of faster editing tempos and 'flashier' presentational styles including the use of logos, sound-bites, rapid visual cuts and the 'star quality' of news-readers.

A stress on immediacy in the presentation of news is a specific and recent development in global news which can be seen most obviously in the 24-hour live coverage of CNN, though it is also a feature of routine evening news programmes. Quite apart from live broadcasts by satellite, Electronic News Gathering (ENG) technology allows television to bring edited accounts of global and local events to the screen almost as they happen while lightweight cameras, digital video editing and the multi-skilling of television personnel allow for speed and flexibility. Global television has thus shortened the 'threshold' time of what constitutes news. This stress on immediacy may, as we shall see with regard to the Gulf War, be to the detriment of context and explanation as well as furthering an ideology of transparency. For example, CNN transmits a good deal of 'live' or lightly-edited footage which depends on its mimetic quality and so obscures its construction in terms of camera angles, voice-overs and rapid editing.

Political coverage in particular has come to rely increasingly on the staged sound-bite. Politicians go to some length to provide a resonant phrase or telling image for the purposes of television. A stress on the smart, compact sound-bite arguably downplays explanation and interpretation while strengthening the hand of those able to manage the news by providing newsworthy 'events' and footage. While this would usually favour the powerful – business, politicians, lobbyists – there is some evidence of its use by 'alternative' animal rights and ecology pressure groups. Greenpeace for example has proved adept at providing newsworthy footage and its success against the Shell oil company over the Brent Spar oil rig owed much to the television pictures it provided to news organizations. When French marines knowingly seized Greenpeace camera equipment in the South Pacific they dealt the Greenpeace campaign against French nuclear testing a serious blow.

Alongside these developments within the traditional news programme there has been a proliferation of new, popular formats including the tabloid-style news broadcast, the political talk show, the vox-pop audience participation format and the 'infotainment' magazine shows of breakfast and daytime television (Dahlgren, 1995). These programmes rely on a rapid turnover of items, emblematic visuals and a sense of proximity through the location of news in everyday experience (the human interest story). On the one hand popular formats can be said to enhance understanding by engaging an audience unwilling to endure the longer verbal orientation of older news formats while on the other, they arguably work to reduce deeper understanding by failing to provide the structural contexts for news events. We quickly learn what has happened (or at least a version of it) but not why it has happened.

Global News Flows

One of the central media concerns raised by developing nations through the agency of UNESCO and expressed by the McBride Commission's final report (1980) was, and continues to be, the unequal flow of news and information form the North to the South. Masmoudi (1979), a member of the MacBride Commission and leading spokesperson for the establishment of a New World Information and Communication Order (NWICO), argues that there is a virtual one-way flow of news from the northern 'centre' to the southern 'periphery'. News is gathered, selected and controlled by western transnational corporations who treat news as a commodity to be bought and sold, as opposed to the developmental, nation-building and democratic role Masmoudi seeks for it) According to Masmoudi, nearly 80 per cent of world news flow emanates from five major western news agencies, only 20–30 per cent of which involves coverage of developing countries. This is potentially detrimental to developing nations because the news coverage supplied by the transnational news agencies has emphasized negative news values (for example disasters and corruption) and promoted western cultural and political interests (consumerism, US foreign policy, etc.). Further, the lack of accurate and perceptive coverage of development issues in the western media has hampered an understanding of the needs of developing nations within the northern hemisphere.

The domination of news flows by western news agencies is significant because they supply 'spot news' and visual reports (often without commentary) which are the 'factual' basis upon which finished news productions are based. They are thus important agenda setters for world news. Only a handful of agencies have the economic resources to maintain a world news service and these are western owned and controlled. They are Associated Press (AP), United Press International (UPI), Reuters and Agence France-Presse (AFP). Some commentators would include the former soviet agency Telegrafnoye Agenstvo Sovetskovo Soyuza (TASS). Set up within the context of colonial expansion, these agencies continue to bear traces of their history; thus, Reuters and AFP are strongest in Africa while AP and UPI are more geared to Latin America. While these agencies were originally suppliers of news and information to the press, they also form the base for television's world news coverage as well as an increasing role in the supply of electronic information to the corporate community. Two large western television services, Visnews and WTN, are powerful forces within television news while the BBC's monitoring service and the US-based Cable News Network (CNN) have increased their significance as suppliers of international news. While the role of agencies is largely a matter of news and data supply to indigenous television and newspaper organizations in the North and South, there is also an emerging direct supply of finished news products to audiences via satellite television, most notably by CNN, the BBC and News Corporation with the latter looking set to outstrip its competitors by virtue of its increasing willingness to disseminate news in local languages from more local sources. As direct news broadcasters CNN, and to some extent the BBC, are hampered by the English-language base of their material.

The ascendancy of the western news agencies is buttressed by the 'barriers to entry' faced by any agency located in the developing world. Samarajiwa (1984) argues that the high costs of market entry, notably capital expenditure, telecommunications and personnel costs, mean that any new entrant would have to sustain considerable losses before its revenue base matched that of the established players. Further, it is unlikely that a Third World agency could develop such a base in the face of transnational agencies' (TNAs) ability to set differential price structures. Thus the TNAs, having already covered costs in their profitable domestic markets, can afford to charge local markets only what they can bear. No agency based in the developing world would have such a market and would therefore be unable to compete in terms of price. It would also be extremely difficult for a Third World agency to break into the western market by supplying development news to the western media since not only do some western news organizations distrust the governmental role in developing nations agencies, but the western agencies are vertically integrated with press and television news buyers. The supply of news to integrated media organizations is seen as a 'service' input and there is no incentive for western media to look for other sources. In addition, the technological lead of western agencies, which gives them far greater reliability and speed, constitutes further barriers to a fledgling Third World agency. Samarajiwa concludes that 'there is very little likelihood of a Third World based news agency entering the world market in news as presently constituted and surviving as an economically viable entry' (Samarajiwa, 1984, p. 130).

The UNESCO-inspired debate about a proposed New World Information and Communication Order (NWICO) prompted the formation of a number of news agencies and news exchange mechanisms throughout the developing world, prominent amongst which have been the Latin American oriented Inter Press Service (IPS), the Non-aligned News Agencies Pool (NANAP), the Broadcasting Organisations of the Non-aligned Countries (BONAC), the Pan-African News Agency (PANA), the Caribbean News Agency (CANA) and Caribvision. Most of these, with the notable exception of IPS, are government-sponsored inter-agency co-operative ventures rather than independent associations of journalists or commercially-viable news agencies. Boyd-Barrett and Thussu (1992) surveyed these organizations between 1987 and 1990 on behalf of UNESCO and argued that:

(a) News exchange mechanisms (NEMs) have improved inter-regional and intra Third World information flow.
(b) Some agencies, particularly IPS, have helped to change the way

news is defined and give it a more developmental focus.
(c) All the agencies operate under severe financial and technological handicaps in relation to their western rivals.
(d) Some of the agencies were open to manipulation by Third World elites.
(e) It has proved very difficult for NEMs to establish a foothold in North America and western Europe.

This led them to conclude that:

> NEMs do not appear to have had a significant impact on the structures of media imperialism over the past two decades. The development and maintenance of local and regional centres of news exchange does not in and of itself indicate a weakening in the global market hold of the major western transnationals. (Boyd-Barrett and Thussu, 1992, p. 141)

Musa (1990) argues that the increasing involvement of news agencies in global financial activities has strengthened the western agencies agenda-setting features. Using Reuters as his example, Musa suggests that the profitability of news agencies is increasingly dependent on supplying a wide range of computerized financial data to specialized corporate customers. To facilitate the speed necessary in today's global financial markets, most customers access the data on a Reuters-supplied dealing system, the consequence of which for NEMs is that not only does this increase the capital expenditure on technology required to enter or sustain oneself in the market, but most potential customers are already tied to Reuters. To survive, it becomes increasingly necessary for the NEMs to link up with the western agencies in partnership deals exchanging regional financial information. Thus the Caribbean News Agency (CANA) has forged just such a link-up with Reuters. On the one hand this provides the hard-pushed NEMs with much needed financial resources, but on the other hand it ties them to western agencies and subordinates the public information role of news agencies to the provision of information as a commodity. On a more positive note, Musa argues that as news information in the Third World is increasingly marginal to the profitability of western agencies, so they are more responsive to demands to place less emphasis on negative news, accidents and disasters, and more on other story-types like politics.

The possible consequences of western domination of news agencies and news production can be seen in the case of the 1990/91 Persian Gulf War where US and European oil interests were clearly at stake. Indeed Cummings (1992), following the postmodern arguments of Jameson and Baudrillard, sees the Gulf War as the first television war. Not because this was the first war to be covered by television but because this was a war so wholly managed by television and understood through television that television was 'the event' rather more than actual military activity in the Persian Gulf.

The Television Gulf War

The 'Gulf War' represents a significant moment for global television news for a number of reasons. First, the war was itself a series of events with global economic, political and military implications and can be seen as a Third World war in the sense that it was fought primarily by western powers against a Third World country. A widespread view within the developing world was that the objective of the war was not simply to liberate Kuwait from Iraqi occupation but to demonstrate western power to all Third World countries in order to 'keep them in their place' (Frank, 1992). Second, the Gulf War was a global television war seen all over the world and marked the arrival of Cable News Network (CNN) as a world-wide news service. CNN was received in 100 countries across the globe and facilitated 24-hour coverage of the war much of which was 'live' television. Third, the news coverage of the war was a highly-managed affair. Global television news covered a series of events with global implications, including possible planetary survival, in an extraordinarily selective way.

The CNN coverage of the Gulf War was unique in its live 24-hour format. The ratings success of this style had already been established by the channel's reporting of the explosion of the space shuttle Challenger and the 1989 suppression of the democracy movement in Beijing. In a study of CNN's Gulf reporting, Vincent (1992) argues that the channel employed the following forms of presentation:

1 Press briefings, speeches and staged events.
2 Tapes and interviews supplied by government agencies and the military.
3 Press pool stories.

4   Re-caps, sound-bites, journalist reports.
5   Use of consultants and 'experts'.
6   Non-elite sources.
7   Original stories based on current or related events by staff reporters.
8   Events in which news personnel are allowed to become the story.

The striking feature of these presentational styles is the predominance of studio-based coverage and stage-managed events. Morrison's (1992) content analysis of CNN, Sky news and UK terrestrial television confirms that over half of the coverage of the war was studio-based and most of the images that were not from a studio were of military press conferences so that only the pictures of Scud missile attacks could really be seen as 'live'. As he argues, this is 'hardly the action of battle'. Morrison goes on to document evidence that only 3 per cent of the news coverage was of 'the results of military action in terms of human casualties' and only 1 per cent of the visual images of television were of 'death and injury'. The impression given by news coverage, particularly by CNN, of immediacy and comprehensiveness was just that, an impression. A second conspicuous feature of Vincent's list of CNN techniques is how open they are to management and manipulation by the military authorities of the 'Desert Storm' coalition, since staged press conferences and tapes supplied by the military authorities are clearly open to manipulation by their originators. The experts deployed were for the most part military or pro-war consultants and even the stories featuring non-elite sources were centred on ordinary people in support of the war. Original investigative pieces of war journalism were few and far between.

The organization of the 'press pool' requires further discussion since it was critical to the management of the media by the authorities. Journalists from the press and television were not able to move and report freely during the Gulf War, their numbers were limited and those that were present were carefully shepherded by the military in a technique developed by the British during the Falklands conflict (Morrison and Tumber, 1988). Priority was given to journalists from coalition nations and many countries were unable to send journalists because they were not given visas. For example, no Swedish prestige paper had visa applications accepted (Norhrstedt, 1992). Once in the Gulf, journalists were escorted by troops and all copy and footage was vetted by military censors, journalists who did not accommodate themselves to such management were threatened with loss of accreditation or even arrest. According to the American television reporter James LeMoyne, the pool officials,

> decide which American units can be visited by reporters, how long a visit will last, which reporters can make the visits and, to some extent, what soldiers may say, what television cameras can show and what can be written. (cited in Cummings, 1992, p. 111)

The restrictive rules of the pool forbade interviews with soldiers without permission or the presence of military authorities so that no images of patients suffering or undergoing treatment were allowed (Ottosen, 1992). While it was made clear that CNN reporter Peter Arnett's stories from Baghdad were subject to censorship by Iraqi authorities (and it is worth noting that Arnett was vilified in some quarters for even being in Iraq) the extent of coalition news manipulation and use of disinformation was never made clear.

I have concentrated on the overt management of the news by military authorities because it was so marked in the Gulf War, but in recognizing this we should not overlook the cultural biases of western journalists who, with few exceptions, could be expected to support the war. The influence of these western journalists extended well beyond the boundaries of the USA and Europe. For example, Sainath (1992) reports the attraction of CNN to Indian elites and the domination of Indian press and television by western pro-war sources. Indian journalists were not encouraged to apply for visas to the Gulf and while Indian papers carried anti-war editorials the rest of the papers were filled with news reports exclusively from western news agencies. While state television did introduce an element of debate they suffered from the domination of the screen by images supplied by the coalition authorities so that:

> On television, India's one international affairs programme 'The World This Week', found itself imprisoned by its footage – all from western sources. Many of the journalists working on the programme were clearly against the war, but the footage was not. (Sainath, 1992, p. 71)

News management by the military means of course that television news was presenting a specific kind of 'truth' and constructing a very particular 'reality'. Perhaps the most enduring motif of the television Gulf War was that of technologically 'smart' weapons able to hit targets with pin-point accuracy thereby confining the war to military engagements and minimizing casualties. Viewers of CNN could hardly fail to be mesmerized by the sight of cruise missiles snaking through high-rise blocks to reach their military targets or the video images beamed directly from the nose cone of an air-to-ground missile as it left the jet and destroyed another Iraqi munitions dump. As Robins and Aksoy (1992) argue, this smart technology was equated with 'good', 'reason' and 'morality'. This was depicted as a well-ordered and managed war fought against a robust 'fourth largest army in the world' which achieved its military and political goals without needless civilian suffering. That the war needed to be fought at all was explained, as the content analysis carried out by Morrison shows, in terms of the need to 'liberate Kuwait', 'uphold international law', and check 'Hussein's expansion capacity'. Responsibility for the war was placed firmly at the door of Iraq for its invasion of Kuwait and in particular on the shoulders of Saddam Hussein who was cast in the role of 'evil emperor'. Morrison confirms that Hussein was the political leader most referred to by television and where a quality was associated with him, 90 per cent fell into a negative category.

However, there is another version of 'truth' and 'reality' in relation to the war presented by 34 authors from 18 countries in the book *Triumph of the Image: The Media's War in the Persian Gulf* (Mowlana, Gerbner, and Schiller, 1992). They claim that:

1   Only 7 per cent of the tonnage dropped was 'smart' and of this 10 per cent missed its targets.
2   Iraq was subjected to carpet-bombing involving a greater tonnage than that which was dropped in the entire Second World War.
3   The infrastructure of Iraq was destroyed, returning it to a pre-industrial era.
4   Over 150,000 civilians were killed and total Iraqi casualties approached a quarter of a million.
5   The Iraqi army was largely made up of unwilling conscripts who did not live up to the image of the 'Elite Republican Guard'.
6   Coalition forces slaughtered the retreating Iraqi army in what some pilots called a 'turkey shoot'.
7   Western powers looked away as troops loyal to the Iraqi leadership massacred Kurdish and Shi'ite opponents.

If accurate, this is a damning indictment of western governments and the media's complicity with them, but perhaps worse was television's deficiency in providing an adequate explanation for the war. Rather 'the event itself – war – appears to swamp the news and did so at the expense of discussion about either the initial invasion of Kuwait in August 1990, or the presentation of a historical perspective on the war' (Morrison, 1992, p. 68). By concentrating on the 'glamour' of high-tech weaponry and the immediate military objectives of the war television obscured the reasons that lay behind the conflict.

Few of the western critics of the war would want to condone the Iraqi invasion of Kuwait. Thus, Noam Chomsky and Edward Said appeared on US television and supported the UN economic sanctions against Iraq which followed the offensive. However, the reasons for the Iraqi invasion and the precise justification for a western military response did not appear to be fully explored on television or in the press. There is, for example, an argument which suggests that Iraq was the victim of a deliberate policy by the USA, Saudi Arabia and Kuwait to drive down the price of oil. Further, there is evidence that the US ambassador to Iraq told Saddam Hussein that any action taken by Iraq against Kuwait was an internal Arab affair which would not lead to any American response. This is in direct contrast to arguments suggesting that the US president George Bush had decided on a military solution to predicted Iraqi action and that at no time was the US administration committed to allowing economic sanctions to work. Indeed, it has been argued that Bush quickened the drive to war at the very moment when an Iraqi withdrawal threatened at least to stabilize the situation without the need for western military activity. The continued rationale that the war was a necessary response to unwarranted use of force against a neighbour arguably obscured the USA's own use of force in, amongst other places, Panama and Grenada, not to mention Vietnam. Nor was television keen to highlight the undemocratic and despotic nature of the regimes in Saudi Arabia and Kuwait.

If television had made such arguments more widely available and explored the evidence in support of them, the western public would perhaps have been less enthusiastic in its support of the war. If television is to contribute to the creation of a public sphere and assist in the development of the rights of citizens to participate fully in the life of society, then as Murdock (1991) argues, it must provide people with the full range of information they need to make personal and political judgements, engage in the greatest range of contemporary experience and offer the broadest possible range of viewpoints on the experiences it represents. With respect to the Gulf War televison fell short of this view of the public interest.

Hopkinson (1992) represents one journalist's argument that images of the rout of fleeing Iraqi forces may have influenced President Bush's decision to stop the Gulf War short of a full-scale invasion of Iraq. The President is said to have feared that images of slaughter would turn public opinion against the war as it was thought to have done in Vietnam. If so, it was a decision based on political rather than military considerations. While Hopkinson points out that there were other political and military reasons why Bush could have made that decision the claim does highlight the potential that television has for playing an illuminating role. Television news is not always as carefully controlled as in the Gulf War and it would be foolish to ignore the very real ability news has to inform and educate us. Electronic media have indeed widened our horizons and my discussion of the Gulf War was not intended to deny this. Rather, I hoped to contrast a discussion of the ideological policing of television news with my earlier, more populist, discussion of soap opera.

Conclusions

Television can be said to be global in that similar narrative forms circulate around the world. Soap opera and news can be found in most countries. Further, we saw that similar narrative themes and structures occur within those forms, thus open-ended story development and a focus on the private sphere are markers of a global soap. We also encountered evidence to suggest that news across the world tends to originate from the same western mould.

In contrast to this globalizing tendency we also explored countervailing forces towards localization of global forms so that news, even where the sources are the same western agencies, is frequently tailored to local cultural contexts. Likewise, telenovelas, while sharing some characteristics, are not the same as western soap operas, indeed the Latin American format has almost eclipsed their Anglo-American counterparts in terms of exports. While there is an undeniable push towards standardized, western-originated global television narratives we need be careful not to over-generalize. Rather, we must explore global television in terms of a global–local dialectic.

Although I have, in this chapter, approached television in terms of genre this is not necessarily a reflection of viewers' experience. The global multiplication of communications technologies has created an increasingly complex semiotic environment so that television produces and circulates an explosive display of competing signs and meanings. This creates a flow of images which fuses news, views, drama and reportage. The variety of juxtapositions of images and meanings in television creates a sort of electronic bricolage which occurs both within and across channels. Multi-channel diversity and the ability of viewers to zip and zap, channel change and fast forward, adds to this bricolage effect. We might, therefore, ask whether there is a global television culture which is developed across the range of television forms. This will be the theme of chapter 5.

However, before we explore that issue we need to consider whether identified textual meanings are the ones which actual audiences take up. We need to consider the relationship between programmes and audiences and how the latter use television and its texts in everyday life. This issue forms the substance of the next chapter which again concentrates on soap opera and news.

4

Television and Global Audiences

This chapter centres on the relationship between television and its audiences and begins with a general discussion of how to conceptualize audiences before reviewing what is known from empirical research about viewers of soap opera and news. This is followed by a discussion of the structuring influences of television on the domestic routines of daily life and, in particular, those connected to 'the family'. The chapter concludes with a discussion of audiences, ideology and identity. This chapter will be confined to issues of individual identities while chapter 6 will explore the influence of television on whole cultures with particular reference to collective national identities.

Constructing the Passive Audience

Given the sheer volume of research into television audiences it is not possible to summarize or do justice to it all. My account is necessarily selective and concentrates on a theme which has been central to television audience research since 1980: the 'active' audience. To understand the significance of the phrase 'active audience' we need to establish the ways in which the audience has been conceptualized as 'passive'. By 'passive' I mean a sense that the meanings that television has for audiences are determined by the texts themselves. In my account the audience has been seen as a passive consumer of a powerful television message by:

- Early television 'effects' researchers.
- Television companies.
- Some writers who see the audience as subject to an ideological 'effect' through television.

Early research into the television audience was undertaken within an empirical framework which conceptualized the audience as a large mass composed of isolated and unknown individuals. That was the thinking of a group of researchers in the USA who employed a series of experimental and statistical methods in search of the 'effects' of the media. These effects were conceived of as behavioural ones subject to measurement. This paradigm, often referred to as the 'hypodermic model' by its detractors, has been the subject of considerable criticism. Firstly, the model concentrates on short-term behaviour rather than considering the meanings that audiences construct and deploy. Secondly, it fails to differentiate between social groups and the meanings they bring to television. As Williams (1961) remarked, there are no masses, only ways of seeing people as masses. Above all, the research failed to demonstrate the expected effects of television.

There remains a significant attachment amongst some television researchers to a numerical approach. Thus 'ratings', so important to television organizations in their quest to measure and control audiences and attract advertising revenue, are constructed using a mixture of surveys, diaries and electronic 'people-meters' to give increasingly sophisticated mathematical representations of audience behaviour. These represent the efforts made by advertisers and programme producers to track and shape the audience as part of an ongoing form of surveillance. We are constructed as an audience by an industrial and commercial process that seeks to measure, analyse and produce us in increasingly sophisticated ways in order that we consume certain products be they soap powders or television programmes (Gandy, 1990). Television can be seen as part of a world-marketing strategy whether that be a soft drink or a political party. In either case, television is at the centre of a calculated strategy to control people's habits and routines (Robins and Webster, 1985). In essence, the gathering of information about television audiences has been an attempt to regularize both the audience and the institution (Ang, 1991).

Television is concerned with the construction and interpretation of meaning, and although it is only one of the many ways in which we seek to explore our world it is unique in its ability to standardize and share common cultural meanings with virtually all members of society. It has been argued (Williams, 1973, 1979, 1981; Hall, 1977, 1981) that while any given culture is constructed in terms of a multiplicity of streams of meaning there is nevertheless a strand of meanings which can reasonably be called dominant. The process of making, maintaining and reproducing the dominant set of meanings and practices we can, after Gramsci (1968), see as cultural hegemony. It should be noted that hegemony is never total nor static, rather, hegemony represents a *temporary* stabilization of social conflicts which is always open to challenge and change. Television can play a part in the construction of hegemony through the circulation of a restricted range of ideological discourses and representations. By ideology is meant discourses which, while they purport to be universal truths, are maps of meaning which support the power of a particular social group,whether that group is class, sexual, ethnic or nationally constituted. Ideology, at least in this account, does not imply 'false consciousness', rather, ideologies are world-views which are both effects of power and maintain that power.

To argue that television is ideological is to suggest that a restricted range of representations and discourses is on offer. For example, depictions of the family, the heartland image of television, can be argued to represent a limited repertoire of images and social situations. As Cantor and Cantor (1992) remark, even with the development of off-beat families in American sitcoms problems are always resolved in terms of family values of caring, togetherness, love and peace. A complementary approach on a more global scale is to examine textual meanings and ideologies in order to establish the case for media imperialism. This is the stance of Dorfman and Mattelart (1975) in their analysis of the world of Walt Disney. The author's aim is to locate the values within the Disney universe and to demonstrate the ideological assumptions which support American imperialism. This consists in persuading people that the American way is the 'best way'. Dorfman and Mattelart create an inventory of ideological themes including the racial and cultural stereotyping of Third World nations, the image of developing countries as full of wealth waiting for western explorers to legitimately elevation of money and consumption to the highest levels of personal ambition and the depiction of capitalism as inevitable and necessary.

In the more rigid versions of the 'dominant ideology' thesis the audience is conceived of as passive so that media discourses are unproblematically inscribed in them. In some ways this is no more than a recycled version of a 'hypodermic' model. However, by the end of the chapter we may, given a flexible conception of ideological hegemony, consider that it is possible to retain both the idea of the active audience and the concept of ideology. This is where hegemony is seen in terms of the flux and play of social forces, rather than monolithic domination, and in which 'ideological effects' require our active participation.

Theorizing the Active Audience

It had largely been assumed that meaning lay in the text and was associated with authorial intent. More recently, critics have challenged this view on two counts: firstly on the grounds that authorial intent is not in principle recoverable from within a text and secondly, and more significantly, even if it were identifiable the intentions of the author are unable to police the meanings created by readers/audiences. For Gadamer (1976), understanding is always from the position and point of view of the person who understands. The relationship between the text and the audience for Gadamer would thus be an interactive one in which the reader approaches the text with certain expectations and anticipations which are modified in the course of reading to be replaced by new 'projections'. This relationship between text and reader takes the form of a kind of question and answer session in search of understanding. Critically, this process of understanding involves not merely reproduction of textual meaning but *the production of meaning by the readers*. In other words the audience plays an *active* role in the construction of meaning.

For Iser (1978), an understanding of the act of reading cannot remain with the text but must concern itself with actual acts involved in responding to a text. A text as such is only a set of possibilities which have to be realized by actual readers so that in the reading act the words on the page are given life by the reader. Conceived as such, the text may structure aspects of meaning, it guides the reader, but it cannot fix the meaning which is the outcome of the oscillations between the text and the imagination of the reader. The text is poly-semic, that is to say it has the possibility of a number of different meanings to be constructed from it. As such it contains 'indeter-minacy' and 'gaps' whereby the reader moves through the text and engages in a process of 'gap filling' and meaning construction by which expectations are modified in a dynamic process of interaction between the reader's anticipations and the texts schematic instructions and invitations.

Wilson (1993) applies these concepts to the small screen and, con-sistent with the work of Iser, argues that all readings of television are productive of new meaning though the text may structure a 'pre-ferred meaning'. For Wilson, watching television involves the attempt to construct coherent sense-making narratives from the uncertainties of the text involving the attempt to make sense of the text and to construct a kind of unity of meaning. The audience speculates about the enigmas (questions posed in the text) and indeterminacies (absence of meaning in audience understanding which may have its sources from within or without the text) with which they are confronted. At the heart of this experience is the recognition of the familiar and the different, and a consequent 'com-muting' between involvement and distanciation. Television tries to construct a familiar family-centred world, for example the chatty family-oriented breakfast television, but there will always be a dif-ference between the *general* life-world attributed to the audience and the *specific* horizons of a real audience. As Wilson puts it, 'reading is always appropriation of meaning from a position of greater or lesser semiotic difference' (Wilson, 1993, p. 21). Audiences thus move between similarity and difference, and identification and distancing.

Radical relativist versions of reception theory locate meaning only in the readers' active production so that there would be, in principle, as many readings as there are readers. However, this is not a position taken by the writers discussed above who recognize that while readers are able to construct meaning the act of production is situ-ated both textually and historically. We can thus examine the ways in which texts seek to *position* readers through a series of textual invitations. Buckingham (1987), in his exploration of *EastEnders*, draws on some terminology developed by Iser to explain the textual structuring of the serial and shows the way in which the text offers clues to recall past events (retension) and to invite speculation about the future (protension). The text also invites us to engage in lateral reference, that is, to compare characters and to speculate about the past and future in relation to those characters. Here we are not left simply to invent characters out of thin air, rather it supplies us with a series of clues dispersed throughout its length from which we are able to construct character. Soap operas like *EastEnders* are, as we noted in chapter 3, very 'open' texts, there is plenty of room for differential readings but that does not mean that such readings are limitless (unless one includes totally aberrant readings), rather the text seeks to structure certain boundaries of meaning.

A different theoretical account of the 'active' audience can be found within 'cultural studies', most obviously within the encoding/decoding model developed by Stuart Hall (1981). Hall conceives of the process of television encoding as an articulation of linked but distinct moments – production, circulation, distribution, reproduction – each of which has its specific practice which is necessary to the circuit but does not guarantee the next moment. In particular, the production of meaning does not ensure consumption of that meaning as the encoders might have intended because television messages, constructed as a sign system with multi-accentuated components, are polysemic. In short, television messages carry multiple meanings and can be interpreted in different ways. That is not to say that all the meanings are equal among themselves, rather, the text will be 'structured in dominance' leading to a 'preferred meaning'. The audience is conceived of as composed of clusters of socially-situated individuals whose readings will be framed by shared cultural meanings and practices and, to the degree that these frameworks are also those of the encoders, then the audience will decode the messages within the same framework. However, where, as a result of being situated in different social positions, the audience is constituted in different discourses then they are able to decode the programmes in alternative ways. Hall proposed, after Parkin, a model of three hypothetical decoding positions: a dominant–hegemonic encoding/decoding, a negotiated code (which acknowledges the legitimacy of the hegemonic in the abstract but makes its own rules and adaptations under particular circumstances) and an oppositional code in which people may understand the preferred encoding but reject it and decode in contrary ways.

In summary, there has been a resurgence of interest in audience research since 1980 driven by the active audience paradigm and although there are theoretical differences between writers in the field discernible trends can be identified:

- From a concern with the general to an interest in the particular.
- From a concern with numbers to a concern with meaning.
- From viewing the text as having a single meaning to seeing multiple meanings within it.
- From concentration on the text to a focus on the audience.
- From seeing the audience as an undifferentiated broad mass to trying to understand the specificities of particular audiences under definite circumstances.
- From a conception of the audience as passive to a notion of the active audience.

These being the general theoretical stances of the 'active audience' paradigm, let us now consider some of the empirical research from within the field with particular reference to soap opera and news.

Global Television and Soap Opera Viewing

As Miller argues:

> Soap opera seems to form a triumvirate with Coca-Cola and McDonalds as the key symbols of the global expansion of American culture. (Miller, 1995, p. 213)

The study of soap opera viewing is, thus, a useful entry point into the empirical evidence regarding global television audiences and has been the focus of a number of studies for the following reasons. First, it is a very popular television form. Second, it is, as we have already noted, a world-wide television genre. Third, as one of the more exported television forms, the viewing of soaps in countries other than the originator raises all the questions of potential cultural imperialism. Fourth, the genre has traditionally attracted a large female audience and a number of women writers have been interested in why that has been the case. Fifth, as a traditionally 'low' culture product with a very large audience soaps have raised questions about the relationship between quality and popularity.

In turn, no soap has raised all of those questions more acutely than *Dallas* which was extremely popular on a global scale, attracted a significant female audience and was exported world-wide. To many, including the French minister Jack Lang, it became a symbol of American cultural imperialism and critics fears of 'wall-to-wall *Dallas*' was symbolic of the whole process of the globalization of television and American television in particular.

One much discussed examination of *Dallas* and its audience was carried out by Ien Ang (1985) amongst women viewers in the Netherlands. The study involved placing an advert in a women's magazine asking people to write letters about why they enjoyed watching *Dallas* followed by an analysis of the letters which she describes as 'symptomatic' that is, searching for the attitudes which lie behind the letter as a text. Ang begins by exploring the tension between ideas of an active audience and the potential structuring of meaning by the text as cultural product. She argues that the audience plays an active role in the production of meaning and of pleasure thereby creating a variety of responses but that the range of responses is not infinite given that *Dallas* is structured using specific codes and conventions requiring shared cultural knowledge.

Ang's central argument is that *Dallas* viewers are actively involved in the production of both meaning and pleasure and that these take on a range of manifestations which are not reducible to either the structure of the text, an 'ideological effect' or a political project. Fiction she says is a way of enjoying the here and now and involves playing with feelings in a movement between involvement and distance, and acceptance and protest. It is also an experience which is mediated by the 'ideology of mass culture' which places *Dallas* in an inferior relationship to other cultural activities leading viewers to adopt a range of viewing positions; some felt guilty about watching *Dallas*, others adopted an ironic stance to stave off the contradiction of both liking *Dallas* and seeing it as 'trash', one group argued that it was acceptable to watch the programme if you were 'aware of the dangers' while others, informed by an ideology of populism, defended themselves on the grounds that they had the right to like what they liked.

Other studies of the soap opera audience confirm both the general genre competencies of the audience and the placing of television viewing within a social–domestic context including a sense of a collective, collaborative network of viewing. Thus Seiter et al. argue, based on ethnographic research in the USA, that:

> soap texts are the products not of individual and isolated readings but of collective constructions – collaborative readings, as it were, of small social groups such as families, friends, and neighbours, or people sharing an apartment. Most viewers report that they have made it a habit to rely on other people in order to compensate for gaps in their comprehension. (Seiter et al., 1989, p. 233)

Thus a network of women viewers emerge in Seiter's study who use each other to keep track of the complex plot developments over a long period of time. This network is often family-based – mothers and daughters – or neighbour-centred and topics of discussion included speculation about future developments and moral–ideological judgements about characters and their actions or potential choices. Not that this is in and of itself a new discovery, a good deal of the current interest in soap audiences was pre-empted by Hobson's (1982) work on the British soap *Crossroads*, a much-maligned programme regarded by many as the very definition of trash television. Hobson argued that it had a special place in the lives of its mainly female audience whose very competencies in the interpersonal and domestic sphere, allied to various kinds of programme and genre knowledge, allowed them to take an active role as audience members and to share this with other audience members.

Much of the work done on soap audiences has assumed an adult female audience but this need not be the case since the re-emergence of soap in updated form has seen the introduction of themes, issues and characters intended to create a wider audience including more men and young people. Such a programme is the UK soap *EastEnders*. Buckingham (1987) followed up his textual analysis of *EastEnders* with an audience study involving school-aged children and confirms a shared and collaborative viewing process. *EastEnders* is a programme that is talked about in a way which puts the re-telling of narrative secrets and speculation about plot developments at the heart of the pleasure involved in watching the serial. Discussing the programme was an occasion for moral debate and judgement, sometimes from within the terms of the narrative and sometimes from outside the text, that is from within the children's own moral stance. This involved debate about issues of class and race, but above all of gender. Buckingham stresses the active and critical role of the children and the playfulness of their viewing involving a shifting of responses from within and without of the rules of the game, from fiction to reality and back again.

While Ang's work illustrates the active role of the audience and denies the implied 'hypodermic effect' of mass cultural products, Liebes and Katz (1985; 1986; 1988; 1989) set out to explore the reception of *Dallas* as a US-made programme amongst viewers from a range of cultural and ethnic backgrounds. They argue that *Dallas*, far from being simplistic trash, is a very complex programme in terms of the elaborate sets of relationships between characters, the interweaving of stories and the 'staccato' narrative style which requires considerable skill to understand.

What makes the Liebes and Katz *Dallas* project of particular interest is its exploration of the *cross-cultural* dimensions of viewing since the study involved 65 focus discussion groups from various ethnic groups. These constituted Arabs, Russian Jews, Moroccan Jews, and Israeli Kibbutz members in Israel plus a group of Americans and Japanese situated in their country of origin. The study was looking for evidence of different readings of *Dallas* in terms of understanding and critical ability and it was assumed that members of the groups would discuss the text with each other and develop interpretations together based on mutual cultural understanding.

Liebes and Katz argue that their study does, indeed, provide evidence of different readings of the narrative based on different cultural backgrounds and cite the case of the Arab group who 'misinterpreted' Sue Ellen's actions in terms of their own expectations and understandings regarding families. In particular, they explore the differences between 'referential' and 'critical' approaches to the programme across different groups. By 'referential' they mean an understanding of *Dallas* which fundamentally takes the programme as referring to 'reality' and discusses the programme as if it were real. By 'critical' they mean an awareness of the constructed nature of the programme and a discussion in terms of the mechanisms of narrative construction and the economics of the television industry. Overall, referential statements outweighed critical statements three to one. However, they argue that there were distinct differences between ethnic groups in the levels of each type of statement and conclude that:

1 Americans and Russians were particularly critical.
2 Americans have a greater understanding of the form and underlying business of television.
3 But, Americans are less critical in terms of themes/content and tended to assume *Dallas* has no themes and ideology but is merely entertainment.
4 The Russians by contrast were critical of the 'politics' of *Dallas*.
5 Arab groups had a high sensitivity to the 'dangers' of western culture and of western 'moral degeneracy'.

Liebes and Katz try to explain what they call the 'near universal popularity of programmes like *Dallas*' in terms of 'primordiality' and 'seriality', which are essentially textual determinations, while at the same time arguing that 'for better or worse, real readers insist on behaving more ambiguously than the roles that theory assigns them' (Liebes and Katz, 1988, p. 123). Therein lies the significance of their work and the enigma of global television. On the one hand there are 'near-universal' elements in the text with a global appeal and yet on the other there is a range of culturally-specific decodings. A potential criticism of Liebes and Katz' *Dallas* study is that this kind of cross-cultural research assumes that there is a neutral position or meta-language from which it is possible to make cultural judgements. As Penacchioni (1984) suggests, when Brazilians from the north-east of the country laugh at television how can we know they are laughing at the same thing as us and, indeed, how is it that they may laugh at moments we consider inappropriate. However, the issue is really one of degree; the relativism of Pennacchioni would lead us to question long-held assumptions about how American television is received across the world. That is to say, it would lead us to question or reject the argument for cultural imperialism based on a 'hypodermic model' of audience reception, a position which a reading of Liebes and Katz would also lead us to.

The use of soaps to talk about, explore and test out the boundaries of moral and social life in a cultural context which does not share some of the central assumptions of the text itself is further explored by Gillespie (1995) who discusses the way that young people in Southall (London) of Punjabi cultural background use *Neighbours* to articulate their own emergent norms and values. In particular, the rules surrounding male–female relationships and teenage romance are the subject of discussion. While *Neighbours* makes such relations a core part of its narratives these relationships are taboo within the 'parent' culture. The programme becomes a site for discussion amongst young people themselves and a point of contact, exploration and confirmation of values between parents and children. This is especially significant for girls since *Neighbours* portrays young women with a far greater degree of freedom than many British Asian girls can themselves expect so that the programme both offers the pleasure of seeing more assertive women and provokes discussion about gender roles. Elsewhere, Gillespie (1989) documents the way in which Asian parents, especially mothers, use imported Hindi films on video as a didactic opportunity in which they can highlight the virtues of traditional cultural practices. Thus, *Neighbours* is incorporated into the lives and cultural practices of the Southall Punjabi community in varying degrees with varying levels of acceptance and for different purposes.

There is a growing body of studies about soap opera audiences outside the Euro-American axis, an interesting example of which is Miller's (1995) study of the consumption of *The Young and the Restless* in Trinidad. Miller argues that we would be mistaken in regarding *The Young and the Restless* simply as the export and consumption of American culture or as the unproblematic carrier of modernity and consumer culture. Instead, he recounts the ways in which the soap opera is 'localized', made sense of and absorbed into local practices and meanings. He demonstrates the social and participatory nature of soap opera viewing alongside a sense of the relevance of the narrative content for moral issues in Trinidad. In particular, the gossip and scandal, specifically that of a sexual nature, which are core concerns of the soap opera's narrative, resonate with the Trinidadian concept of Bacchanal, which, according to Miller, is a deeply-rooted folk concept that fuses ideas of confusion, gossip, scandal and truth. The concerns of the soap thus 'collude with the local sense of truth as exposure and scandal' (Miller, 1995, p. 223). Such collusion includes clothing and style which play a significant part in the formation and maintenance of identity within Trinidad where, contrary to western notions, external display is not seen as superficial but as an expression of the true public self. Thus, *The Young and the Restless* provides models and talking points for the discussion and imitation of fashion. Miller's work is significant because it suggests that the study of the formal characteristics of narratives is insufficient and stresses the need to understand local processes of absorption and transformation which, by their very nature, will be specific, contingent and unpredictable.

In a review of 26 studies of what they call 'the most watched television genre globally', Latin American *Telenovelas*, McAnany and La Pastina (1994) argue that we can draw out 'findings that are apparent across a number of studies and are not or rarely contradicted by others'. They conclude that:

1 *Audiences are active and derive a variety of meanings from telenovelas*. The studies confirm the active involvement with narratives and the variety of meanings that audiences derive from the stories.

2 *Audiences make application to their lives*. Notwithstanding the fact that audiences watch telenovelas for reasons of pleasure, McAnany and La Pastina argue that the studies corroborate the claims that telenovelas are talked about by audiences in ways which seek to connect the narrative to their own lives, whether this be economic change, class and gender roles, or interpersonal problems.

3 *Audiences recognize the fictional nature of the genre and the functioning of its rules*. The fact that audiences may relate telenovelas' narratives to the circumstances of their own lives does not mean that they are confused about the fictional nature of the programmes. On the contrary, the studies reviewed by the authors suggest that audiences not only have no trouble in recognizing the dramatic character of telenovelas but have often developed sophisticated genre competencies.

4 *The contextual variables of family, class, gender, and neighbourhood qualify audiences' reaction*. The investigations surveyed substantiate the arguments that local organizational and cultural configurations mediate the understandings of soap operas generated by audiences. For example, McAnany and La Pastina argue (based on their reading of a study by Jacks which they cite) that Gaucho culture of Southern Brazil, which includes a sense of territoriality, machismo, traditionalism and local pride, is implicated in viewers' readings. Further, Leal and Oliven's (1988) study of class interpretations of the Brazilian telenovela *Summer Sun* suggests that working-class accounts of telenovelas are mimetic, they repeat narratives in detail, while upper-class

accounts of telenovelas are more synthetic and thematic in orientation. Working-class discourses on telenovelas tended to treat them as realistic and always involved moral judgements whereas upper-class groups treated novelas as unrealistic and fictitious, but used them to explore questions of emotional fulfilment in relationships. They argue that these differential interpretations depended on very different notions of survival and marriage; for the working-class group marriage was an alliance and a division of labour, which does not necessarily mean emotional and sexual satisfaction, while in the upper-class group emotional satisfaction in the context of stable relationships was the main focus of attention.

Lopez (1995) argues that telenovelas have, above all, created a tele-visual 'national' allowing audiences to 'live' the nation in everyday life. In addition to a sense of national community generated by a sense of simultaneous viewing, she suggests that specifically national themes and symbols are woven into the narratives and recounts Martin-Barbero's description of the way Colombian tele-novelas have 'provided the beleaguered nation with a self-image that differs markedly from the violent narco-trafficking for which it is known throughout the rest of the world' (Lopez, 1995, p. 263). In the case of the large US Spanish-speaking market, Lopez argues that the telenovela 'is making "nation" where there is no coincidence between nation and state' (Lopez, 1995, p. 266). US Latinos, she suggests, recognized themselves in the variety of telenovelas carried in the Spanish-language networks, Univision and Telemundo, and identified with a pan-national Spanish-speaking 'imagined community'.

While telenovelas need to be understood, according to Martin-Barbero (1995), in terms of the variety of meanings generated on the national, regional and transnational planes, their overarching significance lies in 'the field of transformations which make it possible for the urban masses to appropriate modernity without abandoning their oral culture' (Martin-Barbero, 1995, p. 276). Specifically, telenovelas present new social arrangements and ways of thinking in line with modernity. This extends beyond the bounds of nations towards a pan-Latin American identification, required and encouraged by exporting strategies which cannot address the cultural specifities of nations too closely. In short, telenovelas are the site of mediations between production and consumption in which local cultural habits and thinking are responded to, while being recast within hegemonic discourses by the imperatives of commercial television.

The global–local tension which is manifested in telenovelas and which is crucial to the theme of modernity, is not of course unique to telenovelas for there is a similar global–local tension in the production and reception of news.

Watching News

A 'classic' account of 'watching news' is Morley's (1980) research into the audience of the British news 'magazine' programme *Nationwide*, a study based on Hall's encoding/decoding model discussed earlier. The project aimed to explore the hypothesis that decodings varied according to socio-demographic factors (class, age, sex, race); cultural frameworks, identifications and competencies; contexts of viewing; and the topics in the programmes. Though not without its methodological problems the study confirms both a multitude of readings and a clustering around key decoding positions.

In accordance with the schema generated by Hall, Morley identifies the Dominant, Negotiated and Oppositional decodings of sections of the audience which involved a response both to the programmes content and its style. Dominant decodings were made by a group of print managers who held radical conservative views and accepted both the preferred reading and style of *Nationwide*, and also by a group of traditionally conservative bank managers who, while accepting the 'preferred reading' at the level of discourse, rejected the populist style. Negotiated readings were made by a group of trade union officials who, while happy with the populist style, rejected aspects of the content or discourse of the programme and, in particular, the programme's stance to an industrial dispute. Their readings remained negotiated rather than oppositional because they were specific to a particular dispute while remaining within the general discourse that strikes were a 'bad thing for Britain'. According to Morley, oppositional decodings were made by a group of shop stewards whose own political perspectives led them to reject wholesale the discourses of *Nationwide*, and by a group of black further-education students who felt alienated from the programme by virtue of its perceived irrelevance to their lives. (The implications of this for global television are that western news programmes would be decoded by audiences according to their own cultural backgrounds in ways which would undercut the ideological effect of western news within other cultures)

The core criticism of the *Nationwide* study is that the concepts and categories used are insufficiently sensitive to the complexities of the processes involved in watching television so that Morley (1992) himself questions whether the notion of decoding isn't too crude, encompassing as it does a set of processes (e.g. attentiveness, relevance, comprehension and interpretation) which need to be examined in more depth. Morley further acknowledges the criticism that the study stressed class over race or gender and that the sample and settings used in the study were restricted and artificial. In summary, he argues that subjects are more contradictory (interdiscursive) and contexts more important than the conception of the *Nationwide* project allowed for. Nevertheless, he continues to argue for the significance of a sociological orientation to the understanding of audiences so that one can neither 'read' the audience from the text nor assume a limitless range of readings.

While Morley stresses the active nature of the *audience* and the significance of their socio-economic position in shaping a range of decodings, Lewis (1985) demonstrates the importance of the *text* in enabling or constraining the audience's engagement with news. His research involved 54 interviews with audience members regarding the decoding of British news programme *News at Ten* and argues that the audience's ability to understand news programmes depends on the narrative structure of the text. By understanding he means not simply information recall, but the interpretation of news items and their placing within a narrative context so that an understanding of a government minister's speech involves not only what was said, but why it was said and in what context. Lewis goes on to argue that such understanding is facilitated by news which is structured as a chronological narrative, posing enigmas or questions which draw the audience into an engagement with the text. Interestingly, he argues that the audience's understanding of news is enhanced by news narratives which allow the audience to enjoy the satisfactions of being active, of taking part in decoding. Where the structure of news does not encourage this, and Lewis suggests that generally it does not, then possession of prior contextual knowledge is required for audiences to understand news. The implications of this view for global television are double-edged: on the one hand it asserts the significance of the text, implying that the global circulation of western news agendas is significant in re-producing western hegemony for audiences in the north and south, while on the other it suggests that a culturally-specific news may constitute a barrier to engagement for audiences from different cultures so that non-western audiences may simply disengage from western news.

The work of Morley and Lewis depends on staged interviews with audience members who have watched British news programmes and who broadly share the cultural paradigm within which it is set. In contrast, Gillespie (1995) provides us with useful evidence about the nature of news talk amongst Asian youth in Southall (London); these are British young people who also have cultural knowledge and competencies drawn from the Punjabi Sikh community and, like many others across the globe who watch western-originated news, bring a degree of non-western cultural understandings to bear on it. Unlike Morley and Lewis, Gillespie does not rely on formal inter-views alone but draws on a ten-year ethnographic study which enables her to place television viewing within the broader contexts of the viewers' lives. Overall, the relationship between the young people and news is one of ambivalence. Parents are keen on en-couraging their children to understand news from India and in part the young people co-operate in this, both to please adults and because of their own interest in the continent of their parents' birth. Ambivalence remains though, since many of the Southall youth stressed the greater importance to them of *here*, Britain, rather than *there*, India. Ambivalence also marked the young people's discus-sions of news about the Gulf War. As one might expect these young people displayed a humanitarian concern with respect to the death and injury which war brings but also became bored with war news after a period of time. The most deep-rooted response was one of insecurity and ambiguity 'concerning definitions of self in relation to "significant" others'. On the one hand, the young people were drawn to seeing the Gulf War as a war against Islam and, for some, their own religious affiliations led them to identify with an Islamic nation under attack. On the other hand, they regarded themselves as British and westernized and did not want to put themselves outside those cultural boundaries. Above all, the questioning of the loyalty of British Muslims in the media and the rise in racist attacks under-mined their sense of security and raised questions for them about how they fitted in *here* and *there*. One of Gillespie's subjects expressed it thus:

> The news talks about the anger of British Muslims and their loyalty to Islam but what is a British Muslim? Is he more British or more Muslim? You can't exactly have an equal choice of both, it's diffi-cult to say but I think I'm more westernised, I wouldn't say I'm British because we're in two societies at the same time, one is Islamic society, but not to the true extent, and the other is western-ised society, but bearing away from it. If you look at the small things in these societies they are totally different, like your behaviour, your duties and your role in the family. (Gillespie, 1995, p. 138)

News is thus a resource for young people to talk about their identi-ties and is both a source for the construction and confirmation of identities as well as an unsettling, disturbing phenomenon which leads them to question their selfhood. While I have concentrated here on ethnicity as a mediating factor in the understanding of news we should also note that Gillespie documents differences within these same young people which centre on age, gender and class. Gillespie's work confirms that watching and decoding news is a complexly mediated affair the understanding of which requires us to grasp the way television talk is embedded in the routines of everyday life.

The work of Morley, Lewis and Gillespie all stresses the interplay between programmes and actors' cultural competencies, though the different angles from which they approach the issues places greater or lesser emphasis on the determinations of audience, text and context. This highlights a debate which is both substantive, it is about the relative significance of texts and audiences, and method-ological, it reflects the approaches of researchers. The tension between textual and extra-textual determinations is further illus-trated by two pieces of research about audience responses to the Gulf War news. Morgan, Lewis and Jhally (1992) provide evidence that the more American viewers watched television news the less they understood the war. News was an impediment to understanding but a useful vehicle of propaganda: the more people watched the more they supported the war. For example, heavy viewers of television were twice as likely to think that Kuwait was a democracy and supporters of the war were twice as likely to think that Kuwait was a democracy. Thus, heavy television news-watching correlated with both misunderstanding, Kuwait is not a democracy, and with support for the war. The clear lesson is that news as a text, structured audience understandings. Shaw and Carr-Hill (1992), in suggesting that 82 per cent of their sample endorsed the idea that the coalition missile attacks were precision strikes, seem to confirm the influence of the television version of the war. However, they also point to a 'critical tendency' in the audience which expressed concern for Iraqi casualties and saw media coverage as 'glorifying war'. This represented a departure from the television news orthodoxy and asserts again the ability of audiences to bring alternative discourses to bear on the interpretation of television news.

The discussion so far has assumed that the role of news is one of information transfer and that audiences rationally process this information in ways which are more or less determined by the text itself. Dahlgren (1985; 1988) is critical of the 'information processing' notion of news on the grounds that only one of the communicative modes of news is referential or informational, news also has a poetic mode concerned with image and style and a phatic or ritual mode concerned with the act of communication itself conveying a sense of belonging or participation. He suggests that audiences watch news in different ways which he describes as an *archival* or information mode of reception, an *associational* mode which draws on viewers' pre-existing knowledge and frames of reference and a *subliminal* mode where the realm of the cultural unconscious comes into play. Dahlgren downplays the informational side of news by pointing to a body of empirical and psychological evidence suggesting that 'viewers often have great difficulty comprehending and even recalling news items' (Dahlgren, 1988). Instead, he argues that the significance of news lies not so much in specific items of information but in the organization of collective perception so that television news is understood as a form of cultural discourse which is ritualistic, symbolic and ultimately mythic. It is, thus, the broad sweep of cultural and ideological understanding which is key to news rather than specific pieces of information. For Dahlgren, the ritualistic watching of news integrates us with wider ideologies and practices and does so in ways which activate cultural and symbolic aspects of the unconscious.

In a complementary approach, Jensen (1990) also displaces the rational informational role of news. He argues that watching the news helps to situate viewers in relation to a range of political concerns and contributes to the audience's sense of social identity. However, this is primarily a matter of *feeling*, watching the news gives us a sense of community and of ourselves as competent political subjects. For Jensen, news has a hegemonic role in legitimating the political institutions of democracies and giving us a sense of citizenship, it does not however lead to political activity, not least because there are few institutionalized channels for citizens to be politically active in and through. Oppositional accounts are not used as a resource for oppositional action.

Both Dahlgren and Jensen are suggesting that while official discourse on news treats it as an important source of information enabling political activity, in practice our relationship to news is a symbolic and affective one which draws from and legitimates the wider parameters of our culture. News viewing is ritualistic, symbolic and a matter of feeling as much as information. This is important because there is a tendency in audience research, including in my own account, to regard the engagement with television as a rational, cognitive process and to underplay the aesthetic and emotional.

The *act* of watching news, which appears to be a marker of status, most notably as an adult and a citizen, is as significant as reflecting on its informational content. Gillespie (1995) reports that while news is the most viewed television genre amongst Southall youth, on the whole they do not enjoy it, rather, watching news is encouraged by adults because competence in understanding news is regarded by parents and youth alike as a marker of the transition to adulthood. Monteiro and Jayasankar (1995) recount an interview with a male Indian viewer living on the outskirts of Bombay who developed an interest in news when he acquired his own house. Watching the news supported his identity as male, head of the household and citizen of the Indian state since news watching was associated by him with the serious male-oriented public sphere and he regarded his watching of the news as a significant difference between himself and his wife. Watching the news was also a marker of difference between his conception of himself as an educated urban dweller and the rural poor. In sum, news may help position subjects on the child–adult continuum, as citizens of a particular state and as participants in a male-dominated political realm.

Nevertheless, Dahlgren continues to argue that different cultural groups refract ideology 'through its own prisms' and that specific individuals mobilize different forms of news discourse (for example, official or more personal discourses) in different settings. Thus, it is one thing to watch BBC news in Britain or CNN in America, it may be quite another to do so in Bombay or Baghdad. Whether it be rational information processing or a matter of feeling and identification viewers continue to have different resources to draw on. Whether western news in India or Iraq encourages identification or alienation is a moot point requiring empirical investigation.

Regrettably, I am aware of few empirical investigations of cross-cultural consumption of news and there is no study of news which would parallel the Liebes and Katz investigation of *Dallas*. However, Chaffee's (1992) review of survey studies of news does provide us with some empirical evidence and he reports that women in China who watched western television were more likely to espouse individualistic values than those who did not. However, the statistical correlation is stronger in relation to entertainment programmes than news. Chaffee also discusses a survey of young people in Belize which suggests that viewers of western television were more likely to want to emigrate to the USA than those who did not watch television as much. Again, the correlation is stronger with entertainment television than news. Indeed, readers of news magazines were less likely to want to emigrate. Chaffee speculates that this was a result of the images of crime and violence connected to the USA, in such magazines, in contrast to the more glamorous image of the USA derived from entertainment. In any case, these studies should be regarded only as indicative rather than conclusive.

What sense can we make of these apparently contradictory accounts of news and its audience? Does news shape an audience's understanding of the world or does the audience make of news what it will? Is the understanding of news a rational cognitive process or is it an emotional and symbolic one? It may be trite to say so but there is no one sense that can be made of news, what news means depends both on the structuring of the text and the cultural competencies of the audience. Those competencies are themselves socially, historically and geographically differentiated; in particular, questions of class, gender, age and ethnicity are crucial in shaping our responses to news. Nevertheless, the content and style of news does matter since it is the raw material with which we as an audience work. If the news continually legitimates a particular political system or world-view, an audience will have to have alternative discursive resources available in order to come to different or competing conclusions.

Of course watching television, be it soap opera, news or any other genre is not only a matter of meaning but of the place of television within the rhythms and routines of everyday domestic life. As Giddens (1984; 1989; 1991) argues, the study of everyday life is of major importance to any sociological understanding since it is day-to-day routines and interactions which both occupy most of our time and give structure and form to what we do. Further, the studying of everyday life illuminates our understanding of larger social systems and institutions since they depend on the patterns of social interaction engaged upon in the course of daily life.

Television and Everyday Life

Watching television is a complex set of practices linked to other social, and particularly domestic, activities so that the meanings produced by audiences need to be understood as embedded in the general set of routines surrounding television viewing. As Morley argues:

> Television as 'text' and television as technology are united by their construction, their recontextualisation, within the practices of our daily lives and in the display of goods and cultural competence, both in private and in public. (Morley, 1992, p. 182)

Thus, Morley and Silverstone (1990) argue that the text-reader model requires further reworking to take into account the way meanings generated by audiences are not confined to the viewing situation but are generated and sustained by the wider activities of everyday life. We need to understand, they argue, the kinds of attention and inattention which characterizes the relationship to television as a domestic medium subject to the rhythms of everyday life by placing television in a network of much wider acts of meaningful consumption.

Of relevance here is Morley's (1986) study of *Family Television* in which he seeks to understand how television is interpreted and used by different families with a specific focus on power and gender. He focuses on the levels of attentiveness; the different programmes watched; the spatial arrangements involved in viewing; the relationship between television and other family activities, together with the relationship between television and other domestic technologies; and of course the meanings and significances generated by the audience in relation to television programmes. From his qualitative interviews with 18 south London working-class families he draws the following conclusions:

1   Power and control over programme choice lies mostly with adult men.
2   Men have more attentive viewing styles than women who are engaged in other domestic activities.
3   Men tend to plan their viewing more systematically than women who tend to watch what is on at any given moment.
4   While men deny talking about television women use it as a conversation piece.
5   The use of the video is controlled by 'dad'.
6   Women express guilt over their viewing preferences especially 'solo' viewing habits.
7   Drama and fiction feature more in the preferences of women than men for whom sport and news are more central.
8   Women prefer local to national news.

There are acknowledged limitations to this work in terms of the restricted range of families both in terms of number (only 18) and composition (exclusively white, London working-class) but it is nevertheless suggestive of the kinds of work that can be done in relation to television in a domestic setting.

Television is bound up with our everyday conceptions of time since, as Scannel (1988) has argued, broadcasting is 'profoundly implicated in the temporal arrangements of modern societies'. In particular, television sustains routines which are significant aspects of the reproduction of social life since they serve both to provide actors with ontological security and are a mechanism for the reproduction of wider social structures. Thus, broadcasting brings major public events into the private worlds of viewers and in doing so constructs a kind of national calendar which organizes, coordinates and renews a national public social world. In Britain such events would include, for Scannel, sporting occasions such as the FA Cup Final, the Grand National and Wimbledon, but might also include political events like the opening of Parliament, party conferences and royal birthdays. On a more local and private level television contributes to the organization of social life through its scheduling practices which partly reflect, but also create, domestic family routines such as the positioning of 'tea-time' in relation to *Neighbours*. Broadcasting also 'unobtrusively but no less remarkably, re-socialises private life by providing ritual social events in which families or groups of friends watch together and talk about the programme before, during and after' (Scannel, 1989, p. 155). Soap operas tend to figure prominently in such a role.

While television plays a role in the construction and reproduction of domestic time, since families mesh their activities with those of the TV schedule, they nevertheless do so to varying degrees and Bryce (1987) relates distinct conceptions of time within families to the way they use television. Thus, families with a linear and sequential orientation to time will tend to plan television viewing and watch it as a singular activity so that television is watched between other activities. Families with a polychronic orientation to time, that is to say one involving multiple simultaneous activity with little reference to clocks, will view television as one of a number of concurrent activities and do so without much pre-planning. Finally, Behl (1988) reports that television in India is transforming some rural Indian families' routines by shifting their primary time orientation away from 'nature' and towards the clock and television.

One of the more in-depth ethnographic explorations of watching telenovelas was carried out by Barrios (1988) in Venezuela who studied 13 families' viewing habits from amongst the wide ethnic, class and family formations of Venezuelan society. Although 51 per cent of the programmes to be seen on Venezuelan television are imported, and it is possible to watch American serials like *Dallas*, *Dynasty* and *Falcon Crest*, the five hours of telenovelas broadcast each day remain the most popular shows.

> [Telenovelas] are one of the few shows broadcast by the television system here where Venezuelan people can watch characters that live, dress, speak, suffer, and enjoy in the same ways audience members do in their everyday lives. (Barrios, 1988, p. 77)

Barrios's study focuses on the mutually-constituting way that television viewing and the organization of family life are intertwined.

In particular, the economic and spatial resources available to families combined with the politics of the family to establish patterns and modes of watching television; families with more space (e.g. more rooms) valued television viewing more, but watched it as a communal family event less than those with only one 'television room'. Television viewing was integrated into the daily routines of life: getting up in the morning, meal times, homework times, returning from work and so forth. Of particular significance was the ritual sacred space created around the two blocks of telenovela time in which interruption was frowned upon. This was especially important to women, whose lives centred on domestic labour, but also played a part in the lives of men and children. Indeed, questions about who watches what on television, when and where, were at the heart of family politics both encouraging and disrupting communication between family members. Barrios again authenticates the centrality of post-transmission talk to the telenovela experience since, as one teenage girl expressed it, 'in this way I can talk with my friends at school tomorrow about what happened tonight' (Barrios, 1988, p. 69).

The connections between television and daily routines in China are explored by Lull (1988) who regards television as an agent of modernization. Limited domestic space means that the introduction of a television set into a household has considerable impact. When the television is on it cannot be escaped so that watching television has to be a collective family experience; family routines now include a specific time to watch TV. The arrival of television has altered family relationships including potential conflict over what is watched, when and by whom. The regulation of children's viewing was a particular issue. Lull also suggests that television has significantly altered leisure patterns by reducing film-going and other outside activities in favour of more private domestic viewing.

Audiences, Ideology, Identity

There is now a good deal of work on television audiences within the ethnographic and cultural studies traditions. The striking thing about these studies is the repetition of the broad parameters of their findings. These can be summarized as follows: first, the audience is conceived of as an active and knowledgeable producer of meaning not a product of a structured text. Second, those meanings are bounded by the way the text is structured and by the domestic and cultural context of the viewing. Third, and following on from this, audiences need to be understood in the contexts in which they watch television both in terms of meaning construction and the routines of daily life. Fourth, audiences are able easily to distinguish between fiction and reality indeed they actively play with the boundaries. They move in and out of degrees of involvement and distance, and engagement and inattention. Fifth, the processes of meaning construction and the place of television in the routines of daily life alter from culture to culture and in terms of gender and class within the same cultural community.

It has often been assumed that the active nature of the audience undercuts the role of ideology in television making reception, for example of western-originated programmes in non-western contexts, less problematically tied to textual construction and issues of power. While I concur with the argument that audiences are active and that ideology is not unproblematically injected into them, I would counsel a note of caution. While evidence suggests that television viewers understand a good deal about both the grammar and production processes of television, and on the level of television *form* individuals are extremely sophisticated and literate, that does not necessarily prevent them from producing and reproducing forms of ideology. For example, Liebes and Katz's (1989) study of *Dallas* suggests that while American viewers offer the most critical statements, more for example than Russians, these critical comments refer more often than not to questions of television form and production. Americans were far less likely than Russians to offer critical comments that related to the ideological messages of *Dallas*. On the contrary, they regarded *Dallas* as entertainment with no particular ideological stance, a view which is itself ideological.

My own research (Barker, 1995, 1996c), carried out amongst mainly British Asian teenage viewers of soap opera and centred on post-transmission talk, suggests that they are both active *and* implicated in the reproduction of ideology about the family, relationships and gender. The young people in the study were indeed an 'active' audience, they moved easily between discussions centred on the plots, as if it was the *real world*, to recognition of the constructed nature of the text within a television production context. They were able both to play the game of plot prediction and at the same time discuss plot inconsistencies and episodes from the past (screened in the present) thereby demonstrating their understanding of the constructed nature of soap opera. In other words they had a sound grasp of the *TV world*. For example, in the sequence below three 15-year-old girls discuss possible plot directions in *EastEnders*:

C: Apparently Natalie commits suicide.
B: Yeah, that's what I heard, you told me I think someone told you and you told me.
A: I heard that.

The phrase *apparently Natalie commits suicide* refers to a future story-line and thus acknowledges its construction outside of real time. Further, the role of previous soap talk is acknowledged, *that's what I heard*, from which we can infer recognition of the fictional nature of a narrative already prepared for screening on television. At another moment it is quite clear that the nature of soaps, in this case *Neighbours*, as fictional constructions of television is understood by the same speakers:

A: She [Helen] has survived a stroke, she's been gassed, fallen down stairs, broken her arm she . . .
B: They should kill Helen off.
A: No, listen right how far are they ahead of us in Australia, how far.
B: Meanwhile about 10 million people have come and left and she's been in it from the start.
A: I've been watching the old ones on UK Gold, I'm waiting for Daphne to get killed.

In this sequence the girls seem to be hinting at the unreality of *Neighbours* in terms of the number of accidents that have befallen Helen. The phrase *They should kill Helen off* acknowledges that the programme is capable of being altered by 'they'. It is a made-up story! The fictitious nature of the soap is underlined by the observation that the episodes are screened in Australia ahead of the UK showing. The ability to watch old episodes on the satellite channel UK Gold and wait for a known event, further underscores the narrative as fiction.

While the participants recognized soap opera as fiction, they are not fooled in to thinking that the *soap world* is the *real world*, nevertheless, as Hodge and Tripp note 'The closer the message is judged to be to reality by the receiver, the more it will be responded to both emotionally and cognitively as though it were reality' (Hodge and Tripp, 1986, p. 116). The perceived realism of soaps was certainly an issue for the participants since criticism of particular soaps was frequently introduced with the phrase *it's not realistic enough* and British soaps were consistently held to be superior to Australian soaps by virtue of their greater realism. Realism was a high-status phenomenon for these young people and was one of the character-istics of valued soaps associated with the serious over the trivial. However, as we have already noted, the participants know full well that soaps are fictitious. Realism for these young people does not simply mean unmediated reality, rather, it is possible to identify five uses of the concept which I want to explore further here.

1   Mimetic realism whereby the soap is deemed to be a 'copy' of the *real world* by virtue of the fact that it looks and sounds like everyday life.

C: Do you think that's real, like the story?
A: I don't know, it sounds, it looks kinda real.

2   Naturalism or literal realism which involves not only questions of the appearance of physical reality but crucially the plausibility of action and linear causation in terms of the 'regime of signification' (Abercrombie, Lash and Longhurst, 1992) of everyday life. The judgement as to whether a given event does or does not happen in 'real life' was the touchstone of naturalistic realism.

B: Those are realistic things.
A: Yeah realistic.
C: Those kind of things could happen.

3   Narrative realism or *soap world* realism whereby action and causation are plausible within the bounds of the soap narrative and characterization. This is essentially a question of internal narrative consistency and came to the fore most often in its negative form, as a criticism of Australian soaps in particular.

B: Yeah you know Cody in Neighbours, she went to America.
A: She was in Todd's year.
B: Yeah and came back and Todd.
A: Todd would probably have been twenty.

B: Yeah if he was still in it and imagine back in the beginning a sixteen-year-old.

A: Now she's supposed to be the same age as Michael and that lot, doesn't that mean she's actually lost.

A&B: About three years.

A: 'Cos when she left she was supposed to be about fifteen.

4   Emotional realism, as identified by Ang (1985), whereby the narrative while not necessarily conforming to the rules of naturalism or even narrative realism does appeal to a recognizable array of personal and interpersonal 'problems' to which we respond and identify emotionally. This is where the classic central concerns of soaps: marriages, divorces, affairs and pairings, come to the fore. The young people never say 'this is emotionally realistic', but it is clear that many emotional and moral dilemmas in soaps are discussed as being relevant to their lives. That is, they are realistic and plausible emotional situations. For example, the girls below discuss dancing and sexuality as it relates to Vikram, an Asian male character in *Neighbours*, in a way which suggests that aspects of the situation bring the girls' own sexual and emotional dilemmas to the fore. The question of what is acceptable dancing and sexual behaviour is clearly linked to the identities of the speakers as Asians and girls. The feeling of being *left out* contrasted to the dangers of getting a *bad reputation* appears to be an emotional dilemma which these girls orientate towards.

B: You know Vikram, he's a hypocrite cos do you remember when it was that party, I can't remember when, and he was dancing with Philip's wife Julie, and he can't talk that his daughter, I mean sister.

A: No but he didn't fancy her.

C: He didn't fancy her, that was just a normal dance.

A: He doesn't mind her having friends like, normal friends, but not like you know, boyfriends and trying to have it off with them.

B: Yes I think that's wrong, it's the influence of everybody around her, you know Lahta she doesn't want to feel, you know, left out.

A: Yes that's why Asians do this stuff sometimes.

B: Yeah, sometimes, yeah.

C: Why not Asians, most girls.

D: Get a bad reputation and that stuff.

5   Mythic realism. As Miller argues in relation to a study of the consumption of *The Young and the Restless* in Trinidad:

it is clear that the 'realism' with which it is identified has little to do with the environmental context of domestic presentation; the scenes cannot look like Trinidad. Realism rather is based on the truth of the serial in relation to key structural problematics of Trinidadian culture. It is the realism of myth. (Miller, 1995, pp. 219–20)

This realism is not the realism of verisimilitude rather it embodies a form of depth ontology by which reality is equated with forms of deeper truth. The creation of mythic realism, whether it is intended by producers or not, is ultimately an aspect of localization in consumption and depends on the audience perceiving the 'deeper truth' and its relevance to their lives.

B: I think it's [EastEnders] urm, I think it's the most realistic programme I see on TV nowadays.

C: It's got a lot to do with us right.

B: Yes, it talks about racism, relationships, urm, women not getting jobs and really everything.

This kind of realism was frequently associated with the handling of social issues in a way which connoted seriousness and which was also a marker of the superiority of British realist soaps over Australian fantasy. '*Yeah, and another thing, the AIDS issues that they do in* EastEnders *and that are much more realistic than the one with Michael* [in Neighbours].'

To accept that a character, story-line, or viewpoint is realistic by any of these versions of realism is to legitimate them. That realism takes a number of forms, that it is in a sense plastic and malleable, underlines the complexity of the process. Nevertheless, in examining aspects of the young people's talk within my research it is difficult, while agreeing that they are active, not to regard the discussions about relationships as implicated in the reproduction of gender ideology. Thus, a recurrent mode of talk employed by the group participants centred on favourite characters and through examination of such talk we can identify emerging attitudes towards gender and identity. The *EastEnders* character Grant Mitchell was a frequently discussed 'favourite' irrespective of gender or ethnicity. Consider the following extract from a discussion between three Asian boys:

A: I like EastEnders more, like down to earth, I just like it 'cos it's more realistic. My favourite character is, from there is, Grant because, did you see when the BNPs came and like he was the main man to sort 'em out like, but they made him a jerk since the affair, now the story-lines gone a bit dull. Pat and her new friend and Cathy's gone off somewhere. Who's your favourite in EastEnders?

C: Well, EastEnders is quite good but, well Nigel in EastEnders is a fat, fat prat.

B: Prat, he's a proper prat.

C: What about when the BNPs were coming and Nigel and the boys.

B: What about Sanjay.

C: Nigel agreed to go and talk to Rod in the pub, he was scared.

Here the speakers construct a model of masculinity around Grant by comparing his admired characteristics with those of less tradition-ally 'masculine' men. Speaker A sees Grant, like *EastEnders* itself, as *down to earth* and *realistic*; he is earthy and the *main man*. His status is based on his physical strength and mental toughness, his ability to *sort 'em out*. Since the participants in the conversation are Asian, we may infer that sorting out the fascist British National Party (BNP) is of particular significance. Interestingly, Grant's appearance – tall, muscular, cropped hair – is not a million miles from the stereotyped BNP skinhead and its associated version of masculinity. We may conclude that it is not just physique that makes Grant appealing to this young man but his moral position also. Grant's masculinity is, of course, a feature of the public sphere – sorting out the BNP – while in the private sphere, centred on his relationships with women, *they made him a jerk.*

The achievement of masculinity occurs through comparison of Grant with other characters, for example Nigel, who is seen as both *fat* and a *prat*. The most obvious point of contrast between Nigel and Grant is one of physique: Grant is hard, powerful and muscular while Nigel is soft and rounded. These physical appearances become metaphors for attitudes: Nigel is a more considerate person, more attuned to interpersonal relationships than the bullish male, public-oriented Grant. Further, while Grant is generally regarded with admiration for his fearlessness and willingness to *sort out* the BNP Nigel is mocked for being *scared* of them.

In another conversation a white boy compares Grant to Geoff: *Grant makes me laugh, he's the best actor in it now* but in direct contrast suggests that *Geoff was a prat.* Having 'a laugh' is one way boys survive the school environment and seek to subvert it (Willis, 1977). That Grant is able to do this is a major asset for the boys in the sample. However, Geoff was not a character with whom it would be possible to have a laugh, on the contrary, he was the very icon of the serious, educated, controlling middle-class. Again, physical differences embody important values for the participants: Geoff, as a slightly flabby middle-aged person has more in common with Nigel than Grant.

Disliked characters are equally revealing in terms of these particular boys' images of masculinity.

A: Who do we individually hate from soaps? I hate what's his name, Ricky, he's a loser, a proper loser.
B: Mechanic.
A: Yeah, look, he doesn't even know what's going on.
B: His girlfriend pushes him around!
A: Pushes him around man!
B: And they go, her friends they say to Ricky, are you coming?
A: She's a saucy cow, Bianca is.
A: I know man.
C: I say Ricky should be better off with someone else.

According to these boys Ricky displays characteristics which are quite undesirable in men since he is regarded as a *loser* when, by implication, as a man he should be a success, a theme which reoccurs elsewhere in the conversation. The reason that Ricky is regarded as a loser in this instance is because of his relationships with women, Ricky allows himself to be *pushed around* by his girlfriend and treated as a subordinate by her friends. In turn, the girl in question, Bianca, is regarded as a *saucy cow* with all its implications of unacceptable sexual assertiveness in women. Such a relationship appears to these boys as the world turned upside down, as speaker B later remarks, *It's stupid, the girl taking the boy.*

The construction of masculinity centred on Grant is not just a matter of 'boys' talk' and the tapes reveal an equal fascination with the character amongst the female participants.

B: I like EastEnders best, I like Grant.
C: Grant in EastEnders.
A: I love Grant our [sister] fancies Grant like mad.
B: . . . I like all the Dickheads.

D: Oh I really liked Grant. I didn't want him to go, even though he was the violent type. I didn't like him before, in like, before, but once he came out of jail, I *really* liked him.

For these girls Grant stands in a tradition of rebellious men characterized by strength, energy, self-assurance and the ability to stand alone, and his 'wayward' status as a *Dickhead* is admired. These are characteristics which, as we shall see later, are less tolerated in women. A contrasting approach adopted by girls was to express a growing interest in Grant as he became more embroiled in plots centred on romantic, marital and interpersonal themes. While girl D formally disapproves of the *violent type*, the character is *really liked* later when his altered position in the text makes it more acceptable. It is relevant to say that this girl was especially committed to the conventions of love and the 'quest romance' so that most soap pairings were allowable *as long as they love each other.* Grant's positioning in story-lines that connect with this theme makes him more agreeable.

That girls appropriate Grant in different ways, on the one hand as a symbol of rebellion and on the other as a more sensitive figure located in discourses about love, expresses a tension in 'girl culture' between attraction to the traditional private world of interpersonal relationships, traditional both to women and soap opera, and the desire to take up more assertive characteristics in the public sphere. Some of the tensions within 'girl culture' manifest themselves in discussions that centred on two other *EastEnders* characters: Natalie and Bianca.

B: I like Natalie, I think her and Ricky should get together.
A: Yeah well, they, they can like relate to each other and Natalie's a much nicer person, she cares for other people, she doesn't just think about herself and, I don't know, she's been there for Ricky more than Bianca has.
C: What about Bianca's dress [Laughter] did you see that [Laughter].
A: Bianca's Bianca's dress it was pink it clashed with her hair.
C: She makes me laugh she's so stupid.
B: She's so stupid.

Natalie is constructed as a *nice person* in contrast to Bianca. Natalie is a *nicer person*, she can *relate* to Ricky, she *cares for other people* and *doesn't just think about herself.* These qualities are constitutive of the traditional identity of women, skilled in the private world of interpersonal relationships, but excluded from more assertive roles in the public domain. This is an identity to which these particular girls seem to be orienting towards, for these are the very same girls for whom all is forgiven *if you do love the person.*

Bianca was universally disliked by the participants and was described by one group of girls as *a right slag* and *a bit of a cow.* In describing Bianca in these terms the girls appear to be attacking her in two ways. First, for being over-assertive, pushy and self-centred and second, for her confident sexuality. The term *slag* suggests the perception of inappropriate sexual behaviour for women. Given the apparent sexual nature of the assault on Bianca it is significant that some speakers attack her appearance, what is deemed to be Bianca's 'bad taste' is a cause of mockery and marks her out not only as different but as trashy and even *tarty.* Elsewhere, the hint of forbidden sexuality is more overt, *Urm, what do you think of her walking into the pub like that, she's practically wearing a slip.* Many of these girls do not accept assertive women in the same way as they warm to assertive men, readers may recall that Grant's wayward-ness was an admired feature.

While there are other examples of what might be seen as tradi-tionally sexist judgements, Cody from *Neighbours* was criticized (by girls) for having *a weird voice, a deep voice* and *a rough voice*, we would be mistaken to see these discussions as simply re-enforcing tradi-tional gender postions. The tension to which I have already alluded, between tradition and a desire to be more assertive, continues to manifest itself, thus one girl criticized Helen, also from *Neighbours*, for her apparent commitment to domesticity. *All Helen does is sit there baking casseroles, giving advice.* In a not dissimilar vein, Beverley from *Brookside*, having been criticized for her social pretensions, was praised for her assertive past, *But she's changed, remember when she first, she came in, she was like, urm, sort of like, urm, a man-eater* [laughter]. One could interpret *man-eater* as a derogatory term, however, in this context it can also be seen as a form of praise for her self-assurance and sexual confidence.

Of course, it is not watching television soap opera *per se* which introduces gender ideology into the equation. The young people bring previously formed ideas to their viewing experience and subsequent talk. Clearly there is a complex process involved, in which discourses are circulated and modified, and it is crucial to the active audience argument that everyday routine experience is more significant to audiences than media representations. As Tomlinson (1991) has suggested, 'we can view the relationship between media and culture as a subtle *interplay of mediations*' in which, for example, the images of love within soap opera are constantly mediated by people's lived experience of love. Thus, resistance to the ideological work of television depends on the range of discursive resources and cultural competencies available to us from outside and beyond television itself.

In my view the argument that resistance to ideology works on the basis of alternative discursive resources being available to people is stronger and more felicitous if linked to a view that 'human beings are centerless networks of beliefs and desires and that their vocabularies and opinions are determined by historical circumstance' (Rorty, 1991, p. 191). Thus, Rorty suggests that we see the self as a 'weave' with no centre, which is constantly having new strands woven into it as others are discarded. Of course, this runs counter to the current western 'regime of the self' which conceives of persons as unified and possessing an inner core identity. As Gergen (1994) argues, a romantic view of identity based on the notion of a unified 'deep interior' remains one of the central means by which people in everyday life justify themselves. However, he argues that identities are not the product of individual minds but of relations amongst persons formed within the shared social resource of language.

Indeed, there can be no god-like vantage point from which the self can integrate and organize itself, no grounding for a self which is its own subject and object. Only within discursively-constructed communal traditions do identities have any meaning. Language, which does not acquire its significance from individual mental states but is a shared social resource, is used by people in carrying out social rituals and activities within relationships where they are used to praise, admonish, achieve unity and invite forms of social action. 'One participates in the cultural forms of action as in a dance or a game . . . languages are among the resources available for playing the games and participating in the dances of cultural life' (Gergen, 1994, pp. 103–4). In this view the self is made up of beliefs, attitudes, emotions, etc., which are linguistic guides to action and not representations of independently existing entities.

If, along with Rorty and Gergen, one contends that the discourses of the self are not integrated into a unified whole but remain fragmented and decentred this helps us explain how resistance to ideology is possible. Ideology as a form of power/knowledge circulates both through television texts and the discourses produced and disseminated by parents, peers, schools, and other sites and agencies, for the production and distribution of ideas. Of interest is the way in which discourses which form the self in one site are articulated with discourses from another site inviting mutual support, or contradiction and resistance enacted through talk. For, as Rose has argued, people

> live their lives in a constant movement across different practices that address them in different ways . . . the existence of contestation, conflict and opposition in practices which conduct the conduct of persons is no surprise and requires no appeal to the particular qualities of human agency . . . in any one site or locale, humans turn programmes intended for one end to the service of others. One way of relating to one's self comes into conflict with others. (Rose, 1996, pp. 140–1)

Thus, discourses encountered in one site of human activity provide the basis for resistance in another and since the self is now conceived as a series of discourses, a weave, it is quite possible for individuals to be constituted by contradictory discourses. This is of particular significance to global television where discourses produced in one cultural context are articulated with discourses and practices which embody an entirely different set of cultural assumptions and orientations thus providing the basis for resistance.

While this may explain how resistance is possible it does not guarantee that it will happen. For if the print media was instrumental in summoning up the 'imagined community' of the nation (Anderson, 1983) then so do the electronic media contribute to our understanding of an 'imagined social reality'. Though audience members are active, their activity will be resistant only when alternative discourses are available and drawn upon. Thus the self becomes a site of ideological struggle. We need perhaps to differentiate between subjects and subject matter where routine discursive experience is of more or less help to us in mediating the media. Where global television brings 'distant' events into our front rooms there may be less 'lived experience' or alternative discourses to act as mediation than for domestic events in a local context. Alternatively of course, local discourses and practices may form the basis for the rejection of specific ideological formulations because the discourses of television are simply alien to and jar with local meanings.

In short, there has been a tendency to see the reproduction of ideology as associated with passive audiences and to link the active audience with resistance to ideology. The research which I have been discussing suggests that audiences are, as Silverstone (1994) argues, *always* active but that this is not necessarily a form of resistance. Of course the active audience may well be resisting certain ideological formations, but this is something to be determined empirically in given cases and not to be taken for granted.

Conclusions

A key tension involved in understanding television audiences is between the pressures towards institutional and ideological control on the one hand and the critical abilities of active audiences on the other. We have explored examples of both. That global television could be a vehicle for cultural homogenization, elite control and western values seems undeniable, though whether it actually is depends on specific circumstances. In particular, we have noted the abilities of viewers to bring their own cultural competencies to bear and to decode programmes in ways which depart from the dominant textual ideologies. In any case, television is one of the significant resources for identity construction under conditions of globalization and late modernity. The construction of multiple selves, of the self as a series of discourses, underlines the possibility that discourses constituting the self in one site may contradict or resist other discursive identities. By this means, audiences can actively resist the ideological formulations of television. However, activity does not always involve resistance: the discursive resources of the self may also be supportive of the discourses of television.

While such an approach stresses the explicit understandings of audiences, the influence of television can also be understood in terms of material practices and in particular the routines of domestic life. The organization of time is of particular significance and we noted the connections between television, time and modernity. We also noted the connections between television, in this case telenovelas; the desirability of consumer goods; and the reproduction of a global consumer culture. There are, thus, areas of television influence which may be missed by a concentration on individual decodings and it is to questions of how television is implicated in the wider parameters of cultural life that we now turn. In chapter 5 we will explore the involvement of television in 'promotional' and 'postmodern' culture while chapter 6 will centre on issues of cultural identities and cultural imperialism.

Part III

The Cultural Politics of Global Television

5

Global Television Culture?

This chapter centres on issues surrounding the cultural impact of global television that are not confined to specific programmes but are identifiable in the broad flow of images. First, the rise of trans-national television as a commercial phenomenon has made advertising both a core source of revenue and a major component of the flow of television. We shall explore the question of whether global television culture constitutes a promotional culture. Second, given that the flow of global television has been understood as a bricolage of juxtaposed images we shall examine the question of whether television promotes a postmodern culture.

Raymond Williams (1974) was one of the first to draw the question of flow to our attention. Flow, as understood by Williams, can take different forms according to that which is designated as the unit of flow. One type of flow is that of discrete programmes used as a scheduling device to capture audiences for significant periods of time. However, flow also includes the movement between programmes, including trailers and adverts, which since they use similar techniques, flow into and out of the programmes rather than just filling a space in between.

It may be even more important to see the true process as flow: the replacement of a programme series of timed sequential units by a flow series of differently related units in which the timing, though real, is undeclared and in which the real internal organisation is something other than the declared organisation. (Williams, 1974, p. 93)

Flow, argues Williams, corresponds to the actual experience of watching television. In his analysis of an American commercial station he points to the disjointed fusion of news, views, drama and reportage which tumble one over the other. He notes that this flow of consumable reports and products is marked by speed, variety and miscellaneousness wherein, he argues, the 'real' meaning lies.

Newcomb (1988) extends this argument, describing television as a cultural forum of competing ideas and images, an open text in which a primary unit of textual analysis is the 'strip text'. By this he means a chosen viewing route across a specified time period and through a variety of programmes, adverts and channels. In his analysis of nine hours viewing of American television on a Thursday night he calculated 81 possible paths counting only those paths that change at programme breaks. In one specific strip – *Magnum PI*, *Cheers*, *Night Court* and *Hill Street Blues* – a combination of CBS and NBC, Newcomb argues that there are resonances across the programmes which create and activate a set of discourses about gender, sexuality and the moral base of law which occur both in and across distinct programmes. Newcomb argues that the entire history of television forms part of its scheme, making the notion of text both synchronic and diachronic.

The notions of flow and strip text are significant because they allow us to highlight patterns of signification that occur outside the boundaries of individual texts. This idea is central to the concepts of promotional and postmodern culture, ideas whose efficacy rely on the identification of accumulated patterns of meaning embedded in the flow of television. For example, advertising is important to the question of flow not only as a discrete element but also as part of a more general set of promotional meanings embedded in the flow as such. This occurs as trailers, product placement and hoardings at sporting events as well as in the general promotional ethos of consumer culture. Indeed, the music video which forms the core of MTV can be regarded as at one and the same time both entertainment and promotion. MTV has also been cited as a prime example of the bricolage of juxtaposed images from different times and places, which constitutes postmodern television. This bricolage of images occurs not only as flow across an evening but frequently within a given music video.

Finally, the issue of promotional and postmodern flow is important to an understanding of global television in terms of the overall direction which television is taking within national systems across the world and because transnational television is globalizing a postmodern televisual culture setting up competition with more traditional forms and relativizing all cultural meaning.

Is Global Television Culture a 'Promotional Culture'?

Since the mid-1980s there has been a rapid increase in commercial television channels across the globe reflecting the world-wide trend towards de-regulation. The advertising industry was both a prime lobbyist for de-regulation and one of the leading beneficiaries of it. For example, between 1980 and 1990 the total expenditure on advertising in Europe tripled. In 1993 levels of advertising investment in the press, television and radio, and on hoardings were estimated to be four times higher than 1980 levels (Sanchez-Tabernero, 1993; table 5.1). Indeed, there has been a world-wide growth in the percentage of GNP spent on advertising.

Sanchez-Tabernero argues that:

> It is clearly the audio-visual industry, and television in particular that has benefited from the transfer of a part of advertising investment from the printed press towards vision and sound . . . television's share of total advertising expenditure increased from 15.6% in 1980 to 25.1% in 1990 and will rise to 27.1% in 1993. (Sanchez-Tabernero, 1993, p. 127)

Table 5.1 *Evolution of advertising expenditure compared to gross domestic product*

	1980	1990	1993 (estimate)
Germany	0.75	0.82	0.83
Italy	0.37	0.62	0.64
France	0.48	0.78	0.80
United Kingdom	1.11	1.37	1.31
Europe	0.70	0.91	0.92
Japan	0.95	1.12	1.13
United States	1.32	1.51	1.40

Source: Zenith Media Worldwide: Adapted from Sanchez-Tabernero (1993).

He predicts that the total level of advertising expenditure in television could double again between 1990 and the year 2000. Satellite TV in Europe will account for 5 per cent of total advertising revenue and 20 per cent of television advertising revenue by the end of 1999. The advertising journal *M & M Europe* argued in July 1995 that 'the advertising economy picked up in 1994 and we are bullish in our expectations of growth into 1995 – especially for television'.

One obvious outcome of this growth in advertising on television is that audiences see more of it so that advertising can be understood as an increasing cultural form. Another outcome may be on the programming mix of channels. The model feared by some critics in Europe is the American one of television dependency on the advertising industry, thus it is argued (Blumler, 1986) that advertising-financed television on the US model develops pressures to maximize audiences and programme popularity above all else. Advertisers develop a sense of their right to have their interests served by producers and networks whose business becomes not making and transmitting programmes but delivering audiences to the advertisers. A linked concern is that many of the 'new' television channels who are funded by advertising will not be committed to making programmes but will import relatively cheap, largely American, audience-maximizing programmes. However, a counter trend is the concern of advertisers to target specific audiences in terms of 'life-styles' a move which has been supportive of some kinds of 'quality' programming attracting smaller audiences with high disposable incomes. In an increasingly competitive market some advertisers have wanted to be associated with 'quality' programming which has 'stand out' characteristics.

The Globalization of Advertising

The globalization of advertising has two distinct aspects. First, the spread of advertising practices across the globe and second, the emergence of the global brand. Since the Second World War there has been a marked increase in the role played by multinational corporations across the globe, particularly those of American origin. Sinclair (1987) notes that the value of US private investment overseas increased over sixfold between 1953 and 1973. With this expansion of US-based multinationals, in particular those producing consumer goods, has come the spread of advertising. Of specific interest to us here is, 'The notable tendency for the transnational advertisers to direct most of their advertising into television' (Sinclair, 1987, p. 123).

Coca Cola, Pepsi, Levi's, McDonald's, Nike, Burger King, IBM and *Marlboro* are probably the leading global brand-name advertisers. According to one leading advertising agency associated with the idea of the global strategy:

> We live in an era of global communications. Scientists and technologists have achieved what militarists and statesmen down the ages have attempted to establish but without success – the global empire. There is no doubt that the world is becoming one marketplace. Capital markets, products and services, management and manufacturing techniques have all become global in nature. As a result, companies increasingly find that they must compete all over the world – in the global market place. This new development is emerging at the same time as advanced technology is transforming information and communication. (*Saatchi & Saatchi Annual Report,* 1986, cited in Mattelart, 1991)

The driving forces behind the constructing of world-wide advertising campaigns and global branding are said by Vardor (1992) to be:

- Economies of scale.
- The converging of consumer needs prompted by technological changes.
- The homogenization of consumer tastes through the global media.
- The emergence, as a result of global communications, of a strata of global consumers.

These are themes propounded by Theodore Levitt, a management 'guru' of global marketing, through which production, distribution and communication are to be approached in global terms. Thus, 'The global corporation operates as if the entire world (or major regions of it) were a single entity; it sells the same things in the same way everywhere' (cited in Mattelart, 1991). This growth in a global strategy is paralleled by the significance of global advertising agencies which have aimed not simply to be advertising bodies but global communications and management consultants. The agency most associated with these trends has been the UK-based Saatchi & Saatchi which rapidly expanded to become the largest agency in the world, though it has subsequently been eclipsed.

Advertising of the 'global brand' variety requires a similar product, image, market and consumer segment world-wide, though differences of culture, language, taste, media and regulations make this difficult to achieve. The consumer is always local and there has not been a complete convergence of tastes across the globe. Global advertising of the 'one product, one sell' variety can only work in a small number of cases, mainly in the consumer food, drink and clothes sectors. Many products will require different strategies and campaigns in different markets. The fact that the global brand is a limited case does not mean of course that advertising is not inter-national both in its spread and its co-ordination, a particular product may well be advertised across the world using a set of centrally-planned themes but it will be subject to local adaptation and variation. It will be multi-local rather than uniformly global.

Television is central to both multi-local and global brand adver-tising but particularly to the latter because advertising executives involved with global branding

> generally favoured advertising types that had emotional appeal, showed life styles and product features and were visual, simple and factual, relying less on language, pun and humour [and more on] strong visuals, sound and music rather than lengthy dialogues. (Vardar, 1992, pp. 118–19)

In other words, television is the ideal medium for global brand advertising.

How Television Advertising Works: Current Developments

In exploring the workings of advertising, Williamson (1978) addresses their formal qualities and points to the transformation of the 'use-value' of objects into a value-added 'exchange-value'. Objects in advertisements are signifiers of meaning which we decode in the context of known cultural systems associating prod-ucts in adverts with other cultural 'goods'. While an image of a particular product may denote only beans or a car it is made to connote 'nature' or 'family' so that advertising creates a world of differences between products and life-styles which we 'buy into'. In buying the products we buy the image and so contribute to the construction of our identities through consumption. For Williamson, such advertising is ideological in its obscuring of economic inequality at the level of production by images of consumption.

In Williamson's work the distinction between 'use-value' and 'exchange-value' is retained, while in the work of Baudrillard this distinction is argued to be invalid. For Baudrillard, no objects are seen to have an essential value, rather use-value itself is determined through exchange making the cultural meaning of goods more significant than labour or use-value. These cultural meanings derive from the wider 'social order' and are not a matter of individual preference or needs. Baudrillard argues that the codes of similarity and difference in consumer goods are used to signify social affiliation so that objects speak of a stratified society. Baudrillard introduces the idea of sign-value, whereby commodities confer prestige and signify social value, status and power; a commodity is not just an object with use or exchange value but a commodity-sign. Advertising imagery is significant in circulating commodity-signs so that they 'float-free' from objects and are able to be used in a variety of associations. Featherstone (1991) explains it thus:

> For Baudrillard the essential feature of the movement towards the mass production of commodities is that the obliteration of the original 'natural' use-value of goods by the dominance of exchange value under capitalism has resulted in the commodity becoming a sign in the Saussurean sense, with its meaning arbitrarily determined by its position in a self-referential system of signifiers. Consumption, then, must not be understood as the consumption of use-values, a material utility, but primarily as the consumption of signs. (Featherstone, 1991, p. 85)

While Baudrillard attributes a greater role to imagery and signs than Williamson, they share the idea that advertising plays a role in 'adding' symbolic value to the material object, an idea which is also widely acknowledged in the field of advertising professionals. According to Davidson (1992):

> Start work in an ad agency and the first thing they teach you is the difference between a *product* and a *brand*. This is because it is advertising's job to change one thing into another. Brands are products with something extra. All brands are products, but not all products are brands, and the difference is advertising. That extra is called *added value*. Not just mints, but the elegance and sophistication of

After Eights; not just a hamburger bar, but the fun and optimism of *McDonalds*; not just a cube of artificial flavourings, but the quintessence of *Oxo* family life. (Davidson, 1991, p. 23)

The job of advertising is to create an 'identity' for a product amid the bombardment of competing images by associating the brand with desirable human values. Buying a brand is not only about buying a product but about buying into life-styles and values. The nature of those values and the manner in which they are associated with products are the outcome of a great deal of research by advertisers. The consumption patterns, desires and values of consumers are reflected back through advertising which reflexively utilizes some of the understandings gained about advertising to make it more effective. As Davidson explains, coffee is drunk in the morning to wake up with, during the day as a break, at night as the high point of dinner parties or the pretext for seduction. Advertisers, having researched the social usage of coffee, will reflect these ideas in the brand images attached to a particular coffee. The (in)famous *Gold Blend* television adverts about the growing relationship of a couple, through the medium of enquiring about coffee, clearly utilized the last of these usages. This specific association not only adds value to the product but differentiates it from other coffees. The brand is, thus, positioned in a strategic way in relation to other brands.

Advertising changes its strategies in different periods and can act as a cultural record of its time. Developments in advertising during the 1980s and into the 1990s include (according to Davidson):

- The extension and broadening of advertising from its traditional base in foods and consumer durables to include the less traditional areas of banking, financial services, airlines, leisure industries, political parties and governments, and health campaigns.
- A more definite targeting of specific social groups for particular adverts, connected to the growth of 'life-style' niche-marketing, rather than blanket advertising.
- A move away from advertising based on appeals to rational choice, based on information, towards more visual-based adverts containing minimal information and utilizing a more symbolic and emotional appeal.
- The dominance in the 1980s of 'cool', rather mechanical, 'clever' advertising connected to a brash, self-confident consumerism based on social aspiration.

- The re-emergence in the 1990s of more humanistic, warm, value-based adverts perhaps with 'green' appeal.
- A rise in the cultural status and acceptance of advertising in western cultures allowing us to discuss our 'favourite adverts'.
- The growth of television advertising which promotes itself so that television increasingly promotes its own forthcoming programmes, schedules, etc.
- A stress on design and 'designer labels' so that promotion is built into the product and is part of a wider marketing strategy.
- The blurring of the boundaries between advertising and other more traditional cultural activities such as journalism, drama and musical performance. Thus adverts mimic the style of film and drama, which themselves incorporate some of the style and production values of advertising. As Hebdige notes in relation to the magazine *The Face*:

Advertising – the *eidos* of the market place – is pressed into the very pores of *The Face*. For advertisers as for *The Face*, sophists and lawyers, rhetoric is all there is: the seizure of attention, the refinement of technique, the design, promotion marketing of product (ideas, style; for lawyers, innocence or guilt depending on who pays). *The Face* habitually employs the rhetoric of advertising: the witty one-liner, the keyword, the aphorism, the extractable (i.e. quotable) image are favoured over more sustained, sequential modes of sense making. Each line or image quoted in another published context acts like a corporate logo inviting us to recognise its source – the corporation – and to acknowledge the corporation's power. (Hebdige, 1988, p. 172)

The increased blurring of the boundaries between 'advertising' and 'culture' (which is embedded in the flow of television) is perhaps the most significant development of the 1980s in advertising practices and is a part of what Wernick (1991) calls 'promotional culture'. Wernick argues that advertising does not stand alone but is a part of a wider culture. First, because advertising draws on a wider pool of cultural understandings. Second, because any given advert is a part of a larger campaign. Third, because adverts rely on the previous campaigns and make references to them. Fourth, because promotion is designed into products so that they are conceived from the very beginning as promotional devices. Fifth, because advertising has become a quotational source in cultural life.

For Wernick, advertising is merely a particular example of a wider mode of communication, promotion, which highlights the way in which 'all manner of communicative acts have, as one of their dimensions, and often only tacitly, the function of advancing some kind of self-advantaging exchange' (Wernick, 1991, p. 181). He argues that cultural phenomena which serve to communicate a promotional message of some type or another have become 'virtually co-extensive with our produced symbolic world' (Wernick, 1991, p. 184). The entire 'culture industry' is an inter-dependent complex of promotional activity which manifests itself on the cultural/symbolic level as a new 'regime of signification' (Lash, 1990).

For Wernick, the rise of promotional culture signals an alteration in the relation between culture and economy. To be precise, the take-over of culture by the market, though not without modifications to the economic process itself. Thus, expansion of promo-culture is connected to the transformation of the leading edges of the economy/society relationship from Fordism to post-Fordism (Murray, 1989), and of the emergence of a postmodern culture. The argument is that Fordism involves an economy which is based on mass production of standardized commodities and the consequent mass consumption, which is promoted through mass advertising. The transformation to post-Fordism involves the use of new technology to enable economic small-batch production and customization of consumer goods which stresses niche marketing and life-styling more than mass-based advertising. This has lent weight to the need for promotional designing and targeted advertising.

What's Wrong with Advertising?

Advocates of advertising would argue that it provides the consumer with information with which to make purchasing choices. To the charge that advertising is a manipulative and distorted form of communication it is countered that advertisers have to work hard in terms of resources and research to try and persuade us to purchase their commodities. It would be argued that we are sophisticated and active readers of advertising and, thus, not easily duped. While there is some validity in this argument in relation to *individual* adverts and persons, it does not take into account the wider role of advertising in a commodified consumer *culture* and the promotional meanings embedded in the flow of television. Advertising and promotional culture furthers the commodification of all life undermining the public sphere with a form of communication which aims not to advance the public good or to enhance dialogue and debate, but whose fundamental purpose is to promote narrow commercial interests.

As Mattelart (1991) argues, advertising is taking over those spheres previously reserved for the public sphere. The language of advertising has increasingly adopted social issues like ecology and presented itself as the custodian of responsible public values. Political parties and governments, including those of the 'left' traditionally more hostile to advertising, have made it a central plank of their strategies for both electioneering and of government. For example, the British, French and Canadian governments are amongst the largest spenders on advertising in their respective countries. For Mattelart, this infusion of the public sphere by advertising raises three critical problems. First, the traditional language of public debate appeals to 'reason' (albeit often distorted), while the language of advertising depends on symbolic and emotional appeals, particularly the use of imagery. Second, advertising arguably demands not citizenship and active participation but passivity. Third, advertising promotes the reduction of all value to the values of commodity exchange so that the public sphere itself becomes dominated by the language of public management, the market and technical efficiency to the detriment of other values.

For example, health promotion has become one of western culture's unchallengeable public goods and mass media advertising its critical vehicle, yet the very means by which health is promoted turns health into a commodity and a form of social control. An approved version of health is thrust upon us and the humanistic intent of health promotion is lost through the process of commodification. Commodities are marketed and sold: protection from HIV, condoms and private health insurance plans merge into one market transaction. We are being sold not any version of health but a particular vision of what is for the alleged public and private good. The reflexivity of modern culture demands forms of self-management of which health is becoming a key note, not to be 'healthy' suggests both personal and social inadequacy, so that teenage mothers become social pariahs and victims of HIV are regarded as complicit in their own downfall.

The impact and role of television advertising in the west could be argued to be of a different order to that which it plays in the developing world. In the latter context television can be criticized for portraying in its general flow a western consumer culture alongside advertising which, appearing attractive to the peoples of the developing world, supports the integration of the economies of 'developing' nations into global capitalism. The outcomes of such integration it is argued are:

- The skewing of the economy of the developing nation away from the production of much needed essentials towards consumer goods for the emergent middle class.
- The import of western consumer goods with a resultant balance of payments and debt problem.
- The dumping of commodities which are illegal in the west on developing economies.
- The consumption of less healthy foods or medicines as indigenous items are substituted by foreign imports.
- The ideological association of the good life with western capitalism.

It is argued that the advertising employed by transnational capitalism is deliberately deceptive and manipulative, from which flows the overpricing of goods and the sale of wasteful and unnecessary commodities to the poor of the developing world. Thus, it can be argued that 'consumption patterns are being created that lead to a wasteful spending of what little is available' (Hamelink, 1983, p. 14). A strong rendering of this argument comes when Hamelink argues that commodities which address basic human needs, in this case medicines and baby foods, involve the sale of brand names, for which there are cheaper generic alternatives, at inflated prices. Where it can be shown that advertising is misleading on a 'factual' level this argument clearly has merits. It is deplorable that television advertising should be used to sell products which are being dumped in the developing world with negative consequences for health or ecology.

However, it is harder to sustain the idea that the people of the developing world are more gullible in relation to advertising than we are; for how can we say a need is false in the sense that we have failed to recognize what is best for us? There is no independent or objective epistemological position from which to make such criticism stick, we can make criticisms only from our own vantage point. Further, we might ask why we should deny to the developing world the consumerism we accept (Tomlinson, 1991), and whether, in the context of the developing world, advertising and other representations of an unachievable life-style might have revolutionary consequences as Eco (1986) asserts.

We can, with more justification, make the argument that certain choices have undesirable (and possibly unintended) political, economic, social or ecological *consequences* given a previously delineated value position. We could argue that television is the vehicle for the dissemination of a consumer culture, which is ecologically damaging and wasteful of resources through excessive packaging and chemical pollution. Further, if we are sick and need treatment as a result of chemical pollution then our need for medicine is 'false', in the sense of avoidable, but clearly not in the sense of 'mistaken'. Thus, needs are seen to be imposed on people by the conditions in which they live so that modern cities create poverty which breeds illness and, thus, the demand for medicines (Tomlinson, 1991). This, more viable argument, has to be recognized as a specific political-value position. In other words we can make judgements only from our own perspective, which paradoxically is from within western consumer culture (suggesting that it maintains contradictory impulses). Criticisms of the consequences of the promotional culture embedded in the flow of global television may well be valid from within our own ecological, medical or ethical discourses, but if the people of the developing world vote with their feet and embrace consumer goods, as they frequently seem to do, how can we deny them that choice? It is difficult from my vantage point to see why anyone would choose poverty before consumption.

Is Global Television Culture a 'Postmodern Culture'?

The consumer culture discussed above has been identified as a key aspect of the postmodern. Lash (1990) identifies the shift from the 'discursive' to the 'figural' as core to the postmodern turn by which he means that the signifying logics of the modern and postmodern work in different ways. For Lash, the modernist 'regime of signification' prioritizes words over images, promulgates a rationalist world-view, explores the meanings of cultural texts and distances the spectator from the cultural object. In contrast, the postmodern 'figural' is more visual, draws from everyday life, contests rationalist views of culture and immerses the spectator in his/her desire in the cultural object. This 'aestheticization of everyday life' is a theme which links the postmodern 'figural' with a promotional consumer culture. The blurring of the boundaries between art and culture, culture and commerce, allied to the prominence of the image, have resulted in an aestheticization of everyday life and in particular of urban living. Featherstone (1991) argues that this takes three critical forms: first the appearance of artistic sub-cultures which sought to efface the boundaries between art and everyday life, second the project of turning life into a work of art and third the 'rapid flow of signs and images which saturate the fabric of everyday life in contemporary society' (Featherstone, 1991, p. 67). The second and third elements are linked together in consumer culture through the creation of life-styles centred on the consumption of aesthetic objects and signs itself associated with a relative shift of importance in society from production to consumption.

The term 'postmodern culture' refers here to key cultural trends which have become prominent over the last 20 years and does not imply, in this account, a radical rupture with the past. Rather, post-modern culture has to be understood as emerging from the past with its features becoming more prominent. Central to these features is the bricolage of global images which constitutes television as flow. As I argued in chapter 1, postmodernism as a cultural form can be seen as a marker of 'radicalized modernity' and does not have to be regarded as coterminous with a concept of postmodernity as an historical period. I am using the term postmodern culture to describe a qualitatively different set of cultural concerns that have emerged in conjunction with the global time–space compression of late-modernity. While it might be more accurate to describe these circumstances as the culture of late-modernity, I have retained the term 'postmodern' because it is the' banner' under which many of these issues have been described and analysed and helps to demarcate them as specific concerns.

Although a broad perspective will identify common features of the postmodern, a closer view would recognize significant differences across the fields of art, architecture, film, television, life-styles and urban life. The discussion that follows should be read as a set of broad generalizations about the prominence of postmodern forms in western cultures and the juxtaposition of the postmodern with the traditonal and the modern in non-western cultures. That in India traditional patterns of work, family life and religious custom can coexist with MTV, the internet and promotional culture is precisely an aspect of postmodern culture. Though postmodern culture has emerged most obviously in the developed west the globalization of television within the context of modernity makes it of significance across the globe. While certain discrete meanings within television often promote modernity, for example the use of television as a nation-building tool through Latin American telenovelas, the form and style of television is increasingly postmodern, particularly in terms of flow.

Of course, the experience of postmodern culture cannot be assumed to be the same for all people regardless of class, ethnicity, gender, nationality, etc.; a more finely-grained sociological analysis would need to take account of the variable experience of postmodern culture. This would include the central role of the 'new cultural inter-mediaries' (Bourdieu, 1984; Featherstone, 1991); the producers and disseminators of symbolic goods such as designers, writers, academics, television producers and advertisers, in the reproduction both of the experience of postmodernism and the language used to describe it. Further, it can be argued that philosophic post-modernism represents the undermining of western certainties (and the concerns of a set of decentred western intellectuals) as global-ization increasingly involves non-western voices.

Though writers disagree about the nature and determinants of postmodern culture a number of general features have emerged. My account mixes the sources of these ideas (postmodern bricolage?) and necessarily involves repetition of ideas and trends which are linked and overlapping. The contours of postmodern culture can be described thus:

- The decline both in theory and in actuality of a notion of a common culture and the acceptance of a complex, diverse set of cultures and 'life-styles' is a marker of postmodern culture. Increasingly differen-tiated global societies are unable to sustain a common culture, if they ever were. Of particular significance are global migration patterns, changes in class composition and the emergence of new political formations and identifications in breaking up previous consensual or dominant cultures. The 'other' of modernity, those voices which had been suppressed by the modern drive to extinguish difference, have increasingly found ways to speak within postmodern culture(s). Hence the emergence of 'new social movements' and 'life politics' connected for example to ecological or feminist concerns.

Likewise the development of multi-ethnic communities, the disengagement with mainstream politics (especially amongst young people) and the breakdown of consensus party politics all point to the erosion of any common culture.

- A sense of the fragmentary, ambiguous and uncertain nature of living is a core experience of postmodern culture associated with a loss of faith in meta-narratives, the awareness of the centrality of contingency, the emergence of cultural differences and the speed-up in the pace of living. Global time–space compression, which has intensified the experience of a fast-paced world, and the emergence of new voices in the context of fragmented cultures has contributed to a loss of a sense of certainty based on tradition. Without the certainties of traditional religious, class and ethnic communities modern life may appear as a series of proliferating choices to be made without foundations.

- Central to postmodern culture is the perceived blurring and collapse of the traditional boundaries between culture and art, high and low culture, commerce and art, culture and commerce. The rise in visibility and status of popular culture, hastened by the electronic media, has meant that the distinction between high and low culture is no longer viable. As Chambers (1986, p. 194) puts it, 'High culture becomes just one more sub-culture, one more opinion, in our midst'. Alongside this development has been the notable blurring of genre boundaries within cultural products and their double-coding (Jencks, 1986) allowing them to be understood both by the literati and a popular audience. *Bladerunner* and *Blue Velvet* are frequently cited as films which mix the genres of Noir, horror, Sci-fi, etc. in ways which have attracted both critical acclaim and a popular audience. Within the context of twentieth-century capitalism popular culture is produced and distributed along commercial lines and critics from both the political 'right' and 'left' would have argued that such popular culture must be inauthentic, fake, untruthful and manipulative. However, the collapse of high/low cultural distinctions together with the recognition of the active and creative role of audiences have undone the obviousness of such a critique. Indeed, for some critics the postmodern is marked above all by the de-differentiation (collapse and breakdown) of such classical western categories as 'high' and 'low', 'authentic' and 'fake'.

- The postmodern is marked by historical blurring, merging representations of the past and present so that elements from a variety of historical moments are presented together in a kind of bricolage. Indeed, intertextuality and bricolage as a cultural style are core elements of postmodern culture and have been most often observed in architecture, film and popular music video. Shopping centres have made the mixing of styles from different times and places a particular 'trade mark' and MTV is noted for the mixing together of pop music from a variety of periods and locations. While for some writers this is simply a question of playfulness and style, for others it represents a more dangerous loss of a sense of history.

- The circulation of images and simulacra (copies) is central to postmodern culture. Television is therefore of particular importance to the postmodern debate, though the development of theme parks, shopping centres, virtual reality simulations and computer games are part of the same terrain. While for some commentators this simply represents a wide array of images for us to play with and through which to construct a series of multiple identities, for other writers it represents the inability to distinguish between reality and image so that the image is reality.

- The reorganization of time and space and our understanding of them is a key part of postmodern culture which Harvey (1989) relates to the time–space compression of global economy and culture. The development of new electronic communications and the new post-Fordist flexible forms of production have enabled a speed-up of production and communications giving us the sense of a shrinking world. These production techniques, which make small-batch production and customization viable, have been linked to niche marketing and consumer life-styles, while media developments have created a collage of global cultural elements. Globalization and postmodern culture are thus intimately connected. Further, the displacement of western considerations, by which the west is becoming just another region with no privileged philosophical position, is one of the contributors to the crisis of western thinking and in particular of foundationalist philosophy. The global diversity of culture, politics and images is clearly part of the emergence of other voices in the world and of other images of ways to live.

- A heightened sense of social and individual reflexivity is core to postmodern culture. Here reflexivity refers to the use of knowledge about social life as a constitutive element of it. Thus, reflexivity refers to the constant revision of social activity in the light of new knowledge (Giddens, 1991). Increased social and institutional reflexivity is manifested in the desire of modern institutions to know more about the work-force, the customers and the clients. This involves increased forms of surveillance, from cameras in shopping centres and 'quality management' at work, to the increased significance of marketing. In this sense, institutional reflexivity can be seen as a form of social control.

However, reflexivity can equally enable increased possibilities for the self-construction of identity and playful creation of multiple identities. Reflexivity can be understood as 'discourse about experience' (Gergen, 1994, p. 71) and to engage in reflexive identity is, therefore, to partake in a range of discourses and relationships and to construct further discourses about them so that 'with each reflexive reprise, one moves into an alternative discursive space, which is to say, into yet another domain of relatedness'. Reflexivity is 'a means of recognising alterior realities, and thus giving voice to still further relationships' (Gergen, 1994, p. 48).

Reflexivity also encourages an ironic sense of the 'said before', the feeling that one cannot invent anything new but merely play with the already existent. Eco gives a good example of this with the person who cannot, without irony, say 'I love you' but must preface it with the words 'As Barbara Cartland would say'. The thing is said, but the unoriginality acknowledged. It can be argued that media culture, because it encourages a widespread awareness of the history and techniques of cultural production, promotes such irony.

Postmodern Television

Television is at the heart of image production and the circulation of a collage of stitched-together images which are core to postmodern cultural style. As I suggested in chapter 1 the globalization of television as an institution of modernity has had the paradoxical consequence of disseminating western television's postmodern cultural form.

However, we need to make distinctions between arguments that locate television as *institutionally* postmodern and those which identify specific *textual* features of programmes as stylistically postmodern (Connor, 1989). Television can be seen as institutionally postmodern and at the core of postmodern culture because of its central role in the 'proliferation of signs and their endless circulation' (Collins, 1992). Television produces and circulates with ever more technological efficacy an explosive flow of competing signs and meanings. The variety of juxtapositions of images and meanings in television creates an electronic bricolage in which unexpected associations can occur which are connected both to the flow of a given channel and a reflection of multi-channel diversity. The potential and actual ability of viewers to zip and zap, channel change and fast forward, constitutes a bricolage 'strip text' wherein the ability of viewers to sophisticatedly distinguish between elements and to play with them, adopting the 'appropriate' reading attitudes and competencies, is in itself described as postmodern.

Television has a history and repeats that history within and across channels thereby contributing to the blurring of historical boundaries as programmes from different historical periods sit side by side. In the case of the music channel MTV there is a flow of videos in which music from the 1950s to the 1990s is stitched together into a collage. This articulation of styles and histories contributes to the viewer's understanding of TV history and thus 'television produces the conditions of an ironic knowingness' (Caughie, 1990). Though this is, of course, more prominent in western cultures where television has a long history than in cultures where television has arrived more recently; nevertheless, the globalizing of western television means that an ironic sense of history penetrates even more traditional cultures.

A related point is the growth of self-conscious intertextuality, that is citation of one text within another, involving both explicit allusion to particular programmes and oblique references to other genre conventions and styles. For example, explicit reference to a bar in Boston where every one knows your name in both *Hill Street Blues* and *St. Elswhere*, or to *Twin Peaks* in *Northern Exposure*. It may also be seen in the re-working of Noir conventions or those of the 'Road Movie', both much recycled (for example, in *Pulp Fiction* and *True Romance*). This intertextuality is an aspect of an enlarged cultural self-consciousness about the history and functions of cultural products, including television. The core of this argument is extended by Eco so that television has itself as its prime reference point.

The principal characteristic of Neo-TV is that it talks less and less about the external world. Whereas Paleo-TV talked about the external world, or pretended to, Neo-TV talks about itself and about the contact that it establishes with its own public . . . one can spend 48 hours a day in front of TV, so there's no more need to come into contact with that remote fiction – the real world. (Eco, 1986 p. 19)

Consumption and the aestheticization of everyday life is central to postmodern culture and television is economically and institutionally bound up with it both as a purveyor of advertising and of diverse life-styles in a variety of dramas, sitcoms and game shows. It is also intimately connected to niche marketing (which is an aspect of life-style construction) through the location of targeted advertising, relating particular products and images to specific social groups, and in the way in which channels (in the age of multi-delivery systems) tend to segment and specialize.

Stylistically, rather than institutionally, the markers of the postmodern have been seen as aesthetic self-consciousness/self-reflexiveness, juxtaposition/montage, paradox, ambiguity, uncertainty and the blurring of the boundaries of genre, style and history. Ironically, while postmodernism in the arts is seen as a reaction against modernism, postmodern television seems to take on and make popular those very *modernist* techniques such as montage, rapid cutting, non-linear narrative techniques and the de-contextualization of images. Postmodernism in television is more a reaction against realism in a medium where modernism never really took hold so that programmes which have commonly been identified with postmodernism tend to decentre the importance of linear narrative in favour of a new look and feel in which image takes preference over story-telling (Kellner, 1992).

An often cited example of postmodern television is the American series *Twin Peaks* which mixes the genre conventions of police series, science fiction and soap opera together in a way which is sometimes to be taken seriously and at other times to be seen as humorous ambivalent parody. This is accompanied by a series of tonal variations including pathos and camp, seriousness and humour which encourages the shifting of subject position and oscillation of emotional involvement in one series that a 'strip text' might create across an evening. Thus, Collins describes the scene where Dale

Cooper explains his Tibetan 'deductive technique' based on a dream he once had:

> a thoroughgoing burlesque of the traditional final scene of detective novels, films, or television programs when the detective explains how he/she solved the crime, usually through a hyper-rational deductive process. The introduction of the Dalai Lama, dream states, and rocks transports ratiocination (crime solving by rational deduction) into the realm of irrational spirituality, thereby parodying one of the fundamental 'givens' of detective fiction. (Collins, 1992, p. 346)

Twin Peaks is 'double coded', involving a combination of codes which enable it to engage both with a 'concerned minority' familiar with an 'expert' language and a wider popular audience. *Twin Peaks* was a major ratings success, but its association with a recognized film director, David Lynch, and its engagement with debates about postmodernism allowed it to develop a more specialized audience and discourse. A further postmodern feature of the series is its ambiguous temporal coding so that, as with a number of other Lynch works, for example *Blue Velvet*, we are not allowed a clear sense of the time we are operating in. On one level *Twin Peaks* seems to be engaging with the contemporary, at others, as signified through the diner, cars and music, it seems to be set in the 1950s or 1960s. Finally, *Twin Peaks* is a prime example of the postmodern semiotics of excess, the series was brimming over with meanings many of which seem to be 'irrelevant' to the solving of the crime or the forward movement of the narrative but are part of a spectacle or a diversion.

Another favourite example of postmodern television is *Miami Vice* which Kellner (1992) identifies as postmodern in two fundamental ways. First, its aesthetic style and second, its polysemic nature involving shifting and conflicting identities, meanings and ideologies. The lighting, camera work, rock music, bright colours and exotic terrain lead to

> a wealth of resonant images which its producers sometimes successfully weave into the production of aesthetic spectacles that are intense, fascinating, and seductive. The sometimes meandering narratives replicate experiences of fragmentation and of slow ennui, punctuated with images of hallucinogenic intensity. Image frequently takes over from narrative and the look and feel become

primary, often relegating story-line to the background . . . this arguably postmodern style is fundamental to *Miami Vice*. (Kellner, 1992, pp. 148–9)

For Kellner, *Miami Vice* is not simply postmodern depthless surface but a site of multiple meanings, values and subject positions. Thus, the identities of the two main detective protagonists, Crokett and Tubbs, are 'unstable, fluid, fragmentary, disconnected, multiple, open and subject to dramatic transformation'. This is signified through their constantly changing looks, styles and appearances, together with their interchanging identities as cops with undercover roles as rich drug-runners and hip buyers. In assuming those roles Crokett and Tubbs slip in and out of various identities, suggesting that identity is a construction not a given, that it is a game and a matter of style and choice. Postmodern identities are thus signalled as being both unstable and constructed more from the images of leisure and consumption than from the world of work and occupation. Kellner also identifies shifting and conflicting ideological positions in *Miami Vice* which on the one hand privilege white male subject positions and invite viewers to identify with a rich consumer capitalist life-style, yet on the other offers an example of enduring interracial friendship and associates the 'vice' with unbridled capitalism. Drugs are just another commodity being exchanged in a free enterprise mode so that '*Miami Vice* associates wealth with crime, capitalist enterprise with criminality'. The identification of conflicting ideological positions is important to Kellner's argument that while postmodern image culture is multiple, fluid and transitory such images

> are connected to content and values, to specific modes and forms of identity, and that the images of popular culture are also saturated with ideology, so that identity in contemporary societies can (still) be interpreted as an ideological construct, as a means whereby enculturation produces subject positions which reproduce dominant capitalist and masculist values and modes of life. (Kellner, 1992, p. 157)

Evaluating Postmodern Television Culture

For Baudrillard, television is at the heart of a postmodern culture marked by an all-encompassing flow of fascinating simulations and images, a hyperreality in which we are overloaded with images and information. This is a world where a series of modern distinctions have broken down, or been sucked into a 'black hole' as Baudrillard calls it, collapsing the real and the unreal, the public and the private, art and reality.

> It is reality itself today that is hyperrealist . . . it is quotidian reality in its entirety – political, social, historical and economic – that from now on incorporates the simulating dimension of hyper-realism. We live everywhere in an 'aesthetic' hallucination of reality. (Baudrillard, 1983a, p. 148)

The 'hyper' prefix signifies 'more real than real'. The real is produced according to a model so that it is not a given but is artificially repro-duced as real, a real retouched in a 'hallucinatory resemblance' of itself. The concept of 'implosion' is important to Baudrillard's work and describes a process leading to the collapse of boundaries including between the media and the social so that 'TV is the world' and the distinction between the TV doctor and the real one is confused. For Baudrillard, television simulates real-life situations, not so much to represent the world as to execute its own, thus it re-enacts events so that news and entertainment blur into each other. According to Baudrillard, the world of communication saturation represents an over-intense advance of the world upon the conscious-ness of subjects which he describes as 'schizophrenic'. There is an over-exposure, an explosion of visibility, a process by which all becomes transparence and immediate visibility, which Baudrillard calls 'obscenity'. The television screen is the central metaphor as the schizoid subject of 'obscenity' becomes 'a pure screen, a switching center for all the networks of influence' (Baudrillard, 1983b, p. 148).

For Baudrillard, television is implicated in this postmodern culture through its continual *flow of images*, with no connotational hierarchy, leading to the collapse of boundaries between art and consumer culture. Postmodern television is argued to be flat and one-dimensional, it is both literally and metaphorically 'superficial'. Thus Grossberg's condemnation of *Miami Vice* as 'all on the surface . . . And that surface is nothing but a collection of quotations from our own collective historical debris, a mobile game of Trivia' (Grossberg, 1987, p. 29). For Jameson (1984), who draws on the work of Baudrillard, postmodernism is the cultural dominant of late capitalism; he argues that the postmodern era is dominated by a depthless sense of the present and a loss of historical understanding. We live in a postmodern hyperspace in which we are unable to place ourselves; the specific manifestations of which include:

• The cannibalization of all styles from past and present.
• The associated loss of artistic style in favour of pastiche.
• The transformation of representations of the world into images and spectacles.
• The breakdown of a firm distinction between high and low culture.
• The culture of the simulacrum or copy (for which no original existed).
• The fashion for nostalgia in which history is not the object of representation but of stylistic connotation.
• The transcending of capacities of individuals to locate themselves perceptually or cognitively in postmodern hyperspace.

Jameson's description of the postmodern world as one marked by fragmentation, instability, and disorientation, a culture of images and the dominance of the present, is one that has much in common with theorists of postmodernity such as Lyotard and Baudrillard. However, he radically parts company with these writers on the level of explanation. Jameson is at pains to point out that postmodernism has genuine historical reality and that postmodern cultural practices are expressive of developments and experiences in reality which need to be grasped in their positive and negative manifestations. In particular, for Jameson postmodernism is the cultural expression of an as yet untheorized world system of multinational or late capitalism operating in a new *global space*. Late capitalism, it is argued, extends commodification to virtually all realms of personal and social life so that culture is more and more associated with the circulation of commodities and the transformation of the real into the image and simulacrum.

In contrast to these negative evaluations Kaplan (1987) claims a transgressive and progressive role for the postmodern music video so that, in deconstructionist mode, the postmodern music video offers no assured narrative position for the viewer and thereby undermines the status of representation as real or true.

What characterises the postmodernist video is its refusal to take a clear position *vis-à-vis* its images, its habit of hedging along the line, of not communicating a clear signified . . . each element of a text is undercut by others: narrative is undercut by pastiche; signifying is undercut by images that do not line up in a coherent chain; the text is flattened out, creating a two-dimensional effect and the refusal of a clear position for the spectator within the filmic world. (Kaplan, 1987, p. 63)

Likewise, Collins (1992) argues that *Twin Peaks* not only acknowledges multiple subject positions and identities, but actively encourages the conscious moving in and out of positions and playing with meaning and form. Unlike Kaplan and Collins, Paul Willis does not readily embrace a positive notion of the postmodern, though he does explicitly criticize the postmodern pessimism associated with Baudrillard as

a bad case of idealist theorists becoming the victims of their own worst nightmares. Mistaking their own metaphors for reality, they are hoist by their own semiotic petards. They are caught by – defined in professionally charting – the symbolic life on the surface of things without seeing, because not implicated in, the necessary everyday role of symbolic work, of how sense is made of structure and contradiction. They then coolly announce that modern culture is all surface and in danger of collapse. (Willis, 1990, p. 27)

For Willis, contemporary culture is not a meaningless or superficial surface but involves the active creation of meaning by all people as cultural producers. In relation to television, Willis takes the by now familiar line that audiences (and he is talking about young people in particular) are sophisticated readers of images; they have learnt to play with interpreting television codes. Thus, 'young people have an active, creative, and symbolically productive relation to what they see on television'.

Kellner (1992) agrees that television is meaningful and that it does not represent 'a pure noise in the postmodern ecstasy, a pure· implosion, a black hole where all meaning and messages are absorbed in the whirlpool', rather, he argues for the central role of television in the structuring of modern life. For Kellner, television assumes the integrating role of myth and ritual celebrating dominant values and modes of thought and behaviour.

People do model their behaviour, style, and attitudes on television images; television ads do play a role in managing consumer demand; and, most recently, many analysts have concluded that television is playing the central role in political elections. (Kellner, 1992, p. 147)

There are shades of difference between Kaplan, Collins, Willis and Kellner. Kaplan and Collins celebrate the transgressive potential of postmodern television. Willis does not accept the postmodern argument but does argue for the active role of viewers and the progressive potential of television. Kellner, seeing a more orthodox 'management of meaning' role for television, does not accept the idea that it is a superficial void. What they have in common, in opposition to the more pessimistic and apocalyptic versions of postmodernism, is a notion that watching television is a meaningful experience.

One of the markers of the postmodern, seen very clearly in television, is the recycling or re-articulation of styles and meanings from different historical periods. This can be seen, after Jameson, as 'camp' recycling, pastiche, and a loss of historical depth, as well as pure commercialism. However, 'such a view fails to account for the diversity of possible strategies of re-articulation', which range from simple revivalism and nostalgia to 'the radicalised cover versions of pop standards by the Sex Pistols or The Clash, in which the past is not just accessed but "hijacked", given an entirely different cultural significance' (Collins, 1992, p. 333). Postmodern cultural style can be extremely reflexive about its cultural status and conditions of production and consumption thus drawing our attention to the constructed nature of television and the ways programmes circulate and are given meaning. Further, intertextual reference, juxtaposition of apparently diverse styles and the blurring of distinctions between fiction and non-fiction, art and marketing is not just the domain of commercial *Coca Cola* culture but is also a marker of 'quality television' like *Hill Street Blues*, *Northern Exposure* and *Twin Peaks*.

For Baudrillard and Jameson, consumerism is implicated in a 'depthless culture' of signs without referents. From a different perspective writers like Chambers (1987; 1990), Collins (1989) and Hebdige (1988) have discussed the ways in which commodities form the basis for multiple identity construction, particularly in relation to youth and popular culture, emphasizing the active meaning production of consumers so that they become bricoleurs selecting and arranging elements of material commodities and meaningful signs. Indeed, Paul Willis (1990) argues that because the construction of meaning occurs through actual usage rather than being inherent in the commodity, it is possible for a creative 'common culture' to be formed through the consuming practices of young people.

These more positive versions of consumption are tied in with the construction of a variety of life-styles in postmodern culture through the purchase and consumption of consumer goods, reflecting particular tastes and preferences. The postmodern can thus be read as the democratization of culture and of new individual and political possibilities. It can be argued that:

> Postmodernism, whatever form its own intellectualising might take, has been fundamentally anticipated in the metropolitan cultures of the last twenty years: among the electronic signifiers of cinema, television and video, in recording studios and record players, in fashion and youth styles, in all those sounds, images and diverse histories that are daily mixed, recycled and 'scratched' together on that giant screen which is the contemporary city. (Chambers, 1987, p. 7)

The democratic possibilities of postmodern popular culture lie in the legitimacy being accorded to it, since though it is a statement of the obvious, popular culture is popular and can represent a more democratic cultural movement than traditional high culture. Further, the creative play through which such cultural forms are produced and consumed offers democratizing possibilities because, while the production of popular music, film, television and fashion is in the hands of transnational capitalist corporations, the meanings are produced, altered and managed at the level of consumption by people who are active producers of meaning. This is particularly significant in an environment of semiotic excess whereby the widespread circulation of signs with multiple meanings makes it harder for any dominant meaning to stick; the possibility is opened up for people to create their own meanings and styles from a range of signs and sites of activity. People range across a series of terrains, sites of meaning, that are not of their own making but from which they can actively produce sense so that the bricolage of film, TV and architecture is echoed in the patchwork of self-constructed postmodern identities.

The 'making' in question is a production, a poiesis – but a hidden one, because it is shattered over areas defined and occupied by systems of 'production' (television, urban development, commerce, etc.) and because the steadily increasing expansion of those systems no longer leaves 'consumers' any place in which they can indicate what they make or do with the products of these systems. To a rationalized, expansionist and at the same time centralized, clamorous and spectacular production corresponds another production, called 'consumption'. The latter is devious, it is dispersed, but it insinuates itself everywhere, silently and almost invisibly, because it does not manifest itself through its own products, but rather through its ways of using the products imposed by a dominant economic order. (de Certeau, 1984, pp. xii–xiii)

That the circumstances of postmodern culture both constitute and are constituted by fresh possibilities can be seen in the emergence of new voices, of the 'other' of modernity, in new social movements and in new forms of struggles in and through popular culture. This has taken a number of forms: the emergence of feminism and of black politics, the appearance of 'life politics', of ecology and peace movements, the voices from non-western cultures, the challenges to notions of progress and development by new-age travellers, the demands for free movement and public space implicit in 'rave', the 'declaration of independence, of otherness, of alien intent, a refusal of anonymity, of subordinate status' (Hebdige, 1988, p. 35), of certain sub-cultures and the possibility of the creation of a radical plural democracy based on diversity and difference argued for by Laclau and Mouffe (1985). There are no guarantees, no universal foundations, for such a project and it remains only a possibility inherent in postmodern culture (chapter 7).

These are contradictory times. We face increased social control and surveillance, poverty and powerlessness, transnational corporations and mass-produced culture yet we are also learning to value diversity, difference, popular culture and popular meaning construction, the decline of a dominant culture and the potential for new forms of solidarity. Within urban geography one finds the metaphors of the *landscape* and the *vernacular* where the former is the wider terrain erected by multinational urban redevelopers and the latter represents the reshaping of the space on the ground by popular sentiment and practices. This is an apt metaphor for the possibilities of a global postmodern culture and, while the *landscape* continues to be shaped by multinational power in its various mani-festations, the *vernacular* still holds the potential to be shaped by the power of the popular. It is a hope, a possibility, perhaps a utopia.

Conclusions

The development of global television as a fundamentally com-mercial form has placed advertising in the visible forefront of its activities. Television remains the central vehicle for international advertising both in its multi-local and global branding forms; tele-vision's organizational forms and programming strategies are heavily structured by the advertising industry. Though global branding remains a limited phenomenon, television is central to the production and reproduction of a postmodern 'promo-culture' centred on the use of visual imagery to create value-added brands or commodity-signs. While the excitement and brashness of consumer culture has an undoubted appeal, the concern is that it is eroding a public sphere based on the ideal of rational debate. While consumers may be critical decoders of adverts the terrain is shaped by multinational corporations who are not subject to any kind of democratic control and whose prime concern is profit.

The globalization of television both constitutes and is constituted by the postmodern flow of images from different times and places. That is to say, television is postmodern in part because it draws from the ever increasing sources offered to it by the wider processes of globalization, which in turn globalize a postmodern form whose origins lie in the west. Such a postmodern culture is a reflexive and contradictory culture. On the one hand, the institutional terrain and the production of culture is increasingly commodified and controlled by transnational corporations, western culture is almost completely a commercial one, while on the other, we are all increas-ingly reflexive about ourselves, our culture, and the history, conditions and techniques of cultural production. The tensions between a centrally- and commercially-produced culture and an active, knowledgeable audience is at the centre of an understanding of global television and of cultural conditions in general whether that be in New York, Bombay or Mexico City.

6

Cultural Identities and Cultural Imperialism

In this chapter we will be concerned with the production of collective cultural identities, with particular reference to issues of national identity, and the role of television in that process. This issue has received increasing attention as the processes of accelerated globalization, which encompasses television, have cast national identities into doubt, prompting a renewed theoretical and practical interest in the processes of identity production. Stable identities are rarely questioned, they appear as 'natural' and taken for granted. However, when 'naturalness' is seen to dissolve we are inclined to examine them anew. As Mercer (1992) has argued, identity is hotly debated when it is in crisis.

The chapter begins with a review of a well-established paradigm for understanding the impact of global television, the cultural imperialism thesis. I suggest that while it has arguments to commend it, cultural imperialism is an increasingly inadequate concept for understanding television under contemporary conditions because of the incomplete theorization of cultural identity which underpins it. It will be argued that the concepts of globalization and hybrid identities are conceptually more adequate frameworks for explaining contemporary processes than cultural imperialism. However, the adoption of the concept of globalization should not lead us to ignore the strength of the cultural imperialism thesis, namely the importance of power. This journey requires us to depart from a direct examination of global television in order to develop the theoretical concepts required to establish its significance. This in itself reminds us that television cannot be understood in isolation but must be placed within wider global and social contexts.

The Concept of Cultural Imperialism

Much of the debate about international television has been implicitly or explicitly related to concerns about media and cultural imperialism. In relation to television this imperialism is argued to take the form of the purchase of US programmes, international co-productions dominated by American themes, US-dominated information services and local adaptations of American formats for domestic consumption. The outcome is said to be both the limiting of indigenous production capacity and the domination of local culture by foreign values. Media imperialism, which can be said to have both economic and cultural dimensions, is argued to take place across a number of boundaries:

- The USA vs. developing nations.
- The USA vs. Europe.
- The USA vs. Canada.
- The capitalist countries vs. the rest of the world.
- The rich countries vs. the poor countries.

Core to the concept of cultural imperialism is the domination of one culture over another, most commonly posed in terms of nationality. Thus, cultural imperialism is understood in terms of the imposition of one national culture upon another and the media are seen as central to this process as carriers of cultural meanings which penetrate and dominate the culture of the subordinate nation. In the case of television, the processes of cultural production and dissemination are also economic activities of commodity production and marketing, thus cultural imperialism is arguably premised upon economic imperialism. The economic processes of television production are clearly capitalist in form and the logic of the argument can be extended to assert that cultural imperialism as a set of both economic and cultural processes is implicated in the reproduction of global capitalism. This argument, put in its starkest form, produces the equation that global media are dominated by American-owned multinationals who disseminate pro-American and pro-capitalist values. Thus, cultural imperialism becomes a process whereby an imposed culture is in the service of American capitalism.

Glatzer (1976) summarizes the thrust of the arguments and identifies the general characteristics of televisual cultural imperialism thus:

- Ideological support for capitalism in general and imperialism in particular.
- Information monopoly by a few international news agencies.
- The partial or complete dependency of national television on foreign mass culture.
- Foreign, especially US, ownership and control of national television systems.
- The dependence of less developed countries on technical organization and professional skills acquired abroad.

The case for cultural imperialism in terms of textual meaning is put by Dorfman and Mattelart (1975) in their analysis of the world of Walt Disney. The authors aim to locate the values within the Disney universe and to demonstrate the ideological assumptions which serve American imperialism by persuading people that the 'American way' is the 'best way'. Dorfman and Mattelart create an inventory of ideological themes, including: the racial and cultural stereotyping of Third World nations; images of developing countries with wealth waiting for western explorers to legitimately take; the elevation of money and consumption to the highest levels of personal ambition and meaning; and the depiction of capitalism as inevitable and necessary. This is allied to the dependency of developing economies on the USA, and to the advertising and importation of consumer commodities such as Coca Cola, with its implicit praise for the good life to be had through capitalism and the American way.

This kind of argument is also central to the UNESCO-sponsored McBride Report *Many Voices, One World*, and its search for a new world information and communications order. The report seeks to support the notion of national and cultural identity (not necessarily the same thing) in the context of what is argued to be the global domination of communications by western concerns. This argument is further developed by Mattelart, Delcourt and Mattelart (1984) in their book *International Image Markets*. While they argue that a monolithic notion of cultural imperialism is inappropriate, they nevertheless seek to argue that the 'revolution' in communications has projected culture into the heart of industrial and political strategies; this is intrinsically linked to the globalizing of American-dominated capitalism and its associated advertising industry. This promotes a process of cultural homogenization and the limiting of voices that can be heard in the global media so that economics and culture are designated as 'the same struggle'. The 'solution' for them is the creation of regional cultural spaces, for example a Latin cultural space, in which co-operation allows for the development of previously unheard voices.

Thus, a central strand of the cultural imperialism thesis stresses the homogenization of global culture through the spread of capitalist consumerism for which global television is one vehicle. This argument stresses the loss of cultural diversity and the growth of 'sameness', attaching a negative evaluation to this process. According to Hamelink:

> The principal agents of cultural synchronisation today are the transnational corporations, largely based in the United States, which are developing a global investment and marketing strategy. (Hamelink, 1983, pp. 22–3)

The link between cultural homogenization and global capitalism is made explicit and is often dubbed, for obvious reasons, Coca Cola culture. The grounds for being critical of cultural synchronization are posed in terms of a loss of cultural autonomy and diversity. This argument can be sustained as a value judgement but it seems nonsensical to do so in the abstract since one has to say in exactly what sphere sameness is a bad thing and why. For as Tomlinson (1991) suggests, one can argue that the universal dissemination of medicine or education is a good thing. Where the argument has strength, especially in relation to television, is where people are *denied* a cultural experience as a result of homogenization, or fail to be adequately represented as a result of the homogenization of production. Thus, if the economics of global television lead to certain kinds of programmes not being produced, for example local drama, or certain socio-economic groups not being adequately represented, for example a particular ethnic group, that is legitimate grounds for criticism.

An alternative version of the cultural homogenization thesis is put by Meyrowitz (1986) whose concern is with the way in which electronic media alter our sense of place, of the 'situational geography' of social life, so that we inhabit a virtual global space in which new forms of identification are forged. The core of his argument is that electronic media break the traditional bonds between geographic place and social identity since mass media provide us with increasing sources of identification which are situated beyond the immediacy of specific places. Meyrowitz's argument is double-edged: on the one hand electronic media culture is a more democratic culture which has broken down the high/low culture divide and lowered social barriers, while on the other, the iconic nature of visual signs upon which television relies demand affective rather than conceptual responses so reducing the role of television in political discussion. Further, the sameness of global media, as he would see it, contributes to a homogenization of global culture. Though Meyrowitz provides an interesting starting point for debate he does not, as Gillespie (1995) argues, provide any empirical support for his thesis but relies on the assumed effects of television. In addition, as Dahlgren (1995) suggests, the dynamics of power are largely absent from Meyrowitz's work.

We have already encountered significant limitations to the cultural imperialism argument in previous chapters. First, while the economic case for seeing television as American dominated is strong it is so only in a general sense since the dissemination of such television throughout the world is an uneven process, stronger in some parts of the globe than others. Even where it is strong, American-made TV does not usually form the largest segment of screen time nor produce the most watched programme. Second, it is not accurate to see American television only as an ideological monolith in the service of US capitalism for, while there is a case for seeing the general drift of American television as supportive of consumer culture, the values and discourses embedded even in mainstream programmes, for example soap operas, are often contradictory. Some American television is critical of consumer culture. Likewise, while it can plausibly be argued that American television reproduces the cultural values of the nuclear family, male power and the white community this is not itself the culture of America which is far more diverse.

A third significant consideration is the evidence encountered in chapter 4 regarding the active nature of audiences and the multiple decodings of programmes like *Dallas*. Even if it were the case that all TV was US-produced and embodied the same values, these would not necessarily be the values of a diverse global audience; we could expect to see a variety of understandings emerging from the viewing of television. Fourth, while there is on the face of it a strong case for privileging the role of television in cultural reproduction, that case is far from watertight since, although people across the world watch a lot of television, they also do a lot of other things which are part of the processes of cultural and social reproduction. There is, as Lodziak (1986) has pointed out, a tendency on the part of media theorists to overestimate the significance of their object of study. There is also a tendency to regard the influence of television as the same across any given culture not taking into account both the varied amount of time people devote to television, its degrees of significance in their lives, and the range of cultural competencies they bring to the activity of watching television.

Tomlinson (1991) highlights further problems relating to the notion of cultural autonomy inherent in the cultural imperialism arugment. How can a culture be autonomous or impose itself upon others? The notion of autonomy implies agency, the ability to act according to one's wishes, while domination and imposition suggest the reverse. It is difficult, argues Tomlinson, to say that a culture is able to act autonomously. Cultures are not bounded entities but consist of changing practices and meanings; one cannot legitimately endow an amorphous set of practices with ontological identity and agency. Further, Tomlinson argues, at which level are we to locate the national culture which is allegedly under threat from cultural imperialism? Should it be the government? Or a dominant ethnic group? Which set of values within that ethnic group are the authentic ones? At the very least a given ethnic group will be divided along lines of class and gender.

These arguments highlight a fundamental conceptual problem with the cultural imperialism thesis, namely that the very notion of nationally-based cultural domination is problematic. The arguments for media imperialism as cultural domination are centred on assumptions about national cultural identity whereby the importing of foreign programmes into national cultures is felt to threaten the autonomy of that culture. But, as Schlesinger (1991) argues, these assumptions are at least questionable. Many versions of the cultural imperialism thesis take for granted what they should be explaining;

that is, the formation of collective identities in general, and cultural and national identities in particular. The notion of a national cultural identity is assumed as a finished product rather than a process which is constantly emerging and changing. This has led Schlesinger to argue that:

> we now need to turn around the terms of the conventional argument: not to start with communication and its supposed effects on collective identity and culture, but rather to begin by posing the problem of collective identity itself, to ask how it might be analysed and what importance communicative practices might play in its constitution. (Schlesinger, 1991, p. 150)

National Identity and Post-Traditional Society

According to Schlesinger (1991), collective identity involves a dynamic aspect of collective action, the marking of indeterminate boundaries within a system of social relations which require reciprocal recognition. Collective identity involves the accomplishment of perceived commonality, cohesion and continuity and thus the creation of an 'imagined community'. Collective identity is always a provisional and ongoing form of identification which has to be continually produced and reproduced over time and across space. This is achieved through shared lived traditions, collective memory and symbolic identification, as well as a delineation of boundaries, territorial and symbolic, between insiders and outsiders. National identity would be a specific case. As Morley and Robbins (1995) suggest, any potential 'European identity' will entail a produced sense of a common European home and cultural continuity, alongside the mapping of who Europeans are not. That is to say Europeans are not Americans, Arabs or Japanese. It is important to recognize that collective identities are forged and created culturally; they are not givens of 'nature', and are thus tentative and provisional. As Melucci argues:

> Collective identity formation is a delicate process and requires continual investments. As it comes to resemble more institutionalised forms of social action, collective identity may crystallise into organisational forms, a system of rules, and patterns of leadership. In less institutionalised forms of action its character more closely

resembles a process which must be continually activated in order for action to be possible. (Melucci, 1989, pp. 34–5)

It follows that collective identities differ in their degrees of solidification and that television may contribute to the formation and crystallization of some collective identities, while weakening and dissolving others.

Benedict Anderson (1983) argues that national identity is an imagined and constructed one assembled in relation to a territorial and administrative category taking as its reference symbols and rituals intended by administrative authorities to enlist identification. The 'nation' is an 'imagined community'.

> It is *imagined* because the members of even the smallest nation will never know most of their fellow members, meet them, or even hear of them, yet in the minds of each lives the images of their communion . . . The nation is imagined as *limited* because even the largest of them, encompassing perhaps a billion living beings, has finite, if elastic boundaries, beyond which lie other nations . . . It is imagined as *sovereign* because the concept was born in an age in which Enlightenment and Revolution were destroying the legitimacy of the divinely ordered, hierarchical dynastic realm . . . Finally, it is imagined as a *community* because, regardless of the actual inequality and exploitation that may prevail in each, the nation is always conceived as a deep, horizontal comradeship. Ultimately, it is this fraternity that makes it possible, over the past two centuries, for so many millions of people, not so much to kill, as willingly to die for such limited imaginings. (Anderson, 1983, pp. 15–16)

While Anderson traces a number of distinctive forms of the 'imagined community', the importance of communication in the European model is of particular interest. Anderson's central argument is that 'Print language is what invents nationalism, not a particular language *per se*' (Anderson, 1983, p. 122). The mechanized production and commodification of books and newspapers, the rise of 'print capitalism', allowed vernacular languages to be standardized and disseminated providing the conditions for the creation of a national consciousness. For the first time it was possible for the mass of people within a particular state to understand each other through a common print language. The processes of print capitalism thus 'fixed' a vernacular language as the 'national' language and made possible a new imagined national community; hence nation and communication are inescapably linked together. In addition, it is not just the construction of a common language that is facilitated but also a common recognition of time, which, within the context of modernity, becomes an empty universal concept measurable by calendar and clock. People are encouraged by the media to imagine the simultaneous occurrence of events across wide tracts of time and space allowing for both the concept of nation and of the place of states within a spatially-distributed state system.

Anderson's account is useful because it allows us to see how the concept of nation becomes possible, and how a particular form of nation was produced by the processes of modernity. However, it requires qualification and extension. First, he does not discuss the role of electronic media. Second, he privileges the metaphor of 'commune' and does not recognize the potential cultural diversity of the nation; that is, its divisions and conflicts (Tomlinson, 1991).

At both conceptual and empirical levels nation and state should be regarded as separate analytic entities since cultures and national cultural identities do not easily map on to the boundaries of nation-states. Even within these boundaries one can find diverse cultural and ethnic identifications. In the first case, a 'people' with a collective national identity may be spread across the borders of many nation-states so that various global Diaspora come to mind: Afro-Caribbean, Jewish, Irish, Italian, Scots, Romanies and so forth. In the second case:

> the so called 'nation-state' is rarely a true appellation, for few states have ethnically homogeneous populations. On the contrary: most are composed of two or more ethnic communities, jostling for influence and power, or living in uneasy harmony within the same state border. (Smith, 1981, p. 9)

Both the cultural imperialism thesis and Anderson's conception of national identity posit the subject as a whole person and national identity as a unified position so that diversity and difference are subsumed beneath the sign of the nation. To take the debate further we need a more subtle account of what cultural identity is under contemporary conditions. As Hall argues:

> Instead of thinking of national cultures as unified, we should think of them as a discursive device which represents difference as unity

or identity. They are cross-cut by deep internal divisions and differences, and 'unified' only through the exercise of different forms of cultural power. (Hall, 1992, p. 297)

The unity of the nation is constructed in Hall's account through the narrative of the nation by which stories, images, symbols and rituals represent 'shared' meanings of nationhood. Such narratives emphasize the traditions and continuity of the nation, though they may be invented traditions, including the foundational myth of a collective point of origin. This in turn both assumes and produces the linkage between national identity and a pure, original people or 'folk' tradition.

It is core to Hall's arguments that identity production is constituted within representation so that representations of cultural identities do not reflect pre-given identities but are constitutive of them. In providing a significant set of resources for the work of identity production global television is at the heart of these debates since, as we saw in relation to Brazilian telenovelas, television is implicated in the production of national identities. At the same time 'postmodern' global television represents, and is implicated in the production of, a variety of life-styles, beliefs, images and identities which are separate from, or lie outside of and beyond, the nation. It is the coexistence and layering of different notions of time, identity and values which global television encourages, and which is the critical area to be explored.

One line of argument is to see national identities as potentially in decline so that they are replaced by new hybrid identities. The concept of hybrid identities is important because it suggests that the influence of global television cannot be adequately understood in terms of relations between nations. Thus, it is insufficient to argue that electronic communication, including global television in its American form, simply displaces the national identities of audiences in Africa, India or China. The process of accelerated globalization, which includes the globalization of television, is critical to differential and hybrid ethnic and national identifications. Patterns of population movement and settlement established during earlier phases of colonial and post-colonial globalization, combined with the more recent acceleration of globalization, particularly of electronic communications, have enabled juxtapositioning, meeting and mixing. Thus, globalization has *increased the range of sources and resources available for identity construction* allowing for the production of hybrid identities in the context of a post-traditional global society where bounded societies and states, though very much still with us, are cut across by the circulation of other global cultural discourses.

From Cultural Identity to Hybrid Identities

Since identity is constituted in and through discourse it is, by its very nature, not possible to separate identity from ways of thinking about it; Hall (1990) has usefully identified two poles or positions from which identity can be understood. In the first version identity is regarded as the name for a collective 'one true self' and is thought to be formed out of a common history, ancestry and set of symbolic resources. Through such optics it is possible to speak of a 'British identity' expressed through the symbol of the Union Jack, memories of the Second World War and collective rituals such as the cup final, the coronation and the nightly news. The underlying assumptions of this view are that identity exists, that in both its individual and collective forms it is 'a whole', and that it is expressed through symbolic representation. This account of identity is known as 'essentialism' because it assumes that social categories reflect an essential underlying identity. By this token there would be an essence of, for example, Black identity based on similarity of experience.

By juxtaposing 'British' and 'Black' as cultural identities the assumptions of an essentialist argument are immediately made problematic since it might have been assumed that a British identity was a white Anglo-Saxon one. The presence of a substantial black population in Britain makes a nonsense of such an assumption and, indeed, redefines what it means to be British. Being British can involve being Black with the capability to trace one's ancestry back to the Caribbean and then Africa. However, just as the concept of British identity is problematic, so too is that of Black identity since it is possible not only to argue for cultural identifications that *connect* Black populations in Africa, America, the Caribbean and Britain, but also to trace the lines of *difference*. To be Black British is not the same as being Black African or Black American.

The work of Paul Gilroy (1993) is illuminating in this respect. Gilroy introduces two new 'chronotopes', or units of analysis, to understand Black identities. The first is that of the ship travelling back and forth between Europe, America, Africa and the Caribbean. He argues that:

> Ships immediately focus attention on the middle passage, on the various projects for redemptive return to an African homeland, on the circulation of ideas and activists as well as the movement of key cultural and political artefacts: tracts, books, gramophone records, and choirs. (Gilroy, 1993, p. 4)

The second key concept is that of the Black Atlantic. Black identities cannot be understood, argues Gilroy, in terms of being American or British or West Indian, nor can they be understood in terms of ethnic absolutism (that there is a global essential black identity), but rather can be understood in terms of the Black Diaspora of the Atlantic. Blacks, as a result of hundreds of years of subjugation, are both in and outside of modernity, they both partake of modern identities of the nation and are placed beyond it, never fully in it. Cultural exchange within the Black Diaspora produces hybrid identities and cultural forms which are to be understood in terms of similarities and differences between the various locales of the Diaspora. Gilroy argues against essentialist notions of identity; he rightly suggests that Blackness is not a pan-global absolute identity: the cultural identities of Black Britons, Black Americans and Black Africans are different. At the same time he points to historically-shared cultural forms across the Black Atlantic.

Music is Gilroy's preferred example. He points to the European travels of the Black American choir, the Fisk University Jubilee Singers, in the 1870s as bringing the message of the slaves to the world. In a more contemporary vein, Rap and Hip Hop have become prominent musical forms not only of the Black Diaspora but of youth culture in general. As Gilroy suggests, rap/hip hop is itself an American–Caribbean hybrid which has become a point of Diaspora identification within the Black Atlantic. An example, though not one used by Gilroy, might be the group 'Prophets of Da City'; on tour recently in Europe they are a Black rap band who hail from Johannesburg, South Africa.

For Gilroy, Black expressive cultural forms, like music, give voice to the 'contingent and partial, which Blacks enjoy'. While 'Blacks born, nurtured and schooled in this country are, in significant measure, British even as their presence redefines the term', the history of racial subordination prevents complete assimilation and leads instead to cultural syncretism or hybridity, so that Black 'self-definitions and cultural expressions draw on a plurality of black histories and politics' (Gilroy, 1987). It is important to recognize that hybrid Black British identities and cultural forms demand that we develop a new view of British culture and what it means to be British. As such, it deconstructs not only an exclusive white Anglo-Saxon version of British identity but forces us to disassemble all forms of homogenous national identity.

Therefore, Hall's second position from which to understand issues of cultural identity stresses that as well as points of similarity, cultural identity is organized around points of difference. Above all, cultural identity is not seen as a reflection of a fixed, natural state of being but as a process of *becoming*. There is no essence of identity to be discovered, rather cultural identity is continually being produced within the vectors of similarity and difference. Cultural identity is not an essence but a continually-shifting position, and the points of difference around which cultural identities could form are multiple and proliferating. They include, to name but a few, identifications of class, gender, sexuality, age, ethnicity, nationality, political position (on numerous issues) morality, religion, etc., and each of these discursive positions is itself unstable. The meaning of Britishness, Blackness, masculinity and so forth are subject to continual change since, Hall argues (following Derrida), meaning is never finished or completed. Identity then becomes a 'cut' or a snap-shot of unfolding meanings; it is a strategic positioning which makes meaning possible. This anti-essentialist position does not mean that we cannot speak of identity, rather it points us to the political nature of identity production and to the possibility of multiple and shifting identities.

While the account of hybrid and changing identities given by Hall is an interesting and suggestive one, it is pitched on a fairly abstract level; for a more concrete exposition of shifting and multiple identities we may recall Gillespie's (1995) study of Asian youth in Southall. Here we saw how young people constituted themselves, to varying degrees, as British Asian. Under some circumstances this involved identification with Britishness, at others with aspects of Asian culture (itself not a homogenous entity). The circumstances of the Gulf War opened up ambiguities and insecurities around both those points of identification so that these young people were able to shift from one position to another as they determined it to be situationally appropriate. This shifting within and between the discourses of Britishness and Asianness was further complicated by religious and geographical differences within Asian culture and by age, gender and class.

The differences within the community studied by Gillespie prevent easy identification of particular subjects with a given, fixed identity so that the same person was able to shift across subject positions according to circumstances. Thus, an Asian girl might identify herself with Asianness to argue that traditional clothes should be respected or to suggest that Asians are misrepresented on television yet, in the context of a discussion about relationships, she might speak more from a position of western feminism to argue against the traditional patriarchal practices of some Asian men. On another occasion she may more obviously position herself as a young person, irrespective of ethnicity or gender, as she adopts the fashion and music of a specific youth sub-culture. One such range of shifting identity positions is put by a young singer:

> I rap in Bengali and English. I rap on everything from love to poli-
> tics. I've always been into rapping . . . it was rebellious, the lyrics
> were sensational. I could relate to that, I could identify with it. Like
> living in the ghetto and that . . . It's from the heart. It's: 'I'm Bengali,
> I'm Asian, I'm a woman, and I'm living here'. (cited in Gardner and
> Shukur, 1994, p. 161)

To put this in Hall's more theoretical language, the subject positions of this young woman involve the articulation of positions drawn from a variety of discourses and sites. At the very least she has identi-fications with being Bengali, English, a woman, with youth culture and with rap, an American–Caribbean hybrid, now appropriated as Anglo-Bengali. She is involved not only in shifting identifications but in enacting a hybrid identity which draws on *multiplying global resources*.

A further concrete example of the formation of cultural identities in a global context is Parker's (1995) exploration of Chinese identity in Britain wherein he explores a range of identifications amongst British-born Chinese young people. Parker highlights six identity formations which, it is argued, derive their power from what they define themselves against and the form of narrative through which they are produced. The first two are 'defined unitarily through closed and pin-pointing narratives', thus some of the British-born

Chinese defined themselves as British and had little sense of identification with Chinese culture. These young people, who developed
narratives of increased belonging to Britain, tended to have lived in
relative isolation from other 'Chinese', and had relatively low-level
experiences of racism. In contrast, those who had more considerable
Chinese cultural resources to draw on, and who had also experienced greater levels of racism, defined themselves as Chinese. They
drew strength from their Chinese identity and criticized those whose
identification was less strong as having 'lost themselves'. While the
first of these two more closed positions is an assimilationist one,
the latter is built on a definition of Chineseness as an essential and
core part of identity.

Other forms of identity were more open, contingent and combinatory and were, argues Parker, based on 'partial identifications'
and a 'conditional belonging' to Britain. Some of the young people
combined a sense of being Chinese with local British identities by
which they did not identify with Britain as a nation-state but with
the locality. Thus, one young woman strongly identified with
Liverpool as well as with Chinese culture. However, this combination was relatively unstable and left the participants excluded
from both British and Chinese identities. Others saw themselves as
moving between worlds, combining them in a way which they
regarded as getting the best out of both. Specifically, this involved
defining themselves as Chinese within the domestic, private sphere,
but adopting British identity in the public domain. According to
Parker, these young people had not experienced high levels of
public racism, which allowed them to feel relatively comfortable
with a British public identity. Those who were developing
increasing self-confidence and who did not feel the need to assert
strong closed identities were developing combinatory partial
identifications with both British and Chinese identities. These were
not strictly separated into the public and private domains and are
more obviously a British–Chinese hybrid form. Finally, there were
those with very 'open and expansive' forms of identity for whom
national and ethnic identifications were in themselves an insufficient
basis for identity, they defined themselves only partly in
British–Chinese terms and looked to other nodal points of identification. For some this was gender related, or involved political
activity with wider commitments.

As Parker comments, there is much theorizing about new hybrid identities but limited concrete empirical work to support it, though his own work adds much needed evidence. Having said that, he argues that the development of new hybrid forms is a limited case because of the relatively small number of British-born Chinese involved whose social isolation inhibits fluidity and hybridity. Instead, geographical and psychological separation is the more common position.

The work of Gilroy, Gillespie and Parker suggests the need to differentiate *types of hybridity* and to do so with reference to the specific circumstances of particular social groups. Thus, Pieterse (1995) has suggested that we should distinguish between the different contexts of hybridity and argues that we can make a distinction between structural and cultural hybridization. The former refers to a variety of social and institutional sites of hybridity, for example border zones, while the latter distinguishes between cultural responses ranging from assimilation, through forms of separation, to hybrids that destabilize and blur cultural boundaries. Within the cultural domain Pieterse differentiates between a view of culture as bounded, tied to place and inward-looking, and one which is seen as a 'translocal learning process' and is outward looking. Over all he argues:

> Introverted cultures, which have been prominent over a long stretch of history and which overshadowed translocal culture, are gradually receding into the background, while translocal culture made up of diverse elements is coming to the foreground. (Pieterse, 1995, p. 62)

He goes on to argue that structural hybridization, which increases the range of organizational options to people, and cultural hybridization, which involves the opening up of 'imagined communites', are signs of increased boundary crossing. However, they do not represent the erasure of boundaries and we need to be sensitive to both cultural difference and to forms of identification that involve recognition of similarity. This requires us to recognize the range of cultural and national identities which are formed and unformed over time and across a variety of spaces.

Using the axis of introverted – translocal and recognition of difference – similarity we can identify a broad range of possible cultural identities in relation to British Asians (table 6.1). This range of identifications emerged in research (Barker, 1996a; 1996b) into the

Table 6.1   *British Asian teenagers and cultural identities*

	Introverted Culture	Translocal Culture
Difference	1 Two distinct cultural traditions are kept separate in time and/or space. We would define ourselves as Asian or British. This is the domain of nationalism and ethnic absolutism. 2 Two separate cultural traditions are juxtaposed in time and space. We would define ourselves as Asian and British and move between them as situationally appropriate.	3 Cultures are translocal and involve global flows. Hybridization occurs out of recognition of difference and produces something new. We are 'British Asian'.
Similarity	4 Cultural traditions develop in separate locales but develop identifications based on perceived similarity and commonality of tradition and circumstance. For example, an essentialist version of pan-global Black or Asian nationalism. 5 One cultural tradition absorbs or obliterates the other and creates effective similarity. This could involve assimilation (My parents are Asian but I am British) or cultural domination and imperialism (one tradition is wiped out).	6 New forms of identity are forged out of shared concerns along the axes of class, ethnicity, gender, age, etc. This is an anti-essentialist position in which similarity is strategic and created. For example, a strategic alliance in which Black and Asian people share a common anti-racist strategy. Equally, strategic identifications and alliances occur on other axes such as gender or age.

responses of British Asian teenagers to soap opera. Thus, the argument that soaps are not about 'us' (as Asians) because 'we' are not represented in them suggests a degree (by no means complete) of cultural separation. On the other hand, repeated references to the idea that 'Blacks and Asians are the same' suggests a newly-forged post-traditional identification stressing a similar structural position in British society.

Below is data from my research in which a group of girls complain about the inadequate representation of Asian and Black girls in *Neighbours* and implicitly define themselves as Asian. The manner in which they so define themselves suggests a form of hybridity as British–Asian.

B: What about that thingy in Neighbours, Lahta.
D: That is not a typical Asian girl, did you see her with a sari on.
A: That is a joke.
B: And going out with.
C: That Brett.
A: I know, that was taking the er [pause] mickey then, a typical Asian, they're always taking the piss of Asian or Black people, or Chinese.
B: Or when they had lots of Chinese people in.
C: That one had spots all over his face.
B: And how long do they stay in the programme.
A: None of the other races stay in for long.
D: None of the Black people stay in for long.
B: In Neighbours is there one Black?

Thus *Lahta* is seen as *not a typical Asian girl* because, amongst other things, she had *a sari on*. The girls infer that they *are* typical Asian girls but in a way which is different from Lahta. They do not wear saris and would not routinely expect to do so. Their experience of being Asian is unlike Lahta's, who has arrived in Australia directly from India, because they are British and live in the mixed traditions of a British–Asian context. This is underlined by a different group of girls when they suggest that:

B: And the way her [Lahta's] brother was over-controlling her life it's not on, it's not like that in our life.
A: That does not happen.
B: People aren't that strict.
C: And I don't think that brothers act towards their sisters like that.

Thus, the familial relationships experienced by these girls are not perceived to be the same as those of a traditional Indian family or the media representation thereof. Indeed, girl A appears to see the representation of *a typical Asian* as *taking the mickey* and *taking the piss*. Depending on how one reads this line, we could also see them as claiming that Lahta's going out with Brett, a white boy, is also *taking the piss* and could infer that for these girls, going out with a white boy is unlikely. Overall, the girls appear to adopt an Asian identity which may include an inclusive and traditional sense that you do not go out with white boys, combined with a post-traditional view of being Asian: you do not wear saris, you do not get controlled by your brothers. This can be described as a British–Asian hybrid form.

The girls complain that the representation of Asians is inadequate in both quantitative and qualitative terms. There are not enough Asians in *Neighbours* and they are treated in negative and stereotypical terms when they do appear. The girls give expression to the feeling that Asians are both in and out of Australian and British society. Their feelings that Asians are inadequately represented suggest that they should be better represented by virtue of the fact that they are an integral part of Australian (and I think by implication British) society. The fact that they are not so represented engenders and maintains feelings that they are excluded from taking full part in these societies. They assert their British–Asianness but in a way which underlines what they are not, that is, fully recognized participants. Further, these Asian girls forge an alliance with other excluded groups, Blacks and Chinese, in a post-traditional recognition of shared circumstances since *none of the other races stay in for long.*

Globalization and Power

If global television is understood in terms of cultural imperialism we focus on American domination of the media and upon the capitalist homogenization of culture, since the core of the cultural imperialism thesis stresses the domination of one set of nations over another and of sameness over difference. However, the concepts of globalization and hybridity throw the discourse of cultural imperialism into something of a crisis by undermining the very notions of unified national and cultural identities. Hence, the concept of globalization is more adequate than that of cultural imperialism because it suggests a less coherent, unified and directed process than cultural imperialism.

However, while the arguments and evidence of this book are supportive of such a claim this should not lead us to abandon what is core to the cultural imperialism thesis, namely ideas of power and inequality. The fact that power is diffused or that commodities are subversively used to produce new hybrid identities does not displace power or our need to examine it, for, as Pieterse (1995) argues:

> Relations of power and hegemony are inscribed and reproduced within hybridity for wherever we look closely enough we find the traces of asymmetry in culture, place, descent. Hence hybridity raises the question of the *terms* of the mixture, the conditions of mixing and melange. At the same time it's important to note the ways in which hegemony is not merely reproduced but *refigured* in the process of hybridisation. (Pieterse, 1995, p. 57)

For example, the hybridity of the cultural forms produced by the Black Diaspora does not obscure the power that was embedded through slavery nor the economic push–pull of migration. As Hall (1992) argues, Diaspora identities are constructed within and by cultural power. 'This power,' he suggests, 'has become a constitutive element in our own identities' (Hall, 1992, p. 233). Thus, it would be mistaken to think that we are all free to make ourselves as we wish in a society of autonomous agents. Clearly this is not the case, the choices open to rich white men in New York are of a very different order to those of poor Asian women in rural India since choices are bounded by the structural conditions in which they are made available and enacted. Giddens's theory of structuration makes this abundantly clear (Giddens, 1984) as does, from a different perspective, the work of Foucault. Or, to paraphrase Marx, people make history but not under conditions of their own making. In short, decisions are always enabled and constrained by power.

It is a core argument of this book that global television is constitutive of and constituted by the inherently globalizing tendencies of the institutions of modernity. Since power is inherent in this process it behoves us to ask whether the spread of modernity itself is not a western project. Giddens has argued, in relation to capitalism and the nation-state, that:

If, in close conjunction with one another, they have swept across the world, this is above all because of the power they have generated. No other, more traditional social forms, have been able to contest this power in respect of maintaining autonomy outside the trends of global development. (Giddens, 1990, p. 174)

Given that these institutions originated in Europe and have spread outward from this base, we have to say that modernity is a western project. On the other hand, the globalization of modernity 'is a process of uneven development that fragments as it co-ordinates – introduces new forms of world interdependence, in which, once again there are no 'others' and which involves 'emergent forms of world interdependence and planetary consciousness' (Giddens, 1990, p. 175). Though the early phases of globalization involved western interrogation of the non-western 'other', the current phase of globalization is increasingly less one-directional. As Giddens puts it, 'the point is not only that the other "answers back", but that mutual interrogation is possible' (Giddens, 1994).

According to Giddens (1994) high modernity heralds the dawn of a *post-traditional global* society. It is global in the sense that no one is outside it and all traditions, including those of the west, are now open to scrutiny. Though modernity has its own traditions (including invented tradition), tradition is not simply to be understood as a pre-modern static cultural form, nevertheless, 'modernity destroys tradition'. The condition of high modernity involves the excavation and evacuation of tradition on a global scale.

'Excavation', as in an archaeological dig, is an investigation, and it is also an evacuation. Old bones are disinterred, and their connections with one another established, but they are also exhumed and the site is cleaned out. Excavation means digging deep, in an attempt to clean out the debris of the past. (Giddens, 1994, p. 73)

The combination of globalization and radical doubt problematizes all traditions and, thus, all identities, since tradition is 'a medium of identity' both personal and collective. Traditions are juxtaposed to each other, compared, interrogated and required to explain and defend themselves. All tradition is relativized. In a post-traditional order we increasingly encounter the possibility, not yet fully actualized, of what Rorty has called 'the cosmopolitan conversation of humankind'.

Thus, the globalization of modernity is not simply a western project but involves non-western actors, voices and strategies. This view suggests that the current phase of accelerated globalization represents a shift away from the centrality of the west in the global configuration. Further, as Appaduria has suggested:

> The new global cultural economy has to be seen as a complex, overlapping, disjunctive order, which cannot any longer be understood in terms of existing centre–periphery models . . . for people of Irian Jaya, Indonesianization may be more worrisome than Americanisation, as Japanisation may be for Koreans, Indianisation for Sri Lankans, Vietnamisation for Cambodians, Russianisation for the people of Soviet Armenia and the Baltic Republics. (Appaduria, 1993; cited in Housee, 1995)

Discussion of Diaspora identities and of hybridization raise the issue of 'reverse flow', the impact of non-western ideas and practices on the west. Examples of this, which we have already encountered, would include:

- The export of telenovelas from Latin America to the USA and Europe.
- Population movement from developing nations into the west and the creation of ethnic Diaspora.
- The global impact of reggae, rap, hip hop and 'world music'.
- The influence of Islam, Hinduism and other world religions within the west.
- The commodification and sale of 'ethnic' food and clothing within the west.
- The decentring of western perspectives about progress.
- The increasing economic power of newly-industrializing nations.

The fact that these developments have taken place within spaces already configured by the power of western modernity does not negate the impact that they have had and are having.

As Morley and Robbins (1995) argue, nowhere evokes these issues with more force than Japan, which raises problems for the west. The very notion of the west and the orient, and indeed of the Far East, the Middle East and other geographical zones, are human creations of western domination, inscribed within which are notions of the ethnic superiority of white westerners. The Japanese have been amongst the west's 'others', they have been seen as exotic, alien, mysterious, impenetrable and dehumanized. Japan absorbed western technologies and institutions because this was their destiny, reflecting the presumed superiority of western development and progress. Now Japan is putting western modernity into question. Japan has a growing lead in new technologies (technologies through which the west presumed itself to be superior and advanced) and is synonymous with computers and electronic communications technologies. Japanese business owns significant parts of the Hollywood culture industries, has pioneered post-Fordist production techniques and is the largest creditor and net investor in the world. The rise of Japan as a world power has prompted a degree of racist panic in the west, so that the Japanese have begun to occupy that symbolic space occupied by Jews (amongst others). They are feared and denigrated as inhuman, robotic, conformist and inscrutable. The 'yellow peril' revisited. Thus Morley and Robbins argue:

> Japan has come to exist within the Western political and cultural unconscious as a figure of danger, and it has done so because it has destabilised the neat correlation between West/East and modern/pre-modern. If the West is modern, Japan should be premodern, or at least non-modern . . . The scandalous and unthinkable possibility is raised that the West may now have to 'learn from Japan' . . .What Japan has done is to call into question the supposed centrality of the West as a cultural and geographical locus for the project of modernity. (Morley and Robbins, 1995, p. 160)

They suggest that, while modernity is increasingly the condition of all cultures across the globe, the issue is 'on what terms they are inserted into that modernity, and on what terms they will co-exist' (Morley and Robbins, 1995, p. 171). In short, we are all part of a global society, no one can escape its consequences, but we remain unequal participants and globalization an uneven process.

Conclusions

Global television is constitutive of and constituted by the inherently globalizing nature of modernity. Though television as both technology and cultural form is a western-originated project and continues to be dominated economically by western and, particularly, American economic powers, the global spread of television may be inflected and configured in different ways under different local circumstances. The production of the global and the local are the same process. While the production and circulation of television programmes are dominated by the USA there is evidence that audiences decode programmes in sophisticated and multiple ways which reduces the ideological impact of these programmes. The concept of cultural imperialism with its stress on homogenization is inadequate for an understanding of these processes.

That capitalist modernity does involve an element of cultural homogenization seems undeniable since modernity increases the levels and amount of global co-ordination. However, as we have seen, mechanisms of fragmentation, heterogenization and hybridity are also at work so that, as Roberston argues:

> It is not a question of *either* homogenization or heterogenization, but rather of the ways in which both of these two tendencies have become features of life across much of the late-twentieth-century world. (Robertson, 1995, p. 27)

Robertson goes on to argue that much which is considered to be local, and counterpoised to the global, is in actuality the outcome of translocal processes; thus, nation-states were forged within a global nation-state system and the contemporary rise in nationalist sentiment can be regarded as an aspect of globalization not just as a reaction to it. The global and the local are relative terms, the idea of the local, specifically what is considered local, is produced within and by a globalizing discourse, which includes capitalist marketing and its increasing orientation to differentiated local markets. As Robertson suggests, diversity sells so that ethnicity is commodified and sold, sometimes as nostalgia, sometimes as a sign of cosmopolitanism. In any case, an emphasis on particularity and diversity can be regarded as an increasingly global and universalistic discourse so that 'the expectation of identity declaration is built into the general process of globalisation' (Robertson, 1992, p. 175). Robertson adopts the concept of *glocalization*, in origin a marketing term, to express the global production of the local and the localization of the global.

In some instances the impact of global television may be understood as the creation of a layer of western capitalist modernity which overlays, but does not necessarily obliterate, pre-existing cultural forms. Modern and postmodern ideas about time, space, rationality, capitalism, consumerism, sexuality, family, gender, etc. are placed alongside older forms in a way which relativizes both and sets up ideological competition between them. The outcome may be a range of hybrid forms of identity, though it may also involve the defensive production of 'fundamentalist' and nationalist identities. Nationalism and fundamentalism continue to coexist with cosmopolitanism and the weakening of national identities.

The nation is not necessarily the most suitable level to understand the cultural impact of television, rather we need to consider the various levels of cultural identification, action and influence. For example, global television is one contributor to the creation of pan-global identifications, including those of ethnic Diaspora, and constitutes one resource in the production of hybrid identities. Post-traditional and translocal identity formation involves the production of multiple identities or identifications many of which have little bearing on questions of national identity but focus on issues of sexuality, relationships, age, work, etc. Television is one resource, albeit a significant one, in that process.

7

Some Conclusions:
The Politics of Television

The central concern of this book has been to map developments in global television from a number of angles including political economy, textual analysis, audience studies and cultural studies. As I suggested in chapter 1, a description of global television is inseparable from an evaluation, both in principle (as analytic catagories) and in practice, since in asking about the nature of global television as it *is* we inevitably raise issues about what we think global television *ought* to be like. In the remainder of this book I want to explore three issues of cultural politics which flow from the concerns of the text thus far. These concern questions of programming; of organizational principles; and of television's place in the more formal politics of the state in an era of globalization and fragmented identities. However, in order to put these arguments in context, and so they do indeed represent some conclusions, I want to summarize the broad direction of the arguments put thus far.

Previously on Global Television . . . A Summary

- Global television needs to be understood historically and sociologically in the wider context of the globalization of capitalist modernity. Global television is constituted by and constitutive of the inherently globalizing nature of modernity. 'Society' as bounded by place and space is inadequate for the task of describing and evaluating television and, indeed, the condition of humanity in late modernity, rather, we are part of a global post-traditional society from which there is no escape. Globalization involves both homogenizing and co-ordinating tendencies, in conjunction with countervailing forces, towards localization of global forms. The production of the global and the local are the same process.

- Television is a global phenomenon on an institutional level and involves both the configurations of national systems and the development of transnational television. [Advances in television technology have created new distribution mechanisms which, allied to political and industrial support for market solutions, have weakened national regulatory environments.] New transnational commercial corporations have entered into the global television market creating serious competition for public service broadcasters which, while they continue to survive, have lost part of their audience to their competitors. There has been a rise in transnational and monopoly ownership circumventing national regulations so that global television is dominated by commercial multinational corporations.

- Television can be said to be global in that similar narrative forms circulate around the world: soap opera and news can be found in most countries. At the same time, the global multiplication of communications technologies has created an increasingly complex semiotic environment: television produces and circulates an explosive display of competing signs and meanings. This creates a flow of images which fuses news, views, drama and reportage so that a variety of juxtapositions of images and meanings create a sort of electronic bricolage.

- The globalization of television has contributed to the construction of a postmodern collage of images from different times and places. Postmodern culture is a contradictory culture since it is an increasingly commodified culture but also an increasingly reflexive one. Thus, tensions between a centrally- and commercially-produced culture and an active, knowledgeable audience are at the centre of an understanding of global television and of cultural conditions in general.

- The development of global television as a fundamentally commercial form has placed advertising in the visible forefront of its activities. Television remains the central vehicle for international

advertising both in its multi-local and global branding forr
Television is central to the production and reproduction of a po。。
modern 'promo-culture' centred on the use of visual imagery to
create value-added brands or commodity-signs.

- Heterogeneous global audiences are able to bring their own cultural
competencies to bear and to decode programmes in ways which
depart from the dominant textual ideologies. However, while audiences can actively resist ideological formulations, activity does not
always of itself involve resistance. Watching television also involves
material practices and in particular the routines of domestic life and
the dissemination of modern notions of time.

- Television can be educative, informative and entertaining, as well as
ideological and misleading. It is the cutting edge of advertising and
consumer capitalism, but also of democracy, diversity and a liberating form of hybrid identity politics. The ideas and values circulated
by television may be supported or contradicted by other institutions
so that we must beware of both examining television as an isolated
institution and of overstating its place in modern life.

- Television as both technology and cultural form is a western-
originated project and continues to be dominated economically by
western and, particularly, American economic powers. However,
the global spread of television may be inflected and configured in
different ways under different local circumstances. The production
of the global and the local are the same process. Globalization is not
to be seen as a one-way flow of influence from the west to the rest of
the world, rather, globalization is a multi-directional and multi-
dimensional set of processes.

- Television increases the sources and resources of identity production
which can lead to a range of hybrid forms of identity, though the
defensive production of 'fundamentalist' identities is an equally
significant outcome. The nation is not necessarily the most suitable
level to understand the cultural impact of television, rather, we need
to consider the various levels of cultural identification, action and
influence. Post-traditional identity formation involves the production of multiple identities or identifications many of which have little
bearing on questions of national identity.

- To suggest that the multiple and hybrid identities that global television can promote are to be welcomed, that a decline in national
sentiment, if such is the outcome, is not necessarily a loss, does not
mean that all is well with global television. Issues of representation
and misrepresentation do matter, representations of Islam within

global news or of gender relations in soap opera are of ideological
significance, albeit in a less coherent fashion than had been assumed
by some critics. It is always a question of ideological competition
rather than the imposition of a monolithic ideology.

Finally, according to McQuail (1992), the globalization of television, driven by the logic of capitalism, has placed three key
questions on the agenda:

- The growth and/or protection of the television industry within and
  across national borders (see chapter 2).
- The autonomy of national language and culture in the face of fears
  regarding transborder broadcasting (see chapter 6).
- The need to regulate the increased commercialization of television
  with particular reference to dependence on advertising and the
  related considerations of programme range and quality (see chapter
  5 and this chapter).

The Politics of Television

The question of what kind of politics to pursue in relation to television is complicated in conditions of high modernity by a loss of
faith in the idea that 'reason' could offer a sense of certitude and
progress. Reason can at the very least be argued to have turned out
to be selective and unbalanced. The condition of modernity had been
associated with an emancipatory project through which 'enlightenment reason' would lead to certain and universal truths so laying the
foundations for humanity's forward path of progress. However,
thinkers as diverse as Adorno, Nietzsche, Foucault, Lyotard and
Baudrillard have criticized the impulses of modernity for heralding
not progress but domination and oppression (see Bauman, 1991). In
these accounts, the modern world is seen as demanding a rational
explanation of everything constituting what Heidegger described as
a 'will to planetary order'. Indeed, 'enlightenment reason' is
regarded as a totalizing force which seeks to subsume all difference
beneath it, so that 'reason' leads not to alleviation of material needs
or philosophical enlightenment but to control and destruction. From
this stance modernity consists of a set of disciplinary institutions,
practices and discourses. Foucault (1972; 1977; 1980) has been the
most prominent theorist of the disciplinary nature of modern institutions. Specifically the 'regimes of truth' of modernity involve

relations of power/knowledge whereby knowledge is a form of power implicated in the production of subjectivity. Foucault concentrates on three disciplinary discourses: the 'sciences', which constitute the subject as an object of inquiry; technologies of the self whereby individuals turn themselves into subjects; and 'dividing practices' which separate the mad from the insane, the criminal from the law-abiding citizen and friends from enemies.

Recognition of the disciplinary nature of modernity has contributed to a loss of faith in the foundational schemes that have justified the rational, scientific, technological and political projects of the modern world. This is what Lyotard (1984) describes as 'incredulity toward metanarratives'. Lyotard argues that there remain no viable meta-narratives (or elevated standpoints) from which to judge the truth of anything, rather we should resist the totalizing terror of such dogmas in favour of the celebration of difference and understandings from within particular knowledge regimes.

I take the position that no universalizing epistemology is possible because all truth claims are formed within discourse, there being no access to an independent object world free from language, and there is no 'God like' discursive vantage point from which to neutrally evaluate claims. There are no universal philosophical foundations for human thought and action and all truth is culture bound or 'ethnocentric' (Rorty, 1991). Indeed, Rorty suggests that truth has no explanatory power, he recommends that we abandon epistemology and recognize that truth is a form of commendation, at best a degree of social agreement from within a particular tradition.

A sophisticated defence of a postmodern epistemology, its status and the consequences, is put by Gergen (1994) to whom I refer readers who wish to pursue this line of thinking. For now, I want to make two points which I draw from Gergen. First, no epistemological position is able to give universal grounding for its own truth claims and that includes both modern science and postmodernism. Second, the *consequences* of adopting a modern or postmodern epistemology are different. Modern truth claims are universalizing, they assert their truths for all people in all places with potentially disastrous disciplining consequences in which the bearers of 'truth' know what is best for all of us. In contrast, both Gergen's postmodern relativism and Rorty's pragmatism argue that truths are only truths within the language games in which such truths are founded, the consequences of which are to accept the legitimacy of a range of truth claims, discourses and representations of 'reality' which compete for ascendency.

To accept the legitimacy of a range of truth claims is in itself a political position and not an abandonment of politics as critics of so-called relativism imply, indeed, it signals support for pragmatic postmodern cultural pluralism. Further, not only can we not avoid the implications of political inaction but within the terms of our own traditions and cultures we can and do act to improve the human condition as we understand it. The latter half of this sentence clearly indicates the limitations of the project but it does not invalidate it for, as Rorty (1992) argues, we do not require universal validations and foundations to pursue a pragmatic improvement of the human condition on the basis of the values of our own tradition. In doing so we will require a kind of 'utopian realism' (Giddens, 1990). 'Utopian' because it is in the nature of the modern *and* postmodern human mind to contemplate questions of love, death, life and happiness, and to project possible improved futures. 'Realism' because moral convictions pursued without reference to the sociologically grounded and politically possible may not only yield no positive results but may also in fact be counter-productive.

Does 'Global Television' Mean 'Bad' Television?

Critics of commercial global television have argued that a decline in range and quality is the inevitable result of the eclipsing of public service television, others have condemned television's postmodern populist turn. Though the double-coding of *Twin Peaks* encouraged critical acclaim, both *Miami Vice* and MTV (discussed in chapter 5) have been derided as popular 'trash', thus postmodernism, in collapsing the boundaries of high and low culture, opens itself up to the accusation of being 'bad' television.

Critics' judgements about 'good' and 'bad' televison derive from textual analysis, rooted in literary criticism, a paradigm concerned with questions of aesthetic evaluation and the policing of the boundaries of a canon of 'good works'. This has been to the detriment of popular culture which was largely excluded from the canon. With the passing of time, and the increased interest in popular culture, a new set of theorists began to argue that there was no legitimate reason for drawing the line between the worthy and unworthy so that evaluation was not a sustainable task for the critic, rather, the task was to describe and analyse the production of meaning. This had the great merit of opening up a whole new array of texts for legitimate discussion, for example the soap opera, but was also in danger of undermining any kind of evaluation and political project (Brunsdon, 1990).

Paradoxically, the 'new' audience studies have also undermined the legitimacy of making judgements of quality about programmes since it has become commonplace to argue that audiences are much more active, creative and skilled than they had hitherto been given credit for; meaning thus resides with people rather than within texts (chapter 4). Indeed, the concept of a 'text' in television has been challenged on the grounds that the experience of 'watching television' has more to do with segmentation, 'flow' and intertextuality than discrete programmes. At its most extreme we are invited to abandon notions of 'text' and 'audience' altogether in favour of 'moments in television' (Fiske, 1989). This represents a reversal of the traditional question of how the culture industry makes people into commodities that serve its interests in favour of exploring how people turn the products of industry into their popular culture to serve their interests. While moves to understand the processes of watching television in more detail are to be welcomed, 'watching television' is indeed an active and creative process which is not confined to discrete programmes or the actual experience of sitting in front of the set (we make programmes the subject of conversation); it is not necessarily productive to abandon textual analysis solely in favour of audience studies since refusal of any notion of text makes it impossible to discuss notions of programme quality or to differentiate between programme values. As Brunsdon argues, 'what are we going to do about bad television? Nothing if we're not prepared to admit it exists' (Brunsdon, 1990, pp. 69–70)

If we are unable to evaluate texts then, instead of constructing a critical political project, we are left embracing commercial television as the best that is possible precisely because it is popular. However, audiences can only be active creators of meaning in relation to what is on the screen, the production choices are not those of the audience but of people working in television organizations. Some television organizations or systems are more likely to offer a diversity of meanings than others, and an abandonment of 'textual' critique would leave us unable to ask about alternative kinds of systems and programmes.

It is one thing to say that in theory audiences can construct a limitless range of meanings from television but it is another to demonstrate that they actually do so (Morley, 1992). The meanings audiences construct will be bounded both by the text and the audience's own discursive competencies, which will differ according to the multiple identities of that audience. These competencies and identities will have been shaped in and through the operation of power and will be, consequently, unequal. People are not able to construct *any* set of meanings they like out of television, only those which the matrix of text and context enables. Meaning construction is thus bounded and the politics of representation do matter. If television offers racist representations of the world, and this view is supported by similar discourses circulating in society, then it is probable that at least a section of the audience will be supported in racist thinking. Under these circumstances we would want to promote alternative images and discourses on the grounds of solidarity and diversity.

Quality Television?

The problem with asking questions about quality is that they are impossible to answer with any sort of precision. Quality is a relative term which refers to a set of characteristics which satisfy certain standards derived from more or less central (though contested) values and norms (Rosengren et al., 1991). The notion of quality may then be applied at different levels within television whether that be in relation to the overall 'system', a particular organization or a specific programme. Different normatively derived understandings of quality may be utilized by a variety of interested parties including television professionals, academic and popular critics, government agencies, advertisers and of course 'the audience'.

Blumler, Nossiter and Brynin (1986) attempted to address the question by canvassing the views of professional broadcasters who suggested that there were a number of features which they deemed to be expressive of quality. These included non-triviality, anti-simplicity, authenticity and integrity, in essence doing justice to the subject matter by drawing out all the angles and giving the audience something to think about. The subject matter, needing to be of social relevance, should be approached in a way which brings a fresh view and an expressive richness.

However, while the judgements of professionals must have a bearing on issues of quality, they cannot necessarily be taken as a reliable guide to audience perceptions of quality. The above characteristics of quality may be laudable and defensible notions, but they are not the same as those employed when one simply wants to flop in front of the TV and, perfectly legitimately, play 'couch potato'. Nor are professionals' views of quality necessarily the same as those brought to bear by the audiences for the highest rated programmes such as the soap opera. Yet popularity, while it must form part of the criteria for evaluation, must also be suspect as a *sole* measure of quality. Programmes watched by large numbers of people tend to reflect the middle ground and submerge the different and distinctive, which may also be regarded as attributes of quality.

As Brunsdon (1990) argues, there are always issues of power at stake in notions of quality and judgement – Quality for whom? Judgement by whom? Judgements of quality derive from an institutionalized and often class-based hierarchy of cultural taste located in western culture. Such a hierarchy, formed within particular social and historical contexts, is employed by its apologists as representative of a universal set of aesthetic criteria, though these criteria are less well established in the world of television, being both a relatively new and popular medium, than they are in the world of literature, art or even film. Brunsdon argues that in the battle to define television quality there are several central domains to which legitimate appeal is made. These include traditional aesthetic arguments, professional codes and practices, notions of adequacy and objectivity, entertainment codes, and moral paradigms, all of which have coherent arguments, but none of which has been able to lay claim to the sole prerogative. Judgements about quality are always going to be both historically and culturally specific and open to contestation, though that does not mean that we cannot construct ideas which are coherent and just for our own time and place. For Brunsdon, such ideas about quality are going to be forged in the process of public debate and, if they are to have longevity, be embedded in institutional practice.

Is Soap Quality?

In chapter 3 I discussed soap opera as an international television form and for some critics it is the proliferation and global circulation of soaps that have led them to denounce global television as 'trash' television. Can soap opera be regarded as quality television?

As Allen (1985, p. 11) notes, 'Until recently the aesthetic discourse on soap operas has been marked by near unanimous disdain of the form'. The soap was not only not quality, it was the trash that quality was defined against. Allen goes on to argue that this was an outcome of the nature of the mainstream aesthetic discourse and the manner in which the soap departed from its central principles. Thus, the work of art was deemed to be a definable object whose parameters the critic was empowered to specify. However, the soap is an open narrative form with little sense of closure or dramatic unity so that many of the central concepts of the traditional aesthetic discourse – balance, theme, tension, unity, integration – are problematic when applied to a form without an end. The authorial anonymity of the soap (it is a collaborative effort) makes the traditional examination of the work of art in terms of the artist's expressive vision and skill difficult to sustain. Allied to the romantic idea of the 'artistic object', produced by the 'artistic soul', is a sense of the complexity and authenticity of the meanings embedded in the work of art and the necessary skill and work required by the readers to access a genuine aesthetic experience. From within this paradigm the soap opera, as an expression of mass culture, is seen as superficial and unsatisfying.

The problem with associating the aesthetic with artistic quality is that concepts of beauty, harmony, form and quality might be applied as much to a steam train, not usually seen as art, as to an artistic artefact or performance. Further, concepts of beauty, form and quality are culturally relative, beauty in western thought may not be the same as that to be found in other cultures. In this sense a work of art is a socially-created category which has attached itself to certain external and internal signals by which art is recognized, hence the 'art gallery' and the theatre. In this sense art, as aesthetic quality, is that which has been so labelled by western cultural and class elites, and to see art as 'a uniquely different kind of work, with a unique, indeed transcendent, product is a mistaken notion, wrongly generalised and taken to be essential to the value of art' (Wolff, 1980, p. 17). Thus, television in general, and the soap opera in particular, have been bypassed for social as much as 'creative' reasons.

Art is not the outcome of a mystical artistic practice which springs out of thin air into the minds of geniuses, rather, it is a product of work: a human transformation of the material environment through labour. Further, art, like the soap opera, is a collective enterprise rather than the outcome of lone individuals: most forms of artistic practice are social and collaborative ones. Thus, producing a play involves writers, actors, producers, technicians and printers, and even the apparently isolated novelist relies on the collective acts of editors, publicists and readers. Further, all forms of cultural production utilize language, a social form *par excellence*. Art is an industry with its owners, managers and workers operating according to the law of profit every much as is popular culture and popular television. Thus, there are little justifiable grounds for excluding the soap opera from the artistic domain on the grounds that art, that is aesthetic quality, is a different kind of activity. The fact that, even within television, quality is associated with literary source, prestigious actors, money and high production values only points to the social convention surrounding quality rather than any intrinsic 'superiority' of form or content. These arguments undercut a high cultural concern about the global circulation of soaps.

It remains possible to argue that the quality work is that which is formally subtle, complex and the most adequate in its formal expression of content. However, this remains a stance riddled with problems including a form–content division which is hard to sustain since they are two sides of the same phenomenon, indistinguishable aspects of the same object. Alternatively, one might want to argue that the quality work is that which is most adequate and expressive in relation to its referent. This is to employ a realist epistemology (not the same as realist conventions) and to say that drama, for example, does refer to the real world and is able, for better or worse, to illuminate our understanding of that world. Here, within the terms of an evaluative and formal aesthetic, soap opera could still be regarded as quality television since soap opera is a complex and open-ended form with the potential to handle ethical and social issues, and to engage its audience both intellectually and pleasurably.

However, many writers, including myself, would have great difficulty in supporting the realist epistemology which underpins the argument, since television is not a transparent representation of the world but a specific construction of it. Nor am I seeking to defend a set of formal aesthetic judgements since aesthetic criteria alone cannot stand up to scrutiny, they inevitably fall to the forces of relativism, for who is to say a mass audience is 'wrong' in an aesthetic sense. More sustainable are arguments which revolve around the pragmatic social and political consequences of constructing and disseminating specific discursive constructions of the world. This would include evaluative criteria based on *diversity as a political value* and *ideological analysis* as a method so that the role of criticism becomes the development of a more profound understanding of our cultural and symbolic processes and the way in which they are connected to social, political and economic power. Criticism becomes centred on questions of discourse, social relationships, and *power* and its consequences. Interestingly, the idea that we should look at the pragmatic consequences of specific discourses is shared by a Marxist–modernist like Eagleton (1984), a postmodernist relativist like Gergen (1994) and a postmodern pragmatist like Rorty (1992).

From this perspective, it makes little sense to discuss whether television is 'good' or 'bad' in an abstract aesthetic manner, rather, we need to consider, from a political and inevitably value-laden position, the ideological construction and potential consequences of television. As an illustration we may consider the case of 'the family', the heartland image of television. Cantor (1991) argues that the domestic drama on American television is primarily a morality play about how we should live; in particular, about how to bring up children and the appropriate love relationships between a range of types of people. What gets on air, she argues, are mainstream ideals and while there have been changes in the representation of families and an increase in the range of types of families, the ideal remains the married couple/nuclear family. While black families and working-class families have been represented with increased frequency it remains the case, she argues, that the white middle-class family is the norm. There were virtually no situation comedies featuring single women in America until the emergence of the *Mary Tyler Moore Show* in the 1970s.

While recognizing the kind of consensual picture that Cantor paints, Taylor (1991) argues that the networks search for more specialized audiences, particularly amongst the younger educated urban consumers, facilitated a break with a consensual tone and opened up a more varied set of representations. In particular, she notes the breakdown of strict genre boundaries and a fluid intertextuality across which the family remains a continuous discourse. Despite this increase in the range of kinds of families seen on television, in the *Cosby Show*, perhaps the most popular television programme in the USA at this time, an authoritarian, stable, nuclear family remains the centre-piece of a comedy of manners and family etiquette. As Cantor and Cantor (1992) remark, even with the development of off-beat families in American sitcoms, problems are always resolved in terms of the family values of caring, togetherness, love and peace.

The consequences of television's discourse of the family may be to demonize the majority of us who do not live in nuclear families; to support the main institution of the patriarchal oppression of women; to suggest that we seek solutions to *social* problems within the family, for example through 'family therapy' or by placing the responsibility for 'crime' or 'social care' on the family; and to bolster an institution which arguably makes us unhappy or 'insane' (Laing, 1960).

My discussion of 'good' and 'bad' television is caught in something of a dilemma. On the one hand, there is a desire to legitimize popular and non-western culture as valuable in the face of a traditional western high cultural aesthetic discourse, which derives from an elite class and cultural position. On the other hand, I am loath to sanction a position in which we are disbarred from making judgements, because it would mean that whatever was beamed by satellite over the world would be acceptable. We would be unable to argue for one programme over another leaving Rupert Murdoch to make those judgements for us. Hence my argument that discourses of *power* remain the target for criticism. Further, such criticism does not require universal epistemological justification since it is made from within a tradition of cultural pluralism, which values equality and democracy, and is based on pragmatic comparison with other forms of social organization and not on notions of universal reason.

Since quality, both aesthetic and political, is contestable we should seek from television a wide variety of forms of quality, and these forms of quality should be debated in the public sphere. Though it does not answer all the relevant questions about quality, *diversity* is as near a measure of quality as we are going to get in these post-modern times. Diversity needs to be understood in two senses. First, in terms of *diversity of representations*, an issue connected with questions of textual construction. Second, in terms of *diversity of programme types*, an issue connected to questions of the organization of television systems. Diversity as a concept links postmodern ideas about knowledge to the modern conception of the public sphere, so that, paradoxically, the future of the public sphere could and should lie with the acceptance of postmodern cultural diversity; postmodern diversity needs to be supported within a plural public sphere.

Television and the Public Sphere

Pursuing the tradition of critical theory, and arguing that the emanicipatory project of modernity is not yet complete, Habermas (1972; 1984; 1987; 1989) has sought grounds for the validation of evaluative judgement and for claims to human emancipation. He does so by arguing that all human interaction presupposes language and that in the structure of speech we may find the essential grounding conditions for all forms of social organization. When we speak, argues Habermas, we are making four validity claims: comprehensibility, truth, appropriateness and sincerity which, he claims, imply the logical justification of truth and the social context for their rational debate. Habermas postulates the existence of an 'ideal speech situation' in which competing truth claims are subject to rational debate and argument. In an 'ideal speech situation' truth is not subject to the vested interests and power play of truth seekers but emerges through the process of argumentation. This is in contrast to the usual speech situation in which rationality is a tool of power and interest, speech being from a position of vested interest.

The critical point is that, for Habermas, our very ability to make truth claims is dependent on a democratically-organized public sphere where such a sphere approximates, as far as is pragmatically possible, an 'ideal speech situation'. The notion of a public sphere is traced historically by Habermas to a realm which emerged in a specific phase of 'bourgeois society'. It is a space which mediates between society and the state in which the public organizes itself and in which 'public opinion' is formed. Habermas describes the rise of literary clubs and salons, newspapers, political journals, and institutions of political debate and participation in the eighteenth century. This public sphere was partially protected from both the church and the state by the resources of private individuals and was in principle, though not in practice, open to all. Within this sphere individuals were able to develop themselves and engage in rational debate about the direction of society. Habermas goes on to document the decline of the public sphere in the face of the development of capitalism towards monopoly and the strengthening of the state. The increased commodification of life by giant corporations, that is to say the way in which more and more aspects of life are turned into things to be bought and sold according to the logic of the market, helps to transform people from rational citizens to consumers of, amongst other things, the non-rational products of the advertising and public relations industries. In a parallel erosion of the public sphere, the state has taken increased power in both the economic realm, as corporate manager, and the private realm, in terms of the management of welfare provision and education.

The concept of the public sphere in the work of Habermas is both a philosophical, historical and normative one. On the historical level there has been considerable criticism of the historical accuracy of the concept (Curran, 1991) and of the male gender bias of the bourgeois public sphere. More philosophically, some postmodern critics of Habermas have argued that he reproduces a totalizing discourse which reproduces 'enlightenment reason' ignoring its repressive character. Instead, Lyotard and other postmodernists have stressed the importance of articulating and preserving differences to avoid potential repression and manipulation. Honneth (1986) has countered that Lyotard has a mistaken interpretation of Habermas's discursive ethics whose purpose lies not in the final determination of common needs, but in intersubjective agreement about the very social norms which allow different needs to be articulated and realized. By this he means that Habermas is stressing the importance of the democratic process rather than the outcome of that process. Further, even Foucault, commonly seen as a critic of Habermas, rejects the idea of 'playing the arbitrary and boring part of either the irrationalist or the rationalist' and suggests that we have to 'accept this spiral, this sort of revolving door of rationality that refers us to its necessity, to its indispensability, and at the same time to its intrinsic dangers' (Foucault, 1982).

Thus, while recognizing that a public sphere based on accessibility, equality and the consensual search for general norms is, at least in part, a fiction, Habermas has articulated a set of principles which stress the importance of a democratic sphere separate from both economic power and the institutions of the state. Whatever the historical problems with Habermas's work, as a *normative* position the idea of a public sphere retains an appeal. Further, though I think Habermas is mistaken in his attempt to construct a universal and transcendental rational justification for the public sphere, the concept retains immediate and historical political leverage since it can be justified on the pragmatic grounds of cultural pluralism rather than on epistemological grounds. We can argue that the 'public sphere' should in itself be able to accommodate difference as a vital principal. Paradoxically, the emancipatory project of modernity and the public sphere is best served by a commitment to 'postmodern' diversity, tolerance and solidarity. Thus, according to Bauman:

> Postmodernity is no more (but no less either) than the modern mind taking a long, attentive and sober look at itself, at its condition and its past works, not fully liking what it sees and sensing the urge to change. Postmodernity is modernity coming of age; modernity looking at itself at a distance rather than from inside, making a full inventory of its gains and losses. (Bauman, 1991, p. 272)

Within this self-reflexivity, the modern values of liberty, equality and fraternity have, Bauman argues, been reassessed in the light of their contradictions to be replaced by liberty, diversity and tolerance in the postmodern mentality. The uncertainty of the postmodern condition, its ambivalence and ambiguity, open up the possibility of the grasping of contingency as destiny, of our ability to create and re-create our futures. However, to do so we must transform tolerance into solidarity:

> not just as a matter of moral perfection, but a condition of survival . . . Survival in the world of contingency and diversity is possible only if each difference recognises another difference as the necessary condition of the preservation of its own. Solidarity, unlike tolerance, its weaker version, means a readiness to fight; and joining the battle for the sake of the other's difference, not one's own. Tolerance is ego-centred and contemplative; solidarity is socially oriented and militant. (Bauman, 1991, p. 256)

There are no guarantees, no universal foundations, for such a project and it remains only a possibility inherent in postmodern culture, for as Bauman argues, liberty remains truncated, diversity thrives only so far as the market drives it, tolerance slips into indifference and consumers replace citizens. Yet, postmodern culture can also imply the need for politics, democracy, full-blown citizenship and the potential withdrawal of consent from the political edifice of the state. Such a postmodern mentality demands that modernity fulfil the promises of its, albeit distorted, reason.

Some recognition of the plural nature of society, the autonomy of various groups and the dangers of totalizing reason argued by post-modernists, combined with the modern sense of emancipatory politics found in Habermas can be discovered in the work of Laclau and Mouffe (1985). They stress the importance of the articulation of cultural and political identities from diverse elements. Most notably this involves forms of radical democracy.

> A society where everyone, whatever his/her sex, race, economic position, sexual orientation, will be in an effective situation of equality and participation, where no basis of discrimination will remain and where self-management will exist in all fields – that is what the ideal of socialism for us should mean today. (Mouffe, cited in Best and Kellner, 1991 p. 196)

Laclau and Mouffe are more critical than Habermas of 'enlighten-ment reason' and argue that all progressive values must be defended within a pragmatic context of particular moral traditions without appeal to any absolute standards of legitimation. Space for the articulation of what is just or unjust within a particular tradition is precisely the realm of the public sphere.

These abstract principles can be made more concrete and relevant to the media through the values of *diversity, independence, access, solidarity,* and *objectivity.* This represents a selective adaptation of the modernist ideas of McQuail (1992) which derive from a similar tradition of progressive modern European thought as Habermas, though by stressing *diversity* I have given them a more postmodern flavour. The concept of *diversity* suggests that pluralistic media are expected to represent the full range of public opinion, cultural practices and social and geographical conditions. Diversity, thus, relates to the range of persons and groups, as well as opinion, topics, information, etc. Diversity may also refer to the range of formats available and thus to differences of media purpose, that is entertainment, information and education.

There is a strong western democratic tradition of supporting the principle of media *independence* on the grounds that it will foster the expression of divergent points of view and sustain public debate.

Independence may be taken as meaning independence *from* undue influence (of owners, the state, advertisers , pressure groups, etc.) and independence *for* television to adopt an advocacy role, take a critical stance in relation to established power and be creative and original.

The principle of *access* requires that all citizens are able to have access to the television programmes that are on offer. A citizen is not able to participate in the society if they are denied knowledge, information or cultural practice, which is available to others. Access is thus related to the notion of diversity, democracy and the public sphere.

Solidarity suggests forms of sharing and co-operation which are genuine and not enforced, that is, it implies supportive tolerance rather than control. The issue is the degree to which television does, and/or should, promote a sense of shared values in a given community and, perhaps more importantly, given the fragmented nature of the social and global worlds, present diverse values in order to increase levels of tolerance, empathy and solidarity by acting as cultural and social interpreter. Nevertheless, a number of the ideas which flow from this are in potential contradiction. Is it possible, for example, to promote both national identity and international solidarity? Can television act justly in relation to a range of social identities if it preserves a notion of national identity? Exactly who is being educated, by whom and into what values and spheres of knowledge? There are of course no simple answers to these questions.

Finally, though it is a philosophic fiction, the principle of *objectivity* is commonly sought after on pragmatic grounds in relation to liberty (we are not free if misrepresented), equality (we cannot be equal with others if we are perceived inaccurately and treated accordingly) and solidarity (which needs to be forged on the basis of as accurate a view of 'others' as possible). McQuail argues that objectivity can be seen to have two dimensions: that of factuality, the cognitive zone of information quality, and impartiality, the field of the evaluative. However, any concept of objectivity will be culture bound depending on definition, empirical research, and the outcome of debate and conflict. It is, therefore, not so much a question of absolute objectivity but of the intersubjective grounds on which a partial and pragmatic 'objectivity' can warrant limited truth claims.

A legacy of the Habermasian version of the public sphere is a stress on cognitive and rational elements to the detriment of questions of popular pleasure. What Corner (1991) calls the 'public information project' has overshadowed the 'popular culture project' thereby overlooking the way that, while the media may have actually enlarged the public sphere (Giddens, 1991; Scannell, 1989) they have also altered its nature (Dahlgren, 1995). The public sphere is now arguably a media saturated one in which:

- Mediated relationships are more conspicuous than face-to-face encounters.
- The visual has gained in prominence over the verbal.
- Entertainment is as significant as news.
- Advertising and commercial interests are ensconced in the public domain.
- The boundaries between the public and the private are blurred.
- The public sphere enters the domestic sphere via the television set.

However, the values of *diversity, independence, access, solidarity* and *objectivity* are equally applicable to questions of popular taste and culture. In the cultural domain the role of television could then be argued to include: pluralistic education, the promotion of both popular culture and high arts, the reflection and constituting of identities, and the provision of a range of 'quality' services. Further, as Dahlgren (1995) argues, if we talk of 'popular knowledge' and 'public culture' the differences between 'knowledge' and 'culture' are broken down. Popular pleasure is as valid as public rationality. Dahlgren also argues that the attainment and maintenance of a democratic public sphere on the level of the state and formal politics is dependent on a democratic civil society. Popular culture contributes to a diverse, tolerant democratic society as much as formal politics. Soap opera is a model of 'how to live' and is talked about in civil society as much, if not more, than the news.

Driven by the commodity logic of capitalism, and prominent in the dissemination of consumer culture, global television can be argued to be increasingly in contradiction with the principles of democracy and the public sphere. Thus, the circumvention of the nation-state by transnational corporations erodes the potential for democratic control while, for Blumler (1992) the special conditions of television markets mean that commercial television is unable to deliver the public service ideal. Having said that, throughout much of this book it has been argued that global television is not uniform in either its content or its consequences. Thus, television is capable of being an institution of modern social discipline and promoting diversity and tolerance in the public sphere.

Cultural Identities and Citizenship

Chapters 4 and 6 concentrated on questions of reception and identity formation. The general direction of the argument and evidence was to downplay assumptions about the monolithic and homogenizing impact of global television. Rather, global television has been seen to contribute to an increase in symbolic resources for identity formation and thus post-traditional, multiple identities. However, this is not the end of the story for it raises questions about the relationship between identities and citizenship, for if diversity is the key value of my modern–postmodern hybrid form of politics there remains the danger of social fragmentation. As Morley and Robbins comment:

> What is problematical . . . is to combine community as mutuality with community as democratic state; to reconcile the ideal of a 'community of culture' with that of 'political community'. As a consequence, what appears to be happening is that questions of citizenship and questions of identity are becoming dissociated. (Morley and Robbins, 1995, p. 184)

This development raises the issue of how individuals and collectives can cope politically with the proliferation of cultural identities within and without the nation-state. On a philosophical level it is possible to argue, as some postmodernists do, that different life-worlds are simply incommensurable on an epistemological basis: there is no point of mutuality. However this argument is based on a particular interpretation of Wittgenstein's theory of language games which sees different life-worlds and languages as based on in-commensurable rules. But, as Rorty (1992) argues, rules in Wittgenstein's sense are not formal rules to be learnt, they are not knowledge with an epistemological base, but constitutive practices. The question then is not whether rules and language games are incompatible epistemologically but whether in practice people can live together.

Rorty (1992) has argued, correctly in my view, that despite the inability in principal to find a universal foundational epistemology to share, we can nevertheless take pragmatic steps to talk to each other. For example, languages can be said to have no common foundation, there is no exact and direct correspondence between languages. Nevertheless, we can learn other languages and take practical steps to communicate with each other. This is meant both literally and metaphorically, that is to say we can learn to find some pragmatic ways of communicating with each other and building alliances on the basis of perceived mutuality in certain areas. Paradoxically, multiple identity positions can make this easier rather than more difficult if we accept that we do not have to agree on everything but can speak to each other from one identity position though not from another. Rorty suggests that should we find that our life-worlds are incommensurable then we may, or perhaps must, act within the terms of our own traditions, but in doing so remember that it is no more valid than others. This does not preclude the possibility that our values are so far apart, and we find the consequences of the other's actions so objectionable, that we come into conflict. It does however suggest the need for dialogue and underpins the procedural arguments for a diverse and plural public sphere for citizens.

As Giddens argues:

> In the domain of personal life, opening out to the other is the condition of social solidarity; on the larger scale a proffering of the 'hand of friendship' within a global cosmopolitan order is ethically implicit in the new agenda. (Giddens, 1994, p. 107)

Paradoxically, in the post-traditional order of fragmentation, competing claims of truth and 'postmodern' diversity, a commitment to the values of dialogue, tolerance and solidarity is required. That is, the establishment of the intersubjective conditions for particularistic diversity to flourish.

Drawing from a discussion of these issues by Dahlgren (1995) we can see citizenship as a form of identity, one aspect of our multiple identities. While we should avoid a full-blown universalistic notion of citizenship, which subsumes difference beneath a homogeneous treatment of citizens, we can envisage a minimalist position by which the 'identity of citizenship' holds together the diversity of values and life-worlds within a democratic framework. The identity of citizenship may be the only thing we have in common, but a commitment by diverse groups to the procedures of democracy and to the mutual and intersubjectively recognized rights and duties of citizenship in the social, civil and political domains advances democracy and brings together particularistic identity projects. This involves what Mouffe (1992) calls the 'hegemony of democratic values'. Democratic citizenship thus involves alliance building between groups which share a democratic perspective. It does not require us to accept all current versions of what democracy means, rather, the activities of those committed to the project of radical democracy would seek to extend its reach from formal governmental procedures to include economic, organizational and domestic democracy.

Citizenship and democracy are socially constructed phenomena and have to be continually built, renewed and extended. Television can play a significant role in this. Dahlgren argues that television could contribute to the establishment of 'common' and 'advocacy' domains. The common domain stresses those elements which citizens might share while the advocacy domain gives voice to particular identity projects. This conception is not, as Dahlgren readily admits, without its problems. For example, at what spatial levels (global, national, regional, neighbourhood) can or should the common domain operate? Who will decide what is common? Who should have access to the advocacy domain and how should this operate? It is, nevertheless, suggestive of a way forward, though it also points to the limitations of television in this project, namely, that it is organized by transglobal commercial interests and increasingly addresses us as individual consumers rather than as social citizens.

The nation-state, which has been the traditional modern container for political dialogue and practice, is now changing under conditions of accelerated globalization. As Held (1989) has argued, transnational economic and political activity have undermined the state as a self-contained arena of decision making and power so that we may need to think in terms of new transnational modes of political activity. Further, there are grounds for agreeing with Schiller (1985) that the activities of transnational corporations which circumvent the state undermine the possibility of liberal democracy. Others have worried about the fragmentation of television audiences and the influence of cross-border television in breaking up national identity. Thus, Rajagopal (1993) has argued that since television played a vital role in creating a sense of national unity in

India, and thus containing conflicts of religious and ethnic difference, the new fragmented television order may undermine this
unity with undesirable sectarian consequences. In this context,
Collins's discussion of transborder television in Canada is illuminating. He argues that Canada has long been subject to cross-border
television from the USA and that such television is popular, more
popular than most Canadian-produced programmes. However,
this has not prevented national identification nor has it destroyed
the Canadian state as a set of political institutions. He concludes
that democratic political institutions can survive without the
sharing of national symbolic culture. While some Canadians
continue to hold nationalist beliefs and longing for a national home-
land, this coexists with a desire to maintain and forge 'a stable and
decent democratic society that imperfectly satisfies such longings'
(Collins, 1990, p. 343).

This argument is not without problems, as the recent narrowly-
defeated attempt by Quebec to secede from Canada illustrates and
there are no guarantees and no one outcome of globalization
and global television. However, the Canadian experience does
suggest that states can live with transnational television, a decline in
national sentiment and a proliferation of identities. Nor do other
states which contain a range of ethnic groups, and a multiplicity of
television outlets, show signs of disappearing. The US and British
states, while subject to modification in the era of accelerated globalization, are not withering away. Despite mutation, the state is
showing no signs of disappearing. Thus, in the foreseeable future the
state remains an arena of significant political activity and the focus
of democracy, though the processes of globalization also demand
that we extend democratic activity across states and begin to forge
transglobal democratic institutions and activities. Television can
contribute to the process of dialogue within and across diverse states
by developing a plural public sphere and allowing us to hear a multiplicity of voices, though it must be stressed again that the response
to a diverse and multi-vocal society is not necessarily one of openness and dialogue, it may also be one of defensive, inward-looking
and hostile identity politics. For example, will any developing
European identity embrace a range of ethnic identifications or will
it be an enclosed and excluding white western European identity?
As Morley and Robbins (1995) ask, will Muslim Turks be welcome
in the European community?

Conclusions

The arguments of this chapter have been premised on the idea that description of global television is inseparable from evaluation. However, rather than critique global television on the grounds of aesthetic quality I suggested that the criticism of television is more readily to be made in terms of power and the pragmatic consequences of discourse. Based on acceptance of a postmodern cultural pluralism I suggested that the level of diversity of representation was a plausible criterion for judgement.

This formed the grounds for an argument in favour of a plural public sphere based on the key value of *diversity*. I contrasted the vision of a plural and diverse 'public sphere' with the disciplinary power of modern institutions and the commodity orientation of capitalism. My arguments fused aspects of modern and postmodern thinking. Given that cultural diversity has an inherent pull towards social fragmentation, I also argued in favour of *solidarity* based on the 'hegemony of democratic values'. This suggested the need for a minimal level of procedural agreement together with the acceptance of citizenship as a form of identity.

I argued that television on a global scale has the capacity to contribute to democracy (via the principles of diversity and solidarity) through its range of representations, genres, arguments and information. However, the vision of television as a diverse and plural public sphere is seriously compromised by its almost complete penetration by the interest-based messages and images of consumerism (chapter 5). It was further argued that, while the cultural domination of one nation by another may be of declining importance, the significance of global transnational corporations is on the increase (chapter 2), suggesting a need to support and boost local production in order to sustain and enlarge cultural diversity.

Bibliography

Abercrombie, N., Lash, S. and Longhurst., B. (1992) 'Popular Representation: recasting realism' in S. Lash and J. Friedman (eds) *Modernity and Identity*. Oxford: Blackwell.

Allen, R. (1985) *Speaking of Soap Operas*. Chapel Hill, NC: University of North Carolina.

Allen, R. (ed.) (1992) *Channels of Discourse, Reassembled*. London and New York: Routledge.

Allen, R. (ed.) (1995) *To Be Continued . . . Soap Opera Around the World*. London and New York: Routledge.

Althusser, L. (1971) *Lenin and Philosophy and Other Essays*. London: New Left Books.

Anderson, B. (1983) *Imagined Communities: Reflections on the Origins and Spread of Nationalism*. London: Verso.

Ang, I. (1985) *Watching Dallas: Soap Opera and the Melodramatic Imagination*. London: Metheun.

Ang, I. (1991) *Desperately Seeking the Audience*. London and New York: Routledge.

Barker, C. (1995) 'Those Kinda Things Could Happen: Soap World in the Everyday Life of Teenagers.' Paper presented at the 'Shouts From the Street' conference, Manchester Metropolitan University, September 1995.

Barker, C. (1996a) 'Soaps, Teenage Talk and Hybrid Identities.' Paper presented at 'The Linguistic Construction of Social and Personal Identity' conference, University of Evora, Portugal, 25–29 March 1996.

Barker, C. (1996b, in press) 'Television and the Reflexive Project of the Self: Soaps, Teenage Talk and Hybrid Identities.' *British Journal of Sociology*. A shorter version was presented at the 'Cross-roads in Cultural Studies' Conference, Tampere, Finland, 1–4 July 1996.

Barker, C. (1996c) 'Did You See? Soaps, Teenage Talk and Gendered Identity', *Young: Nordic Journal of Youth Research.*

Barrios, L. (1988) 'Television, Telenovelas, and Family Life in Venezuela' in J. Lull (ed.) *World Families Watch Television.* Newbury Park and London: Sage.

Batty, P. (1993) 'Aboriginal Television in Australia' in T. Dowmunt (ed.) *Channels of Resistance.* London: British Film Institute.

Baudrillard, J. (1983a) *Simulations.* New York: Semiotext(e).

Baudrillard, J. (1983b) *In the Shadow of the Silent Majorities.* New York: Semiotext(e).

Bauman, Z. (1991) *Modernity and Ambivalence.* Cambridge: Polity Press.

Behl, N. (1988) 'Television and Tradition' in J. Lull (ed.) *World Families Watch Television.* Newbury Park and London: Sage.

Bekkers, W. (1987) 'The Dutch PBS in a Multi-channel Landscape', *European Union Review,* vol. 38, no. 6.

Benjamin, W. (1973) *Illuminations.* London: Fontana.

Berman, M. (1983) *All That Is Solid Melts Into Air.* London: Verso.

Best, S. and Kellner, D. (1991) *Postmodern Theory: Critical Interrogations.* Basingstoke and London: Macmillan.

Blumler, J. (1986) *Television in the United States: Funding Sources and Programming Consequences.* Leeds: University of Leeds.

Blumler, J. (ed.) (1992) *Television and the Public Interest.* Newbury Park and London: Sage.

Blumler, J., Nossiter, T. and Brynin, M. (1986) *Research on the Range and Quality of Broadcasting Services.* London: HMSO.

Bourdieu, P. (1984) *Distinction.* London: Routledge & Kegan Paul.

Boyd-Barrett, O. and Thussu, D. (1992) *Contra-Flow in Global News.* London: John Libbey.

Brants, K. and Siune, K. (1992) 'Public Broadcasting in a State of Flux' in K. Siune and W. Truetzschler (eds) *Dynamics of Media Politics: Broadcasting and Electronic Media in Western Europe.* Newbury Park and London: Sage.

Brunsdon, C. (1990) 'Problems with Quality'. *Screen,* vol. 31, no. 1

Bryce, J. (1987) 'Family Time and Television Use' in T. Lindorf (ed.) *Natural Audiences.* Norwood, NJ: Ablex.

Buckingham, D. (1987) *Public Secrets: EastEnders and its Audience.* London: British Film Institute.

Cantor, M. (1991) 'The American Family on Television: From Molly Goldberg to Bill Cosby', *Journal of Comparative Family Studies,* vol. 22, no. 2.

Cantor, M. and Cantor J. (1992) *Prime Time Television: Content and Control.* Newbury Park and London: Sage.

Caughie, J. (1990) 'Playing at being American' in P. Mellencamp (ed.) *Logics of Television: Essays in Cultural Criticism.* London: British Film Institute.

Chaffee, S. (1992) 'Survey Studies of News in a Cross Cultural Context' in F. Korzenny and S. Ting Tooney (eds) *Mass Media Effects Across Cultures.* Newbury Park and London: Sage

Chambers, I. (1986) *Popular Culture: the Metropolitan Experience.* London: Metheun.

Chambers, I. (1987) 'Maps for the Metropolis: a possible guide to the postmodern', *Cultural Studies*, vol. 1, no. 1.

Chambers, I. (1990) *Border Dialogues.* London and New York: Routledge.

Chatterji, P. (1991) *Broadcasting in India.* Newbury Park and London: Sage.

Chomsky, N. and Herman, E. (1979) *The Washington Connection and Third World Fascism.* New York: Spokesman Books.

Clifford, J. (1992) 'Traveling Cultures' in L. Grossberg., C. Nelson. and P. Treichler (eds) *Cultural Studies.* London and New York: Routledge.

Collins, J. (1989) *Uncommon Cultures.* London and New York: Routledge.

Collins, J. (1992) 'Postmodernism and Television' in R. Allen (ed.) *Channels of Discourse, Reassembled.* London and New York: Routledge.

Collins, R. (1990) *Culture, Communication and National Identity.* Toronto: University of Toronto Press.

Connell, I. (1981) 'Television and the Social Contract' in S. Hall et al. *Culture, Media, Language.* London: Hutchinson.

Connor, S. (1989) *Postmodernist Culture.* Oxford: Blackwell.

Corner, J. (1991) 'Mass Media and Democracy: a reappraisal' in J. Curran and M. Gurevitch (eds) *Mass Media and Society.* London: Edward Arnold.

Crofts, S. (1995) 'Global *Neighbours*?' in R. Allen (ed.) *To Be Continued . . . Soap Opera Around the World.* London and New York: Routledge.

Cummings, B. (1992) *War and Television.* London: Verso.

Curran, J. (1991) 'Rethinking the Media and the Public Sphere' in P. Dahlgren and C. Sparks (eds) *Communication and Citizenship.* London and New York: Routledge.

Dahlgren, P. (1985) 'The Modes of Reception: for a hermeneutics of TV News' in P. Drummond and R. Paterson (eds) *Television in Transition.* London: British Film Institute.

Dahlgren, P. (1988) 'What's the Meaning of this? Viewers Plural Sense-Making of TV News', *Media, Culture and Society*, vol. 10.

Dahlgren, P. (1995) *Television and the Public Sphere.* Newbury Park and London: Sage.

Davidson, M. (1992) *The Consumerist Manifesto: Advertising in Postmodern Times.* London and New York: Routledge.

De Certeau, M. (1984) *The Practice of Everyday Life.* Berkeley: University of California Press.

Dorfman, A. and Mattelart, A. (1975) *How to Read Donald Duck: Imperialist Ideology in the Disney Comic.* New York: International General.

Dowmunt, T. (ed.) (1993) *Channels of Resistance.* London: British Film Institute.

Drummond, P. and Patterson, R. (eds) (1985) *Television in Transition*. London: British Film Institute.

Drummond, P., Patterson, R. and Willis, J. (eds) (1990) *National Identity and Europe: the Television Revolution*. London: British Film Institute.

Dyson, K. and Humphreys, J. (eds) (1990) *Political Economy of Communications*. London and New York: Routledge.

Eagleton, T. (1984) *The Function of Criticism*. London: Verso.

Eco, U. (1986) *Travels in Hyper-reality*. London: Picador.

Featherstone, M. (1991) *Consumer Culture and Postmodernism*. Newbury Park and London: Sage.

Ferguson, M. (1990) 'Electronic Media and the Redefining of Time and Space' in M. Ferguson (ed.) (1990) *Public Communication: the New Imperatives*. Newbury Park and London: Sage.

Feuer, J. (1992) 'Genre Study and Television' in R. Allen (ed.) *Channels of Discourse, Reassembled*. London and New York: Routledge.

Fiske, J. (1989) 'Everyday Quizzes, Everyday Life' in J. Tulloch and G. Turner (eds) *Australian Television: Programs, Pleasures and Politics*. London and Sydney: Allen and Unwin.

Foucault, M. (1972) *The Archaeology of Knowledge*. New York: Pantheon.

Foucault, M. (1977) *Discipline and Punishment*. Harmondsworth: Penguin.

Foucault, M. (1979) *The History of Sexuality*, vol. 1. Harmondsworth: Penguin Lane.

Foucault, M. (1980) *Power/Knowledge*. New York: Pantheon.

Foucault, M. (1982) 'Space, Knowledge and Power: an interview with Michel Foucault' in P. Rabinow (ed.) *The Foucault Reader*. New York: Pantheon.

Foucault, M. (1986a) *The Care of the Self: the History of Sexuality*, vol. 3. Harmondsworth: Penguin.

Foucault, M. (1986b) 'On the Genealogy of Ethics: an overview of work in progress' in P. Rabinow (ed.) *The Foucault Reader*. New York: Pantheon.

Frank, A-G. (1967) *Capitalism and Underdevelopment in Latin America*. New York and London: Monthly Review Press.

Frank, A-G. (1992) 'A Third World War' in H. Mowlana, G. Gerbner and H. Schiller (eds) *Triumph of the Image: The Media's War in the Persian Gulf*. Boulder, CO: Westview Press.

Gadamer, H-G. (1976) *Philosophical Hermeneutics*. Berkeley: University of California Press.

Galtung, J. and Ruge, M. (1973) ' Structuring and Selecting News' in S. Cohen and J. Young (eds) *The Manufacture of News*. London: Constable.

Gandy, O. (1990) 'Tracking the Audience' in J. Downing, A. Mohammadi and A. Sreberny-Mohammadi (eds) *Questioning the Media*. Newbury Park and London: Sage.

Gardner, K. and Shukur, A. (1994) 'I'm Bengali, I'm Asian, and I'm Living Here' in R. Ballard et al. *Desh Pardesh: The South Asian Presence in Britain*. London: Hurst & Company.

Garnham, N. (1980) *Structures of Television*. London: British Film Institute.

Garnham, N. (1983) 'Public Service versus the Market', *Screen*, vol. 24, no. 1.

Garnham, N. (1990) *Capitalism and Communication*. Newbury Park and London: Sage.

Geraghty, C. (1981) 'The Continuous Serial: a definition' in R. Dyer et al. *Coronation Street*. London: British Film Institute.

Geraghty, C. (1991) *Women in Soap*. Cambridge: Polity Press.

Gergen, K. (1994) *Realities and Relationships*. Cambridge, MA and London: Harvard University Press.

Giddens, A. (1984) *The Consitution of Society*. Cambridge: Polity Press.

Giddens, A. (1985) *The Nation-State and Violence*. Cambridge: Polity Press.

Giddens, A. (1989) *Sociology*. Cambridge: Polity Press.

Giddens, A. (1990) *The Consequences of Modernity*. Cambridge: Polity Press.

Giddens, A. (1991) *Modernity and Self-Identity*. Cambridge: Polity Press.

Giddens, A. (1992) *The Transformation of Intimacy*. Cambridge: Polity Press.

Giddens, A. (1994) 'Living in a Post-Traditional Society' in U. Beck, A. Giddens and C. Lash *Reflexive Modernisation*. Cambridge: Polity Press.

Gillespie, M. (1989) 'Technology and Tradition', *Cultural Studies*, vol. 3, no. 2.

Gillespie, M. (1992) 'Soap Viewing, Gossip and Rumour Amongst Punjabi Youth in Southhall' in P. Drummond, R. Patterson and J. Willis (eds) *National Identity and Europe: the Television Revolution*. London: British Film Institute.

Gillespie, M. (1995) *Television, Ethnicity and Cultural Change*. London and New York: Routledge.

Gilroy, P. (1987) *There Ain't No Black in the Union Jack*. London: Unwin Hyman.

Gilroy, P. (1993) *The Black Atlantic*. London: Verso.

Glasgow University Media Group (1976) *Bad News*. London: Routledge & Kegan Paul.

Glasgow University Media Group (1980) *More Bad News*. London: Routledge & Kegan Paul.

Glasgow University Media Group (1982) *Really Bad News*. London: Writers & Readers.

Glatzer, P. (1976) 'What is Electronic Imperialism?', *Theory and Practice*, vol. 8.

Goffman, E. (1971) *Relations in Public: Micro Studies of Public order*. London: Allen Lane.

Gottlieb, V. (1993) 'Brookside: Damon's YTS Comes to an End' in G. Brandt (ed.) *British Television Drama in the 1980s*. Cambridge: Cambridge University Press.

Gramsci, A. (1968) *Prison Notebooks*. London: Lawrence & Wishart.

Grossberg, L. (1987) ' The In-difference of Television', *Journal of Communication Inquiry*, vol. 10 no. 2.

Gurevitch, M., Levy, M. and Roeh, I. (1991) 'The Global Newsroom: convergence and diversities in the globalisation of television news' in P. Dahlgren and C. Sparks (eds) *Communication and Citizenship*. London and New York: Routledge.

Gurevitch, M. et al. (1982) *Culture, Society and the Media*. London: Methuen.

Habermas, J. (1972) *Knowledge and Human Interests*. London: Heinemann.

Habermas, J. (1984) *Theory of Communicative Action*. Boston: Beacon Press.

Habermas, J. (1987) *The Philosophical Discourse of Modernity.* Cambridge: Polity Press.

Habermas, J. (1989) *The Structural Transformation of the Public Sphere.* Cambridge, MA: MIT Press.

Hall, S. (1977) 'Culture, the Media and the Ideological Effect' in J. Curran et al. *Mass Communications and Society.* London: Edward Arnold.

Hall, S. et al. (1978) *Policing the Crisis: Mugging, the State and Law and Order.* London: Macmillan.

Hall, S. (1981) 'Encoding/Decoding' in S.Hall. et al. *Culture, Media, Language.* London: Hutchinson.

Hall, S. (1990) 'Cultural Identity and Diaspora' in J. Rutherford (ed.) *Identity: Community, Culture, Difference.* London: Lawrence & Wishart.

Hall, S. (1992) 'The Question of Cultural Identity' in S. Hall., D. Held and T. McGrew (eds) *Modernity and its Futures.* Cambridge: Polity Press.

Hamelink, C. (1983) *Cultural Autonomy in Global Communications.* New York: Longman.

Hartley, J. (1982) *Understanding* News. London: Methuen.

Harvey, D. (1989) *The Condition of Postmodernity.* Oxford: Blackwell.

Hebdige, D. (1988) *Hiding in the Light.* London: Comedia.

Hebdige, D. (1990) 'Fax to the Future', *Marxism Today* (January).

Held, D. (1989) *Political Theory and the Modern State.* Cambridge: Polity Press.

Herold, C. (1988) 'The "Brazilianisation" of Brazilian Television: a critical review', *Studies in Latin American Popular Culture*, vol. 7.

Hobson, D. (1982) *Crossroads: Drama of a Soap Opera.* London: Methuen.

Hodge, B. and Tripp, D. (1986) *Children and Television.* Cambridge: Polity Press.

Honneth, A. (1986) 'An Aversion Against the Universal', *Theory, Culture and Society*, vol. 2, no 3.

Hopkinson, N. (1992) *War and the Media.* London: HMSO.

Hoskins, C., McFadyen, S., Finn, A. and Jackel, A. (1995) 'Film and Television Co-productions: evidence from Canadian–European experience', *European Journal of Communication*, vol. 10, no. 2

Hoskins, C. and Mirus, R. (1988) 'Reasons for the US Dominance of the International Trade in Television Programmes', *Media, Culture and Society*, vol. 10, no. 4.

Housee, S. (1995) 'Identity, Self/Other, Migrancy, and the over there', unpublished paper.

Hulten, O. and Brants, K. (1992) 'Public Service Broadcasting: reactions to competition' in K. Siune and W. Truetzschler (eds) *Dynamics of Media Politics: Broadcasting and Electronic Media in Western Europe.* Newbury Park and London: Sage.

Iser, W. (1978) *The Act of Reading: a Theory of Aesthetic Responses.* London and New York: Routledge & Kegan Paul.

Jameson, F. (1984) 'Postmodernism or the Cultural Logic of Late Capitalism', *New Left Review*, no. 146.

Jencks, C. (1986) *What is Post-Modernism?* London: Academy Editions.

Jensen, K. (1990) 'The Politics of Polysemy: Television News, Everyday Consciousness and Political Action', *Media, Culture and Society*, vol. 12.

Kaplan, E. (1987) *Rocking around the Clock: Music Television, Postmodernism and Consumer Culture*. London: Metheun.

Kellner, D. (1990) *Television and the Crisis of Democracy*. Boulder, CO: Westview Press.

Kellner, D. (1992) 'Popular Culture and the Construction of Postmodern Identities' in S. Lash and J. Friedman (eds) *Modernity and Identity*. Oxford: Blackwell.

Kumar, M. (1977) 'Holding the Middle Ground' in J. Curran et al. *Mass Communication and Society*. London: Edward Arnold.

Laclau, E. and Mouffe, C. (1985) *Hegemony and Socialist Strategy: Toward a Radical Democratic Politics*. London: Verso.

Laing, D. (1978) *The Marxist Theory of Art*. Sussex: Harvester.

Laing, R. D. (1960) *The Divided Self*. Harmondsworth: Penguin.

Lash, S. (1990) *Sociology of Postmodernism*. London and New York: Routledge.

Lash, S. and Urry, J. (1987) *Disorganised Capitalism*. Cambridge: Polity Press.

Lash, S. and Urry, J. (1994) *Economies of Signs and Space*. Newbury Park and London: Sage.

Leal, O. and Oliven, R. (1988) 'Class Interpretations of a Soap Opera Narrative: the case of the Brazilian *novela* "Summer Sun" ', *Theory, Culture and Society*, vol. 5.

Lewis, J. (1985) 'Decoding Television News' in P. Drummond and R. Paterson (eds) *Television in Transition*. London: British Film Institute.

Liebes, T. and Katz, E. (1985) 'Mutual Aid in the De-coding of Dallas' in P. Drummond and R. Patterson (eds) *Television in Transition*. London: British Film Institute.

Liebes, T. and Katz, E. (1986) 'Patterns of Involvement in Television Fiction', *European Journal of Communication*, vol. 1, no. 2.

Liebes, T. and Katz, E. (1988) 'Dallas and Genesis: primordiality and seriality in popular culture' in J. Cary (ed.) *Media, Myth, Narrative*. Newbury Park and London: Sage.

Liebes, T. and Katz, E. (1989) 'On the Critical Abilities of Television Viewers' in E. Seiter et al. *Remote Control*. London and New York: Routledge.

Lodziak, C. (1986) *The Power of Television*. London: Pinter.

Lopez, A. (1995) ' Our Welcomed Guests: Telenovelas in Latin America' in R. Allen (ed.) *To Be Continued . . . Soap Opera Around the World*. London and New York: Routledge.

Lucas, M. and Wallner, M. (1993) 'Resistance by Satellite' in T. Dowmunt (ed.) *Channels of Resistance*. London: British Film Institute.

Lyotard, J-F. (1984) *The Postmodern Condition*. Minneapolis: University of Minnesota Press.

Madden, K. (1992) 'Video and Cultural Identity: the Inuit Broadcasting Corporation experience' in F. Korzenny and S. Ting Toomey (eds) *Mass Media Effects Across Cultures*. Newbury Park and London: Sage.

Martin-Barbero, J. (1988) 'Communication from Culture', *Media, Culture and Society*, vol. 10.

Martin-Barbero, J. (1995) 'Memory and Form in Latin American Soap Opera' in R. Allen (ed.) *To Be Continued . . . Soap Opera Around the World*. London and New York: Routledge.

Masmoudi, M. (1979) 'New International Information Order', *Journal of Communication*.

Mattelart, A. (1991) *Advertising International*. London and New York: Routledge.

Mattelart, A., Delcourt, X. and Mattelart, M. (1984) *International Image Markets*. London: Comedia.

Mattelart, M. and Mattelart, A. (1992) *The Carnival of Images*. New York: Bergin and Garvey.

Mazzoleni, G. and Palmer, M. (1990) 'The Building of Media Empires' in M. Ferguson (ed.) *Public Communication: The New Imperatives*. London and Newbury Park: Sage.

McAnany, E. and La Pastina, A. (1994) 'Telenovela Audiences', *Communication Research*, vol. 21, no. 6.

McBride, S. (1980) *Many Voices, One World*. Paris: UNESCO.

McGuigan, J. (1992) *Cultural Populism*. London and New York: Routledge.

McQuail, D. (1992) *Media Performance*. Newbury Park and London: Sage.

McQuail, D., De Mateo, R. and Tapper, H. (1992) 'A Framework for Analysis of Media Change in Europe in the 1990s' in K. Siune and W. Truetzschler (eds) *Dynamics of Media Politics: Broadcasting and Electronic Media in Western Europe*. Newbury Park and London: Sage.

Meier, W. and Trappel, J. (1992) 'Small States in the Shadows of Giants' in K. Siune and W. Truetzschler (eds) *Dynamics of Media Politics: Broadcasting and Electronic Media in Western Europe*. Newbury Park and London: Sage.

Melucci, A. (1989) *Nomads of the Present*. London: Hutchinson Radius.

Mercer, K. (1992) '"1968": Periodizing Postmodern Politics and Identity' in L. Grossberg., C. Nelson and P. Treichler (eds) *Cultural Studies*. London and New York: Routledge.

Meyrowitz, J. (1986) *No Sense of Place*. Oxford: Oxford University Press.

Michael, J. (1990) 'Regulating Communications Media' in M. Ferguson (ed.) *Public Communication: The New Imperatives*. Newbury Park and London: Sage.

Miller, D. (1995) 'The Consumption of Soap Opera: *The Young and the Restless* and mass consumption in Trinidad' in R. Allen (ed.) *To Be Continued . . . Soap Opera Around the World*. London and New York: Routledge.

Ministry of Information and Broadcasting India 1991 (1991): *A Reference Annual*. Delhi: Government of India.

Monteiro, A. and Jayasankar, K. (1995) 'The Spectator-Indian: an exploratory study on the reception of news', *Cultural Studies*, vol. 1.

Moran, A. (1985) *Images and Industry: Television Drama Production in Australia*. Sydney: Currency Press.

Moran, A. (1989) 'Three Stages of Australian Television' in J. Tulloch and

G. Turner (eds) *Australian Television: Programs, Pleasures and Politics*. London and Sydney: Allen and Unwin.

Morgan, P., Lewis, J. and Jhally, J. (1992) 'More Viewing, Less Knowledge' in H. Mowlana., G. Gerbner and H. Schiller (eds) *Triumph of the Image: The Media's War in the Persian Gulf*. Boulder, CO: Westview Press.

Morley, D. (1980) *The Nationwide Audience*. London: British Film Institute.

Morley, D. (1986) *Family Television: Cultural Power and Domestic Leisure*. London: Comedia.

Morley, D. (1992) *Television, Audiences and Cultural Studies*. London and New York: Routledge.

Morley, D. and Robbins, K. (1995) *Spaces of Identity: Global Media, Electronic Landscapes and Cultural Boundaries*. London and New York: Routledge.

Morley, D. and Silverstone, R. (1990) 'Domestic Communications', *Media, Culture and Society*, vol. 12, no. 1.

Morrison, D. (1992) *Television and the Gulf War*. London: John Libbey.

Morrison, D. and Tumber, H. (1988) *Journalists at War*. Newbury Park and London: Sage.

Mouffe, C. (1992) 'Democratic Citizenship and the Political Community' in C. Mouffe (ed.) *Dimensions of Radical Democracy*. London: Verso.

Mowlana, H., Gerbner, G. and Schiller, H. (eds) (1992) *Triumph of the Image: the Media's War in the Persian Gulf*. Boulder, CO: Westview Press.

Murdock, G. (1982) 'Large Corporations and the Control of the Communications Industry' in M. Gurevitch et al. *Culture, Society and the Media*. London: Methuen.

Murdock, G. (1990) 'Redrawing the Map of the Communications Industries: Concentration and Ownership in the Era of Privatisation' in M. Ferguson (ed.) *Public Communication: The New Imperatives*. Newbury Park and London: Sage.

Murdock, G. (1991) 'Whose Television is it Anyway?' *Sight and Sound*.

Murdock, G. and Golding, P. (1977) 'Capitalism, Communications and Class Relations' in J. Curran et al. *Mass Communications and Society*. London: Edward Arnold.

Murray, R. (1989) 'Fordism and Post-Fordism' in S. Hall and M. Jacques (eds) *New Times: The Changing Face of Politics in the 1990s*. London: Lawrence & Wishart.

Musa, M. (1990) 'News Agencies, Transnationalisation and the New Order', *Media, Culture and Society*, vol. 12.

Neale, S. (1980) *Genre*. London: British Film Institute.

Newcomb, H. (1988) 'One Night of Prime Time' in J. Cary (ed.) *Media, Myth, Narrative*. Newbury Park and London: Sage.

Ninan, T. and Singh, C. (1983) 'India's Entertainment Revolution', *World Press Review*, vol. 30.

Norhrstedt, S. (1992) 'Ruling by Pooling' in H. Mowlana, G. Gerbner and H. Schiller (eds) *Triumph of the Image: the Media's War in the Persian Gulf*. Boulder, CO: Westview Press.

Ottosen, R. (1992) 'Truth: the first victim of war' in H. Mowlana, G. Gerbner and

H. Schiller (eds) *Triumph of the Image: The Media's War in the Persian Gulf.* Boulder, CO: Westview Press.

Parker, D. (1995) *Through Different Eyes: The Cultural Identities of Young Chinese People in Britain.* Aldershot: Avebury.

Peacock, A. (1986) *Report of the Committee on Financing the BBC.* London: HMSO.

Penacchioni, I. (1984) 'The Reception of Television in Northeast Brazil', *Media, Culture and Society*, vol. 6, no. 4.

Pendakur, M. (1991) 'A Political Economy of Television: state, class and corporate influence in India' in G. Sussman and J. Lent (eds) *Transnational Communications.* Newbury Park and London: Sage.

Pieterse, J. (1995) 'Globalisation as Hybridisation' in M. Featherstone, S. Lash and R. Robertson (eds) *Global Modernities.* Newbury Park and London: Sage.

Pike, M. (ed.) (1982) *Ah Mischief! The Writer and Television.* London: Faber & Faber.

Porter, V. (1989) 'The Re-regulation of Television: pluralism, constitutionality and the free market in the USA, West Germany, France and the UK', *Media, Culture and Society*, vol. 11.

Rajagopal, A. (1993) 'The Rise of National Programming: the case of Indian television', *Media, Culture and Society*, vol. 15.

Robertson, R. (1992) *Globalisation.* Newbury Park and London: Sage.

Robertson, R. (1995) 'Globalization: Time–Space and Homogeneity–Hetrogeneity', in M. Featherstone., S. Lash and R. Robertson (eds) *Global Modernities.* Newbury Park and London: Sage.

Robins, K. and Aksoy, A. (1992) 'Exterminating Angels' in H. Mowlana, G. Gerbner and H. Schiller (eds) *Triumph of the Image: The Media's War in the Persian Gulf.* Boulder, CO: Westview Press.

Robins, K. and Webster, F. (1985) 'Revolution of the Fixed Wheel' in P. Drummond and R. Patterson (eds) *Television in Transition.* London: British Film Institute.

Rogers, E. and Antola, L. (1985) 'Telenovelas: a Latin American success story', *Journal of Communication*, vol. 35.

Rorty, R. (1991) *Objectivity, Relativism, and Truth: Philosophical Papers,* vol. 1. Cambridge: Cambridge University Press.

Rorty, R. (1992) 'Cosmopolitanism without Emancipation: a response to Lyotard' in S. Lash and J. Friedman (eds) *Modernity and Identity.* Oxford: Blackwell.

Rose, N. (1996) 'Identity, Genealogy, History' in S. Hall and P. Du Gay (eds) *Questions of Cultural Identity.* Newbury Park and London: Sage.

Rosengren, K., Carlsson, M. and Tagerna, Y. (1991) 'Quality Programming: views from the North', *Studies in Broadcasting*, vol. 27.

Ryall, T. (1975) 'Teaching Through Genre', *Screen Education*, no. 17.

Said, E. (1981) *Covering Islam.* London and New York: Routledge.

Sainath, P. (1992) 'The New World *Odour*: the Indian experience' in H. Mowlana, G. Gerbner and H. Schiller (eds) *Triumph of the Image: The Media's War in the Persian Gulf.* Boulder, CO: Westview Press.

Samarajiwa, R. (1984) 'Third World Entry to the World Market in News: problems and posssible solutions', *Media, Culture and Society*, vol. 6.

Sanchez-Tabernero, A. (1993) *Media Concentration in Europe*. Hamburg: The European Institute for Media.

Sartori, C. (1986) 'TV around the World', *World Press Review*, vol. 33.

Scannel, P. (1988) 'Radio Times: the temporal arrangements of broadcasting in the modern world' in P. Drummond and R. Paterson (eds) *Television and its Audiences*. London: British Film Institute.

Scannel, P. (1989) 'Public Service Broadcasting and Modern Public Life', *Media, Culture and Society*, vol. 11.

Schiller, H. (1969) *Mass Communications and the American Empire*. New York: Augustus M. Kelly.

Schiller, H. (1976) *Communication and Cultural Domination*. New York: Sharpe M. E.

Schiller, H. (1985) 'Electronic Information Flows: new basis for global domination?' in P. Drummond and R. Patterson (eds) *Television in Transition*. London: British Film Institute.

Schlesinger, P. (1978) *Putting Reality Together*. London: Constable.

Schlesinger, P. (1991) *Media, State, Nation*. Newbury Park and London: Sage.

Seiter, E. et al. (1989) *Remote Control*. London and New York: Routledge.

Seiter, E. et al. (1989) 'Don't Treat Us Like We're Stupid' in E. Seiter et al. *Remote Control*. London and New York: Routledge.

Sepstrup, P. (1989a) 'Research into International Television Flows: a methodological contribution', *European Journal of Communication*, vol. 4.

Sepstrup, P. (1989b) 'Implications of Current Developments in West European Broadcasting', *Media, Culture and Society*, vol. 11.

Shaw, M. and Carr-Hill, R. (1992) 'Public Opinion and Media War Coverage in Britain' in H. Mowlana, G. Gerbner and H. Schiller (eds) *Triumph of the Image: The Media's War in the Persian Gulf*. Boulder, CO: Westview Press.

Shotter, J. (1993) *Conversational Realities*. Newbury Park and London: Sage.

Silverstone, R. (1994) *Television and Everyday Life*. London and New York: Routledge.

Sinclair, J. (1987) *Images Incorporated: Advertising as Industry and Ideology*. London and New York: Routledge.

Sinclair, J. (1990) 'Spanish Language Television in the United States', *Studies in Latin American Popular Culture*, vol. 9.

Smith, A. (1993) *From Books to Bytes*. London: British Film Institute.

Smith, A.D. (1981) *The Ethnic Revival*. Cambridge: Cambridge University Press.

Smith A. D. (1990) 'Towards a Global Culture?' in M. Featherstone (ed.) *Global Culture*. Newbury Park and London: Sage.

Straubhaar, J. (1982) 'The Development of the Telenovela as the Pre-Eminent Form of Popular Culture in Brazil', *Studies in Latin American Popular Culture*, vol. 1.

Straubhaar, J. (1988) 'The Reflection of the Brazilian Political Opening in the Telenovela, 1974–1985', *Studies in Latin American Popular Culture*, vol. 7.

Straubhaar, J. (1992) 'What Makes News: western, socialist, and Third World television newscasts compared in eight countries' in F. Korzenny and S. Ting Toomey (eds) *Mass Media Effects Across Cultures*. Newbury Park and London: Sage.

Taylor, E. (1989) *Prime-Time Families: Television Culture in Postwar America*. Berkeley: University of California Press.

Tomlinson, J. (1991) *Cultural Imperialism*. London: Pinter Press.

Tunstall, J. (1970) *Media Sociology*. London: Constable.

Vardor, N. (1992) *Global Advertising*. London: Paul Chapman Publishing.

Varis, T. (1974) 'Global Traffic in Television', *Journal of Communication*, vol. 24.

Varis, T. (1984) 'International Flow of Television Programmes', *Journal of Communication*, vol. 34, no. 1.

Velganouski, C. and Bishop, D. (1983) *Choice by Cable: The Economics of a New Era in Television*. Hobart paper 96. London: Institute of Economic Affairs.

Vincent, R. (1992) 'CNN: Elites Talking to Elites' in H. Mowlana, G. Gerbner and H. Schiller (eds) *Triumph of the Image: The Media's War in the Persian Gulf*. Boulder, CO: Westview Press.

Vink, N. (1988) *The Telenovela and Emancipation*. Amsterdam: Royal Tropical Institute.

Wallerstein, I. (1974) *The Modern World System*. New York: Academic Press.

Waterman, D. (1988) 'World Television Trade: the economic effects of privatisation and new technology', *Telecommunications Policy*.

Weeks, J. (1990) 'The Value of Difference' in J. Rutherford (ed.) *Identity: Community, Culture, Difference*. London: Lawrence & Wishart.

Wernick, A. (1991) *Promo Culture*. Newbury Park and London: Sage.

White, J. (1991) *Politics and Postmodernism*. New York: Pantheon.

Widdicombe, S. and Wooffit, R. (1995) *The Language of Youth Sub-Cultures*. Hemel Hempstead: Harvester Wheatsheaf.

Williams, R. (1961) *The Long Revolution*. Harmondsworth: Penguin.

Williams, R. (1973) 'Base and Superstructure in Marxist Cultural Theory', *New Left Review*, vol. 82.

Williams, R. (1974) *Television: Technology and Cultural Form*. London: Fontana.

Williams, R. (1979) *Politics and Letters: Interviews with New Left Review*. London: New Left Books.

Williams, R. (1981) *Culture*. London: Fontana.

Williamson, J. (1978) *Decoding Advertisements*. London: Marion Boyars.

Willis, P. (1977) *Learning to Labour*. Farnborough: Saxon House.

Willis, P. (1990) *Common Culture*. Milton Keynes: Open University Press.

Wilson, T. (1993) *Watching Television: Hermeneutics, Reception and Popular Culture*. Cambridge: Polity Press.

Winston, B. (1986) 'Survival of National Networks in the Age of Abundance', *Intermedia*, vol. 14, part 31.

Wittgenstein, L. (1957) *Philosophical Investigations*. Oxford: Blackwell.

Wittstock, M. (1992) 'The Empire Strikes Back', *The Times*, 12 May.

Wolff, J. (1980) *The Social Production of Art*. London and Basingstoke: Macmillan.

Worsley, P. (1990) 'Models of the Modern World System' in M. Featherstone (ed.) *Global Culture*. Newbury Park and London: Sage.

Ten Recommended Texts

For students who wish to read further on global television I suggest the following as useful texts which cover related issues. Clearly this represents a personal view and not an 'objective' judgement.

Allen, R. (ed.) (1995) *To Be Continued . . . Soap Opera Around the World*. London and New York: Routledge.

Anderson, B. (1983) *Imagined Communities: Reflections on the Origins and Spread of Nationalism*. London: Verso.

Dahlgren, P. (1995) *Television and the Public Sphere*. Newbury Park and London: Sage.

Giddens, A. (1991) *Modernity and Self-Identity*. Cambridge: Polity Press.

Gillespie, M. (1995) *Television, Ethnicity and Cultural Change*. London and New York: Routledge.

Hall, S. (1992) 'The Question of Cultural Identity' in S. Hall, D. Held and T. McGrew (eds) *Modernity and its Futures*. Cambridge: Polity Press.

Harvey, D. (1989) *The Condition of Postmodernity*. Oxford: Blackwell.

Liebes, T. and Katz, E. (1989) 'On the Critical Abilities of Television Viewers' in E. Seiter et al. (1989) *Remote Control*. London and New York: Routledge.

Morley, D. and Robbins, K. (1995) *Spaces of Identity: Global Media, Electronic Landscapes and Cultural Boundaries*. London and New York: Routledge.

Tomlinson, J. (1991) *Cultural Imperialism*. London: Pinter Press.

Index